DRAWINGS IN ASSESSMENT
AND PSYCHOTHERAPY

Drawing is a language, projected by children and adults, reflecting their joy and pain. It is used extensively by clinical psychologists, art therapists, social workers, and other mental health professionals in the assessment and treatment of children, adolescents, adults, and couples. This book brings together a renowned group of professionals to analyze the research and application of the most popular assessment and treatment tools. Tests discussed include the Draw-A-Person Test, the House-Tree-Person Test, the Kinetic Family Drawing Test, the Art Therapy-Projective Imagery Assessment, and the Wartegg Drawing Completion Test. Working with sexually and physically abused children, assessing clients with anorexia nervosa, and the influence of osteopathic treatment on drawings are some of the special topics considered. Numerous case studies are also included.

Leonard Handler, PhD.

Antoinette D. Thomas, PhD.

DRAWINGS IN ASSESSMENT AND PSYCHOTHERAPY

Research and Application

Edited by
Leonard Handler and
Antoinette D. Thomas

Routledge
Taylor & Francis Group

NEW YORK AND LONDON

First published 2014
by Routledge
711 Third Avenue, New York, NY 10017

and by Routledge
2 Park Square, Milton Park, Abingdon, Oxon OX14 4RN

Routledge is an imprint of the Taylor & Francis Group, an informa business

Library of Congress Cataloging-in-Publication Data
A catalog record for this book has been requested.

ISBN: 978-0-415-53624-0 (hbk)
ISBN: 978-0-415-72415-9 (pbk)
ISBN: 978-0-203-11017-1 (ebk)

Typeset in Bembo
by Apex CoVantage, LLC

Printed and bound in the United States of America by Sheridan Books, Inc. (a Sheridan Group Company).

CONTENTS

CONTENTS

ABOUT THE EDITORS

Leonard Handler, ABAP, PhD from Michigan State University; is Professor Emeritus, University of Tennessee. He published with others: *Teaching and Learning Personality Assessment, The Clinical Assessment of Children and Adolescents: A Practitioner's Handbook,* and *A Guide to Collaborative/Therapeutic Assessment.* Dr. Handler, Past President of the Society for Personality Assessment, received the Bruno Klopfer award "in recognition of his unique and distinguished contributions" and the Walter Klopfer award for "distinguished contributions to personality assessment". He is an APA Fellow (Division 12) and had the "Outstanding Clinical Educator" award from the Society of Clinical Psychology. Others include the Hans Strupp award from the Appalachian Psychoanalytic Society; University of Tennessee Chancellor's Senior Research and Creative Achievement award; and the College of Arts and Sciences Senior Research and Creative Achievement award. He maintained an active practice in assessment and psychotherapy.

Antoinette D. Thomas, PhD is a graduate of Université de Montréal. She is an eclectic clinical psychologist in private practice, combining behavioral and psychodynamic-psychodynamic backgrounds. She accomplished her personal psychoanalysis with Dr. Clifford Scott, and an advanced theoretical and technical training in psychoanalytically oriented psychotherapy. She held clinical, research, and university teaching positions in Quebec, Nova Scotia, and Egypt. She supervised doctorate candidates in psychological assessment and psychotherapy. Dr. Thomas authored the TAT Affective Scale©, Mutuality in Financial Management Scale©, and two techniques in this volume. She is Past-President of the International Council of Psychologists and coedited two conference proceedings. She is Life Fellow of the International Council of Integrative Medicine, Life Member of the Canadian Psychological Association, and Life Fellow of Society for Personality Assessment.

ABOUT THE CONTRIBUTORS

Achilles N. Bardos, PhD, is a Professor of School Psychology at the University of Northern Colorado. His teaching and research interests include psychological and educational assessment; measurement; treatment effectiveness; and computer applications in psychology. He is the coauthor of the Behavior Intervention Monitoring Assessment System (BIMAS; McDougal, Bardos, & Meier, 2011), author of the Basic Achievement Skills Inventory (BASI-Comprehensive; Bardos, 2004) a multilevel achievement test and the BASI-Verbal & Math Skills Survey (BASI: Survey, 2004). He also coauthored the General Ability Measure for Adults (GAMA; Naglieri & Bardos, 1997) a nonverbal intelligence test; and the Draw-A-Person: Screening Procedure for Emotional Disturbance (DAP:SPED; Naglieri, McNeish, and Bardos, 1991).

Matthew Bernier, MCAT, ATR-BC, registered and board-certified art therapist is an Associate Professor in the Graduate Art Therapy and Counseling Program at Eastern Virginia Medical School. His academic interests include: symbolism; processes and materials of art psychotherapy; theories of psychotherapy, counseling, and art therapy; psychological development; and expressive arts. He is coeditor of (2005) *Puppetry in Education and Therapy: Unlocking Doors to the Mind and Heart.* He served on the Board of Directors of the American Art Therapy Association and the Puppeteers of America. He lectured and taught in the United States, Canada, and Europe on art therapy, domestic violence, and therapeutic puppetry. He is a working artist in puppetry and visual arts. He is completing a PhD in Expressive Arts Therapy and Social Change at the European Graduate School.

Donna Betts, PhD, ATR-BC, is an Assistant Professor in the Graduate Art Therapy Program at George Washington University and President-Elect of the American Art Therapy Association. She has researched, published, and presented on a variety of topics. In 2006, Dr. Betts published her seminal article, *Art therapy assessments and rating instruments: Do they measure up?* She received a GW Columbian College of Arts & Sciences grant in 2010 to fund the International Art Therapy Research Database, www.arttherapyresearch.com. Presently, she is collaborating on a number of projects, which includes her role as Principal Investigator on a Defense Advanced Research Projects Agency (DARPA) funded study that is exploring the use of a computer-based graphic novel authoring tool to help service members express combat-related experiences.

Alessandro Crisi, PsyD is Adjunct Professor at "La Sapienza" University of Rome and is a Fellow of the SPA; he works with Performance Based Personality Tests and mainly with the Wartegg Drawing Completion Test (WDCT). He devised a new methodology for interpreting this test in clinical assessment. Such a methodology has been presented in several International Society of Rorschach Congresses and SPA Annual meetings. Dr. Crisi has written *Manuale del test di Wartegg [Handbook for the Wartegg test]* (2007), numerous articles, and book chapters. Since many years Dr. Crisi has strongly devoted himself to promote his new Wartegg methodology within the scientific world. He has been requested to hold seminars and formation courses in Stockholm, Madrid, Wien, Austin, TX, Tokyo, and Buenos Aires.

Sarah Deaver, PhD, ATR-BC is a registered and board certified art therapist. She has been an art therapy educator, researcher, and clinician for over 25 years. A professor at the Eastern Virginia Medical School Department of Psychiatry and School of Health Professions, her scholarly interests include reflective practice, art therapy educational theory and practice, and art therapy assessment and efficacy research. At EVMS, she is the Research Director of the Graduate Art Therapy and Counseling Program, teaches the program's research curriculum and ethics course, and provides clinical supervision to students. She has presented prolifically in the United States, and has published numerous articles and book chapters. She has been involved in service to the American Art Therapy Association in many capacities and is currently its president.

Maria Doropoulou, PhD is a Research Fellow at the Research Centre for Greek Society in the Academy of Athens.

Denyse Dufresne, DO is a physiotherapist. She specialized in the treatment of children at Glenrose School Hospital Alberta; Hôpital Marie-Enfant de Montréal and Hôpital Ste Justine de Montréal, Québec; and Hôpital orthopédique de la Suisse Romande, Switzerland. She developed a program in pediatric at the Physiotherapy School, Lausanne. She has been an osteopath since 1988 and graduated from Collège d'Études Ostéopathiques de Montréal. She has been responsible for children at Fondation Canadienne pour l'Enseignement et la Recherche en Ostéopathie since 1983 and president since 2001. She has been in charge of the pediatric program in diverse Osteopathic Colleges in Canada, Germany, and Switzerland. She chaired symposia at conferences in Montréal, Germany, Toulouse (France) and pediatric seminars in Strasbourg (France), Buenos Aires (Argentina), and Rio de Janeiro (Brazil).

Deborah Engram, MA is a registered clinical psychologist in the province of Alberta, Canada. For the past 30 years she has worked at a multicultural mental health clinic specializing in the assessment and treatment of people with mental disorders.

Dennis R. Finger, EdD is a licensed psychologist in private practice in New Jersey specializing in individual and couple psychotherapy. He is a graduate of the Postdoctoral Program in Clinical Psychotherapy and Psychoanalysis of New York University. Dr. Finger was formerly a university professor and graduate school psychology program coordinator as well as a school psychologist. He is a recipient of the Distinguished Teacher Award from the New Jersey Psychological Association. Dr. Finger dedicates his chapter to the memory of Dr. Emanuel Hammer, projective drawing pioneer.

John W. Getz, EdD is a clinical psychologist in private practice. His clients are children, adolescents, and adults. His specialty is projective testing, in particular the Rorschach. As the chief psychologist at Upward Bound, he directs a comprehensive ADHD clinic for adults and children and provides cognitive therapy for his patients. Previously, he worked for 20 years at Penn State's Medical College where he was on faculty and worked in a number of clinics including the sleep, the obesity, and the mood disorder clinics. His specialty at the medical college was treating patients with anxiety and depression. His students loved his class on the Rorschach technique. Dr. Getz brings a high level of energy, creativity, and empathy in his work with patients.

Gary Groth-Marnat, PhD, ABPP, is an author, lecturer, researcher, and practicing clinical psychologist and neuro-psychologist. He is a fellow of the American Psychological Association, fellow of the Society for Personality Assessment, board certified with the American Board of Professional Psychology, board certified with the American Board of Assessment Psychology, and a licensed psychologist in California. He is an Emeritus Professor at Pacifica Graduate Institute. Dr. Groth-Marnat is the author of five books (*Handbook of Psychological Assessment; Neuropsychological Assessment in Clinical Practice: A Guide to Test Interpretation and Integration; Integrative Assessment of Adult Personality; Psychological Testing and Assessment; Psychological Report Writing Assistant*) and over 160 journal articles, monographs, and chapters in books.

Juliann W. Hanback, PhD graduated from Northwestern University and has been practicing psychology for over 30 years. Her work with children, adolescents, and adults includes both psychotherapy and psychological assessment. Valuing how assessment and treatment complement each other, Dr. Hanback frequently utilizes assessment techniques in the therapy process and employs therapeutic assessment approaches in her evaluation. A specialist in clinical intervention and diagnostic assessment, she taught cognitive and personality assessment as an adjunct professor in the PsyD program at George Washington University. There she developed an administration and interpretation handbook for several projective assessment techniques. Dr. Hanback is also enrolled in a fine arts program of study.

Charlotte LeBlanc, MA is a licensed psychologist with the New Brunswick College of Psychology. She has over twenty years of experience as a practicing professional psychologist and is currently a member of a strategic intervention team in her school district. She has been a reader on a number of graduate theses in clinical psychology, she is responsible for supervising a number of graduate interns in clinical psychology, and she is an active member of her professional college. Charlotte is a practicing school psychologist in Moncton, NB, Canada.

Yann Le Corff, PhD, is a professor of Psychometrics and Psychopathology in the Department of Vocational Counselling at l'Université de Sherbrooke, Canada. He is a registered vocational counsellor and psychotherapist. His research interests include personality assessment, the association between personality traits and psychopathology, and professional practices in psychological testing. He contributed to French translation of tests such as Achenbach's *Adult Self-Report* and *Adult Behaviour Checklist*. He is coauthor of the book *Tests à l'appui: pour une intervention intégrée de la psychométrie en counselling de carrière* [Integrated psychometric intervention tests in career counselling]. He has published in journals such as *Journal of Research in Personality* and the *Canadian Journal of Psychiatry*.

Eva Fishell Lichtenberg, PhD is a clinical psychologist educated at the University of Chicago and further trained clinically at the Illinois Neuro-psychiatric Institute of the University of Illinois Medical Center. She is in private practice in Chicago and an Adjunct Medical Staff Member of Northwestern Medical School. In addition to psychotherapy, her practice encompasses psychodiagnostic assessment of children and adults for both clinical patients as well as litigants in forensic cases. Her extensive experience in psychological assessment includes not only intelligence and neuropsychological evaluation, but also heavily involves projective testing in which projective drawings have served as an important component. The Draw-A-Person in the Rain Test was first used and developed at Mount Sinai Hospital, Chicago, where Dr. Lichtenberg was Chief Psychologist.

Heidi P. Perryman PhD is a child psychologist and co-founder of "*Acorn to Oak*" in Lafayette, California where she specializes in the assessment and treatment of children. A graduate of the California School of Professional Psychology, she has a particular interest in attachment, trauma, and serious mental illness. She has published in the field of custody of children with special needs and is a regular speaker for family and juvenile law. While pursuing her degree, she worked for 10 years in state-funded daycare, where she had experience with infants, preschool, and school-aged children. Having a firm understanding of normal development, as well as extensive clinical training in multiple backgrounds, has helped her become a more effective clinician.

Sonia Pinard, DO (late) practiced osteopathy from 2001 to 2012. She obtained a bachelor degree in anatomy from McGill University; Montreal, Canada. She was a graduate of the Collège d'Études Ostéopathiques (CEO) in Montréal and a clinical supervisor of students at the CEO. Her thesis in osteopathy in 2006 was on the influence of three osteopathic treatments on the wellbeing of kindergarten children.

Elaine Rivas, PhD, received her doctorate in Clinical Psychology in 2009 from University of Tennessee, Knoxville under the mentorship of Leonard Handler, PhD. She completed predoctoral internship at NYU-Bellevue Hospital Center and currently works as a clinical staff psychologist at the VA Medical Center in Bath, NY. Her research interests have included adult attachment, defense mechanisms, psychological assessment, and personality disorders.

Gabrielle Roberts is director of the psychology program at Hope Children's Hospital in Oak Lawn, IL. She specializes in treating youth who have experienced psychological and physical trauma. She is experienced in working with children and adolescents with severe emotional and behavioral difficulties and has worked with a diverse client population across psychiatric inpatient, outpatient, residential, and medical settings. She earned her PhD in 2007 from the University of Texas at Austin, where she received training in therapeutic assessment and participated on the Therapeutic Assessment Project (TAP). She spent three years treating youth in the New York City foster care system with serious mental illness and managed a hard-to-place semisecure unit for adolescent girls at Leake and Watts Residential Treatment Center in Yonkers, NY.

Justin D. Smith, PhD is a Postdoctoral Fellow at the Prevention Research Center at Arizona State University. He is a former fellow of the Development and Psychopathology Research Training Program, funded by the National Institute of Mental Health, at the Child and Family Center at the University of Oregon. He received his doctoral degree in clinical psychology from the University of Tennessee Knoxville and completed his internship at the University of Colorado, School of Medicine. Dr. Smith is Co-Editor of the Clinical Case Applications Section of the Journal of Personality Assessment. He has received a number of awards for his research on assessment-driven interventions including the Martin Mayman, Mary S. Cerney, and John E. Exner Scholar Awards from the Society for Personality Assessment.

Deborah J. Tharinger, PhD, a graduate of the University of California at Berkeley, is a full professor in the Department of Educational Psychology at the University of Texas at Austin. She teaches graduate courses in Child

Psychopathology, Social/Emotional/Personality Assessment of Children and Adolescents, and Interpersonal Intervention with Children and Adolescents. For the past decade her research and scholarship has focused on the methods and efficacy of Therapeutic Assessment with children, adolescents, and their parents. She has published over 15 articles and chapters on Therapeutic Assessment. She is involved in local, national, and international training in Therapeutic Assessment and is a founding member of the Therapeutic Assessment Institute. Dr. Tharinger is a Fellow of the American Psychological Association and the Society for Personality Assessment.

Shira Tibon Czopp, PhD, ABAP is Associate Professor at the Academic College of Tel-Aviv Yaffo and Adjunct Professor at the Interdisciplinary Center (IDC) Herzliya. She is in the practice of clinical and forensic psychology in Tel-Aviv, Israel. Professor Tibon Czopp is a Diplomat of the American Board of Assessment Psychology (ABAP) and a Fellow of the American Academy of Assessment Psychology (AAAP) and the Society for Personality Assessment, in which she serves as the chair of the Israeli chapter. Some of her recent publications include *The Rorschach inkblot method* in Levesque, J. R. (Ed.) *Encyclopedia of Adolescence* (2012); Invited Commentary: *Applying Psychodynamic Developmental Assessment to Explore Mental Functioning in Adolescents, Journal of Youth and Adolescence* (2012); and *Normative CS data for Israeli adolescents, Journal of Personality Assessment* (2012).

John Tivendell, PhD was born in Quebec. He completed his undergraduate studies at l'Université de Laval, had a M.Sc. and a PhD in Applied Psychology at the University of Aston in Birmingham, England. He has been a full professor for over 25 years, teaching and doing research in applied psychology at l'Université de Moncton's school of psychology. In addition to being a licensed psychologist he is an active member of a number of international professional and scientific organizations and is a Fellow of the Canadian Psychological Association. He continues to work with a number of organizations including the military and the police, and he is a research consultant with Human Factors International in Henly-in-Arden, England.

PREFACE

Why did the editors want to compile a book about projective drawings?

Ever since I (LH) can remember, I have been fascinated by various art forms, such as paintings, drawings, and sculptures. I have wondered what artists had in mind when creating portraits. Such interest probably got me to study figure drawings, more of an unconscious effort during my youth. Now, my home is filled with abstract forms, portraits, and a variety of masks. When I learned to use the Draw-A-Person Test, and other tests, in my graduate classes, I spent considerable time trying to figure out what subjects had in mind. This effort has sensitized me to study various art forms and my patients' drawings. Several professors became role models for me. Faculty members who were physically and emotionally available were flexible, energetic, and concerned with their students' growth.

The City University, in New York, had a two-year intensive but gratifying program in assessment. I learned the Rorschach from a professor who had worked closely with Bruno Klopfer. I learned other projective tests, including figure drawings. I joined the graduate school at Michigan State University. The program included application and research. My four-year training included work with patients at two VA hospitals stressing both assessment and psychotherapy. I learned assessment and therapy at our university counseling center.

The chairman of our psychology department, Lee Winder—a world expert on schizophrenia—implemented "a renaissance" in the program at the University of Tennessee, where I got a position for 40 years, as a faculty member, disregarding offers elsewhere. I established a program to study assessment and psychotherapy, from an object relations viewpoint. We were successful in our effort, and had a large number of students who attended the annual meeting of the Society for Personality Assessment (SPA), and many published their research. I was elected to the Board of SPA, then became President.

Our graduate students were able to absorb much of my enthusiasm; they have enjoyed the process and made excellent contributions to the Society and elsewhere. Two former students, Mark Hilsenroth and J. Christopher Fowler, continue to make excellent contributions in assessment.

When I "devised" the Make Believe Animal and Story-Telling game, I found it rather easy to understand how children and adults experienced their world and the problems it causes for them. Most important, was the way in which I could reach patients/clients, using fantasy "fables" taken from their drawings and stories. This allowed me to craft healing stories for the patient. I call the process the Fantasy Animal and Story-Telling game, or the Make Believe Animal and Story-Telling Game. This technique is described in more detail in a later chapter in this book. The technique has been incorporated in the Therapeutic Assessment (TA) procedure widely employed in the United States. It is included in extensive training for psychologists and presented in conferences.

Knowing that Professor Lewis Meleika—of Stanford—was teaching the House-Tree-Person (HTP) test at another university, the second editor volunteered to learn and participate in his standardization of the test in Egypt. As the first department of psychology in the Middle East, it was totally staffed by foreign-trained professors. Graduate courses elsewhere were taught at the undergraduate level. She was fascinated with this projective drawing test and decided to expand her learning experience about projective techniques in general. In his research held by the UNESCO focusing on "Person," Dr. Meleika supervised her scoring of a Bedouin sample. She was overwhelmed by the uniformity of tiny human figures, reflecting how self is perceived relative to the vast Sahara. He also taught her the Thematic Apperception Test (TAT) and clinical psychology. She obtained another BA, followed by a graduate diploma.

The Chairman, Professor Mostapha Ziwar—of the Sorbonne—the first psychoanalyst in Egypt—mentored her MA thesis based on the TAT. He opened his students' minds to the work of projection and the sub-conscience.

Working six years at the National Center for Social Research—the first in Middle East countries, Dr. Saad Abdelmeguid—of Stanford—taught the Rorschach. His psychology unit translated two basic Rorschach books. She experienced the reflection of her internal self-image through her responses to these projective tests.

Since then she has been dedicated to projective techniques, theory, and application. Unaware of other existing systems, she devised the TAT Affective Scale© a quantitative scoring system, in her dissertation, mentored by Professor Emeritus Stephanie Dudek, of New York University and APA Fellow. It was published in an American textbook and presented in APA credited workshops with the editor, Professor Sharon Jenkins, who teaches the scale at University of North Texas. It is also taught at Masaryk University, Brno, Czech Republic and used in Masters and PhD theses. Two innovative drawing techniques are included in this volume.

She attended an Art Therapy conference and workshop, learning more about projective drawings, in addition to books and conferences. She accomplished personal analysis with late W. C. M. Scott, founding member of the Canadian Institute of Psychoanalysis, followed by "Individual and group psychoanalytically oriented psychotherapy" in a three-year advanced theoretical and applied program. Dr. Ahmed Fayek—training psychoanalyst, author, and lifetime friend—informed her that psychoanalysts are building great hopes on understanding the subconscious psychodynamics through projective techniques.

The first introductory chapter on drawings' historical perspectives displays the assets of the D-A-P and the difference between the terms: Draw-A-Person and Figure Drawings. The term Figure Drawings" incorporates the Draw-A-Person test, as well as other related "figures" such as the House-Tree-Person test (H-T-P) and the Kinetic Family Drawing test (K-F-D).

The second introductory chapter is about detailed instructions for administration of Figure Drawing tests. It describes—in detail—the administration instructions for the Draw-A-Person Test, the House-Tree-Person Test, the Kinetic Family Drawing Test, the Couples Drawings technique (used to assess the quality of marital relationships in marriage therapy), and several other lesser-known drawing techniques, such as Winnicott's Squiggle Game. The chapters contain case material to illustrate elaborations of the techniques discussed.

Well-known Figure Drawing tests are employed in five chapters:

Through the analysis of case studies (chapter 3) the authors demonstrate the use of human figure drawings as they contribute in building a relationship with the child, gaining insight into child and family functioning, and helping parents to take a new (constructive) perspective about their child. This chapter also introduces the use of an integrated holistic *quantitative* scoring system for figure drawings that has demonstrated clinical utility.

Chapter 4 presents an overview of the Draw-A-Person: Screening Procedure for Emotional Disturbance. The *quantitative* scoring system is demonstrated with a case study and a summary about validity evidence over a period of 20 years. Studies using the DAP:SPED with clinical populations, such as emotional disorders, deafness, and sexually abused, are presented.

Study subjects were physically or sexually abused Canadian children and adolescents (chapter 5). Cognitive scores on the Draw-A-Person-Test were statistically significantly lower than Full Scale IQ scores. Qualitative analysis of drawings rendered specific profiles within each abusive category. Results supports a meta-analysis of 12 studies (West, 1998), indicating that HFD discriminated between abused/distressed and non-abused/non-distressed children. A child drew four figures in one session. A high quality human figure represented her therapist, while only part of a peripheral line represented her abuser. It is not "lack of consistency" in Figure Drawings—as advocated by projective drawings critics—rather a reflection of affect attributed to each person in one's life.

The distorted view of one's body image is a hallmark of anorexia nervosa (chapter 6). A blind identification method with 40 HTP sets (Buck, 1966) of which 10 drawing sets belonged to anorexic patients, established a nine-item "Anorexia Profile." A *reliability* study for such characteristics rendered a near perfect agreement (*kepa* 0.83).

Chapter 7 includes two research studies. The first is a blind identification of improvement in the drawings of "person" done after osteopathic therapies, as compared to pre-therapy drawings. The second study dealt with improved physical problems, after three treatments, as reflected in drawings of kindergarten children. The Koppitz Emotional Indicators were used to score the drawings. Blind global correct sequence subgroup was statistically significant in the experimental group.

Lesser known drawing tests and techniques as well as innovative technique are found in eight chapters.

In (chapter 8); an unruly child attempted to control, by acting out, if he did not get his way. Rather than challenging him, the therapist asked him to draw, and tell a story about, a make-believe animal. The story contains a message which shows that he understood, symbolically, how he explained his acting out. Another child perceived adults' dominance, leading to his active resentment. The therapist constructed a story that provided pleasure. Generating better parental images led to more structure, care, and protection in the environment. Each drawing symbolically includes embedded healing messages.

The Art Therapy-Projective Imagery Assessment (AT-PIA; chapter 9) is an art-based clinical interview that was developed by art therapists at Eastern Virginia Medical School in Norfolk, VA. This chapter describes the history of the AT-PIA and the rationale behind including the six drawings of which it is composed. Guidelines for its administration are described as are the art materials used. In addition, approaches to interpreting and documenting the assessment are provided. Finally, a case example is described at length. The chapter ends with a brief discussion of our experience as educators teaching art therapy students how to implement and understand assessees through their AT-PIAs.

Chapter 10 briefly displays the history of the Wartegg Test (Wartegg, 1939, 1953), administration, clinical inferences, and a new methodology within the theoretical context of psychodynamic psychology for scoring and interpreting the test, based on the analysis of thousands of clinical cases (Crisi, 2007). The Italian Army has used this methodology for selection. A case illustration draws links between interpretations of the new Wartegg and the Draw-A-Person Test.

"The Draw-A-Person in the Rain" Test (chapter 11) is a projective technique that can be used in conjunction with the Draw-A-Person Test to increase the latter's interpretive potential, or it can be used by itself. The test can illuminate the amount of stress experienced by the subject as well as the nature of his or her defenses and coping mechanisms. The symbolic stress evoked by rain yields insights into personality dynamics and is helpful in formulating a diagnosis. Guidelines for administration and interpretation are provided in addition to illustrative case examples.

A study of one of the oldest and most parsimonious, yet clinically useful, projective drawing technique is the Tree Test (chapter 12). The historical roots of the Tree Test, characteristics, administration, and scoring procedures are discussed, along with key interpretation guidelines from renowned experts. The chapter also reports on scientific studies supporting the validity and clinical utility of the Tree Test and presents original empirical data supporting its validity in assessing past traumatic experiences. Tree drawings are provided to illustrate empirical results and interpretation guidelines.

Chapter 13 explores the utility of the Squiggle Game in psychodynamic therapeutic assessment. A case study of a 12-year-old boy is discussed in terms of a relational psychoanalytic model in which the clinician plays with the child freely and spontaneously within a context of mutual, though asymmetric, interaction. The analysis of the case study demonstrates the utility of assessment tools that enable playfulness not only for evaluating mental functioning and investigating sources of current difficulties but also for creating effective therapeutic relationships, particularly in adolescents.

The Replacement Technique© (chapter 14) is useful with subjects who do not draw humans or talk. They are asked to draw anything; then they play a game in which they talk about people they know whom these objects remind them of, which provides individualized meanings. "Doodling" and "Free Drawings," were each done by a female patient. Most blind inferences coincided with their diagnosis and information in their files, subsequently reported by their therapist. "What Could it Be?" is a modification of Winnicott's Squiggles. The therapist draws part of a familiar object in one color; the child guesses and draws it when complete in another color, reversing roles. A case study shows its contribution to therapeutic progress of a child of divorce.

Chapter 15 includes two innovative studies. The Symbolic Family Drawing Technique instructs patients to draw their families including themselves in any form except humans. Patients would elaborate: "A cat and a dog are my parents because they always fight." Patients are asked in the second technique, the Abstract Replacement Technique, to draw an abstract representation of themselves and others, such as a heart for love, a computer for being a workaholic. Illustrations are included.

Case studies are found in two chapters.

A dynamic child case study (chapter 16) shows how projective drawings depict dramatic portrayals of the inner world of children and their subjective view of their closest relationships, as well as their usefulness for therapeutic understanding and intervention. This eight-year-old boy had trouble with school, family, and friends.

Chapter 17 includes four case studies about: a multiple-problem adolescent, a boy's persistent castration anxiety, a girl's separation anxiety, and another's psychosomatic reactions.

In the Overview (chapter 18) art therapists and psychologists can benefit from collaborating in the clinical assessment and treatment planning process using drawing-based measures. Recommendations for further refinement of approaches across these two disciplines are presented. Mutually advantageous methods are explored, such as a description of global ratings and formal elements as applied to scoring artwork, and consideration of important moderating variables such as artistic ability and experience with drawing.

Leonard Handler
Antoinette D. Thomas

1

HISTORICAL PERSPECTIVES
Figure drawings

Leonard Handler

Although ancient drawings of people may be found on the cave walls in Southern Europe and in the tombs of nobles in Egypt, modern day use of figure drawings as personality assessment instruments began in 1926, when Florence Goodenough devised and standardized the Draw-A-Man test as a nonverbal test of intelligence. Clinicians soon noticed that these drawings reflected personality traits and issues.

It was not until 1949 that Karen Machover devised the Draw-A-Person test (D-A-P) as a clinical instrument. However, the atmosphere in the past century was focused on understanding the child at a deeper level. Malchiodi (1998) describes this trend in the following quote:

> There has been a growing fascination over the past century with the emotional and psychological aspects of children's art expressions, particularly from the fields of psychology, psychiatry, and art therapy.
> (Malchiodi, 1998, p. 1).

This historical setting has had a predominantly psychoanalytic slant of most projective drawing tasks when it comes to evaluating children. She points out that Machover's assumptions have not held up "under scrutiny." She also points out that projective drawing tests are not sensitive to changes in culture, gender, and class. However, a review of the research of the Kinetic Family Drawing test research (Handler & Habenicht, 1994) found that a large number of studies reflect these cultural differences. Many of them are dissertations, and most have not been published. Scoring systems varied and many of these documents did not have adequate research guidelines.

At that point, drawings had been recognized as one of the most important ways in situations where language could not be used. Malchiodi states, "Children's drawings are thought to reflect their inner worlds, depicting various feelings and relating information concerning psychological status and interpersonal style" (p. 1). She continues on, "Although children use drawings to explore, to

1

problem solve, or simply to give visual form to ideas and observations, the overall consensus is that art expressions are uniquely personal statements that have elements of both conscious and unconscious meaning [to] them" (p. 1).

In the late 1800s and the early 1900s interest also grew in Europe in several other areas, such as the art of the mentally ill and institutionalized adults. Cooke (1985) wrote an early study describing the stages of children's artistic development, and a number of scholars (Ricci, 1887; Harris, 1963) published observations of the drawings of Italian children.

In the fall of 1920 Goodenough collected 4,000 drawings from children in kindergarten through fourth grade to determine differences in structure. Goodenough (1926) and Harris (1963) later explored age norms for human figure drawings, and the scale was published as the Goodenough-Harris Drawing Test (1963) or the Goodenough-Harris Draw-A-Person (D-A-P) Test (Kamphaus, 1993). Goodenough referred to her test as the Draw a Man (DAM) test because the directions ask the child to draw a man. Clinicians soon noticed that the DAM test revealed personality traits in addition to intelligence (Buck, 1948, 1966; Machover, 1949; Koppitz, 1964, 1968; Hammer, 1958).

It was not until the 1940s that clinicians began to realize that drawings represent "internal psychological states" and the term "projective drawings" became popular. Malchiodi (1998) states:

> Projective drawing tests were based on the idea that children's responses through drawing specific figures such as people or common themes such as houses, trees, and figures, would reflect personality, perceptions, and attitudes. Drawing was thought to offer an alternative to self-expression that could bring out information about children that words, alone, could not. (p. 5)

Despite the negative opinions of Machover's book, it has been a major focus in the development of the use of the D-A-P, and the book has been reprinted many (at least 11) times. It fits well with psychoanalytic theory. Machover's basic assumption was, "The human figure drawn by an individual who is directed to 'draw a person' relates intimately to the impulses, anxieties, conflicts, and compensations characteristic of that individual. In some sense, the figure drawn represented the person, and the paper corresponds to the environment" (p. 35).

Although Koppitz's research on children's drawings was focused on intelligence, she was also interested in the evaluation of personality. She created separate scales to determine developmental level, and she also constructed a scale for emotional indicators. Koppitz's list of emotional indicators below is as follows:

List of emotional indicators of human figure drawings of children[1,2]

Poor integration of parts of the figure (Boys 7, Girls, 6)
Shading of face

2

Shading of body and/or limbs (Boys 9, Girls 8)
Shading of hands and /or neck (Boys 8, Girls 7)
Gross asymmetry of limbs
Slanting figure, axis of figure tilted by 15° or more
Tiny figure, two inches high or less
Big figure, nine inches or more in height (Boys and Girls 8)
Transparencies
Tiny head, head less than 1/10 of total figure in height
Crossed eyes, both eyes turned in or out
Teeth
Short arms, arms not long enough to reach waistline
Long arms, arms long enough to reach knee line
Arms clinging to sides of body
Big hands, hands as large or larger than face of figure
Hands cut off, arms without hands or fingers (hidden hands not scored)
Legs pressed together
Genitals
Monster or grotesque figure
Three or more figures spontaneously drawn
Clouds, rain, snow
Omissions: Eyes; Nose (Boys 6, Girls 5);
Mouth; Body; Arms (Boys 6, Girls 5);
Mouth; Body; Arms (Boys 6, Girls 5);
Legs; Feet (Boys 9, Girls 7);
Neck (Boys 10, Girls 9)

Koppitz said she used traditional psychoanalytic theory as her framework, but she also used Harry Stack Sullivan's theory of interpersonal relationship, focusing on interpersonal variables. Malchiodi indicates that Koppitz was interested in children's perceptions of themselves and significant others and their attitudes toward their problems and conflicts.

Projective use of drawings; especially the work of Machover and Koppitz, have come under fire by many researchers and clinicians. She states, "Many take issue with projective drawing findings, noting the problematic aspects of clinical interpretation of children's drawings (Golomb, 1990; Martin, 1988; Roeback, 1968; Swenson, 1968, p. 8).

The tendency to match a specific sign with a specific diagnosis or problem description has resulted in poor outcomes, since it is oversimplified in many ways. Important variables have been omitted and alternative interpretations were not considered. For example, a specific group of children (or of adults as well) were compared with a small group of D-A-P "signs" and were found to have no relationship—no significant findings. The conclusion of the researcher was that the D-A-P is a poor measure of personality functioning. There was no consideration of the accuracy and/or the homogeneity of the research sample. The research design was not considered, which resulted in the findings that could be interpreted in other ways.

When other variables were considered, including the examiner contribution in the interpretation, significant findings were obtained. Maldochi sums up the criticism about some of this research by writing, "The literal interpretation of signs as presented by authors, such as Machover, Koppitz, and others, reduces the understanding [of] drawings to matching details and omissions of singular meanings. This one-to-one approach of associating graphic characteristics with meaning is at best very limited" (Malchiodi, 1998, p.8). One possible reason for this oversimplified research approach is that in the past training programs have not emphasized research with childhood developmental variables, as well as research that takes into account such variables as culture, gender, class and other related factors.

Koppitz focused on the initial variables she studied, combined to form groups of variables, such as *Insecurity/Inadequacy,* slanting figure, tiny head; hands cut off; monster or grotesque figure; omission of arms and/or legs and/or feet. A second group of previous test findings was the group labeled *Anxiety.* It was composed of shading of the face, body and/or legs and/or neck; legs pressed together; omission of eyes; inclusion of clouds, rain, or flying birds.

A third group called *Shyness/Timidity:* tiny figure; short arms; arms clinging to the body; omission of the nose and/or mouth. The final group is labeled *Anger/Aggressiveness.* It is composed of a combination, crossed eyes; presence of teeth; long arms; big hands; nude figure and/or presence of genitals.

A recent book by Lynn Kapitan (2010) titled *Introduction to Art Therapy Research* is a text that is probably similar to those of psychology, psychiatry, and probably social work as well. Most of the graduates from doctoral and subdoctoral programs find their way to clinical practice rather than to research. In a section of Kapitan's book, she has a very interesting section called "Conversations Between Science and Art." She points out that art therapists did not fit easily with scientific research. The same has been said of psychology, psychiatry, social work, and other helping professions. Many training programs in psychology, psychiatry, and some in social work, find that many graduates do not do research or publish after graduation. Kapitan quotes Kaplan, "A distrust of how science could address the complexities of art therapy theory and practices . . . has contributed to 'science neglect'" (Kaplan, 2000, pp. xxii).

Kapitan states, "Interestingly, these 'science versus art' observations in art therapy parallel historic developments in the social sciences in the late 1980s and 1990s when proponents of qualitative research were struggling for recognition. Heated debates pitted traditional scientific research (popularly known as 'quantitative') against new paradigm research ('qualitative')" (Kapitan, 2010, p. xxii). Kapitan highlights a "Top Ten List," referred to as a wish list, for art therapy research: "10. End the Old Debate, 9. No more fear of research, 8. Read more selectively, 7. Ask different questions, 6. Craft better research designs, 5. Consider adding a control group to your design, 4. Report research more clearly and completely, 3. Replicate, 2.Partner up—collaborate, and 1. Do it! Then publish it" (Kapitan, 2010, p. xxvi).The same list is essentially important for psychology, psychiatry, social work, and other helping professions.

Most of the research problems discussed above referred to children's drawings. Research with adults' Figure Drawings are open to the same problems but were treated less empathically. For example; Lombroso (1895) developed the idea that art work of the mentally ill could offer insights into their "inner states."

When I first learned about the D-A-P and the House-Tree-Person H-T-P in clinical work, it was merely to arrive at a diagnosis. Little by little in our work with graphic techniques, there evolved a number of techniques, and the emphasis was designed to not only do diagnosis but to encompass treatment with the same techniques. A number of chapters in this volume are examples of this extension. One reason for designing such a technique that incorporates treatment is the extension of the ability to be trained as a therapist of one kind or another. I remember, for example, when psychologists were not allowed to do treatment, and when they finally got permission to do so, the ruling was to be supervised by a psychiatrist. Many medically oriented practitioners sought specific diagnoses, and they used the results of the psychologist to do so.

We hope the reader will note how the research and case material throughout this book attempt to deal with the reliability and validity issues for both children and adults. For many years projective drawings have been among the most frequently used tests by psychologists in clinical practice (Lubin, Larsen, & Matarrazzo, 1984; Lubin, Wallis, & Paine, 1971, among others), who reported similar findings. I also hope that the reader can see the creative use of figure drawings, especially for therapeutic processes in various therapy settings.

Projective drawings typically are used with children and adolescents to gain an understanding of inner conflicts, fears, perceptions of self and others, and interactions with family members, as well as to generate hypotheses that serve as a springboard for further evaluation (Cummings, 1986).

Notes

1. All of the Emotional Indicators are considered valid for boys and girls age 5–12, unless otherwise indicated.
2. From *Major Psychological Assessment Instruments, 2e* (p. 224), by C.S. Newmark, 1994, Austin, TX: PRO-ED. Copyright 1994 by PRO-ED, Inc. Reprinted with permission.

References

Buck, J. (1948). *The House-Tree-Person technique.* Los Angeles: Western Psychological Services.

Buck, J. (1966). *The House-Tree-Person technique: Revised manual.* Los Angeles: Western Psychological Services.

Cooke, E. (1985). *Art teaching and child nature.* London: London Journal of Education.

Cummings, J. (1986). Projective drawings. In H. Knoff (Ed.), *The assessment of child and adolescent personality* (pp. 199–244). New York: Guilford.

Golomb, C. (1990). *The child's creation of a pictorial world.* Berkeley: University of California Press.

Goodenough, F. (1926). *Measurement of intelligence by drawings.* New York: Harcourt, Brace, & World.

Handler, L., & Habenicht, D. (1994). The Kinetic Family Drawing technique: A review of the literature. *Journal of Personality Assessment, 63,* 440–464.

Hammer, E. (1958). *The clinical application of projective drawings.* Springfield: Charles Thomas.

Harris, D. (1963). *Children's drawings as measures of intellectual maturity.* New York: Harcourt, Brace & World.

Kamphaus, R. (1993). *Clinical assessment of children's intelligence.* Needham Heights: Allyn & Bacon.

Kapitan, L. (2010). *Introduction to art therapy research.* New York: Routledge.

Kaplan, F. (2000). *Art, science, and art therapy: Repainting the picture.* Philadelphia: Jessica Kingsley.

Koppitz, E. (1968). *Psychological evaluation of children's human figure drawings.* New York: Grune & Stratton.

Koppitz, E. (1984). *Psychological evaluations of human figure drawings by middle school pupils.* New York: Grune & Stratton.

Lombroso, C. (1895). *The man of genius.* London: Scott.

Lubin, B., Larsen, R., & Matarazzo, J. (1984). Patterns of psychological test usage in the United States: 1935–1982. *American Psychologist, 39,* 451–454.

Lubin, B., Wallis, R., & Paine, C. (1971). Patterns of psychological usage in the United States: 1935–1969, *Professional Psychology, 2,* 70–74.

Machover, K. (1949). *Personality projection in the drawing of the human figure.* Springfield: Charles Thomas.

Malchiodi, C. (1998). *Understanding children's drawings.* New York: Guilford.

Martin, R. (1988). Ethics column. *School Psychologist, 8,* 5–8.

Ricci, C. (1887). *L'art dei bimbini.* [The art of children]. Bologna: Zanichelli.

Roeback, H. (1968). Human figure drawings: Their utility in the psychologist's armamentarium for personality assessment. *Psychological Bulletin, 70,* 1–19.

Swensen, E. (1968). Empirical evaluations of human figure drawings; 1957–1966. *Psychological Bulletin, 70,* 20–44.

2

ADMINISTRATION OF THE DRAW-A-PERSON (D-A-P), HOUSE-TREE-PERSON (H-T-P), THE KINETIC FAMILY DRAWING (K-F-D) TEST, AND THE TREE TEST

Leonard Handler

The first task in assessment is to establish rapport between you and the client/patient; it is difficult to obtain meaningful data unless rapport is established first. Fischer (Fischer, 1985/1994) defines rapport this way: "I propose that rapport *be regarded as a relationship in which client and assessor have found that they share certain understandings that serve as common ground for joint, give-and-take, exploration of the client's situations and opinion*" (p. 300).

An extreme example of what happens when rapport is not established comes from a novel by John Cheever, *The Wapshot Chronicle*:

> Coverly Wapshot, a teenage boy, went from a little town to the big city, to work in his uncle's carpet factory. Early the next morning Coverly reported to Grafley and Harmer, to be tested . . . He was shown a dozen or so cards with drawings or blots on them and asked by a stranger what the pictures reminded him of . . . The doctor's face was inexpressive and [Coverly] couldn't tell if he had been successful. The doctor's reserve seemed so impenetrable that it irritated Coverly that two strangers should be closeted in an office to cultivate such an atmosphere of inhumanity . . . He would be interviewed by a psychologist the next afternoon . . . A psychologist Coverly felt seemed as strange and formidable [to Coverly] as a witch doctor . . . He was kept waiting in an outer room where many orchids bloomed in pots. He wondered if he was being observed through a peep hole. The doctor was a young man with nothing like the inexpressive manners of

the others. He meant to be friendly although this was a difficult feeling to achieve since Coverly had never seen him before and would
never see him again and was only closeted with him because he
wanted to work in the carpet factory. It was no climate for friendship.

(Cheever, 1954, pp. 122–123)

The D-A-P, the H-T-P, and the K-F-D administration

The client/patient and the clinician discuss just what they want to do to collect
information, to help the client/patient. First, a comfortable setting is located
and the clinician sits next to the client/patient, at a distance that is not too
close or not too far, but just enough to maintain a comfortable interaction.
A place (table or desk, for example) with a smooth surface is used to help the
client/patient obtain an accurate view of the drawing. The materials needed
to administer any of the three tests consists of blank sheets of 8–1/2 × 11-
inch paper and some sharpened #2 pencils, each with erasers. The instructions
should vary according to the test being administered. Some clinicians construct
or purchase a booklet composed of blank pages, which will be used by the cli-
ent/patient. Since one of the advantages of these tests is their lack of structure,
it is important to maintain this lack of structure to compare it, later, to tests that
are structured.

Clinicians should place one of the blank sheets, vertically, in front of the cli-
ent/patient, along with the sharpened #2 pencil and ask the client/patient to
draw a person. Make certain the vertical position is maintained. Most clinicians
ask it this way: "I would like you to draw a picture of a person." No additional
information should be given, because giving information would reduce the
lack of structure. If the client/patient asks for more information, he or she
should not be given any information, except that they should only be given
such information as, "It's up to you; you can do it any way you want." There are
many other requests, such as, "Can I draw my wife? Can I draw just the head?"
and many other questions in order to try to reduce the ambiguity of the task.
They should be told, "It's up to you."

Another popular response of the patient/client is "This is hard for me because I really can't draw," or "I can't draw hands or fingers," or "Can I draw a
stick figure?" The response is typically, "This is not a test of artistic ability and it
does not matter how well you can draw; just do the best you can." If the client/
patient drew a stick figure, he or she should be given a new sheet of paper and
told, "This time I would like you to draw a regular person, not a stick figure."
The same may be done if the person draws only the head; he or she should be
given a fresh sheet of paper and told, "This time I would like you to draw a
whole person." The next step is requesting the client/patient to draw a person
of the opposite sex from the one he or she had drawn: "Now I would like you
to draw a person of the opposite sex." While this is appropriate with adults, it is
not suitable for children:

The clinician might say, "You drew a girl (woman)." or "You drew a boy (man)." What seems to work better is, "You drew a boy (man) before; now draw a girl (woman)." It is important to record all of these attempts to get more information from the person. It allows the clinician/patient to sample the kind of resistance he or she will have to deal with later on. Some clinicians ask their patient to then draw a picture of themselves, on a separate sheet of paper, but most do not do so.

When a patient complains that he or she drew his/her hands behind her back, or draws his/her hands poorly, they emphasize that hands are hard to draw, so the patient says he or she left them out. In a discussion with the patient after the assessment was coming to a close, I asked the patient to take a separate sheet of paper and draw a hand. I was surprised in that the single hand, not attached to a body, was beautifully drawn, with each finger detailed. This led to a discussion about why he could draw an individual hand, but not when it was attached to his/her body.

It is important to get more information about the drawings made by the client/patient and therefore it is important to ask him or her to request making up a story about the person that they drew. The story should be recorded verbatim. Some of the clinicians asked about specific data, but the method of asking individual questions often works poorly.

House-tree-person test (H-T-P)

House

When I first learned figure drawing in graduate school, it was a surprise for me to find both house and tree to be considered as personality measures. The administration is focused, by some experts, as related to the theory of Kohut, and focused with a self-psychology approach (Leibowitz, 1999). Test administration is much like that of the D-A-P, except that the paper is held in a horizontal position, probably to accommodate the spread of a house, and because sometimes trees and other vegetation are included. The client/patient is sometimes told, "I want you to draw as good a house as you can; you may draw any kind of house you wish; it's entirely up to you." A similar approach is made for the tree. The patient is asked to use the vertical position, much like the position for the man and woman, except that the patient is asked to draw as good a picture as he or she can draw (Leibowitz, 1999).

Some clinicians do not ask the patient to draw the very best he or she can draw. It might be interesting to ask the patient to "draw a house" and then ask for "the very best house" after that. Other modifications might be used to facilitate his or her use of writing their thoughts and feelings, to help patients who have trouble in face-to-face communication.

If the H-T-P is being administered, the house and tree are administered first, in the administration of the house and tree, before the person. Many people have constructed a list of questions that will focus on what living in the home is like and how it affects the occupants. For example, it is not enough to translate the chimney as a phallic symbol and just leave it at that. Even if this interpretation is given, and it should not be so without more evidence; it is not enough to talk about experience living in the house and whether phallic issues may or may not be meaningful. The work of Buck (1992) and Handler (1996) have constructed lists of questions, and these vary from time to time, for example:

What kinds of activities go on in the house? What does this house need? What are the weakest and strongest parts of this tree (or of this house)? What does the tree (or house) remind you of, or make you think of? What does this person like most or least to do in the house? What sort of things make the person angry or sad by living in the house?

Unfortunately, there has been comparatively little research on the house, compared with the tree and the person, although more and more work has been done from a Kohutian point of view (Leibowitz, 1999). Although Buck (1948) and much later, Jolles (1971) have constructed or improved a quantitative system, there has been little interest in the scale, probably because there have been many more popular and better constructed scales.

Concerning the house, the relevant features of the house are the door. Can it be easily accessed? Is it present in the drawing? The walkway; the baseline and grounding; the windows; the walls; the roof; the chimney; the surroundings? Evaluation of these variables help to construct items whose presence or absence have differential meaning and from the combination of these variables, such as a view of the deeper meaning of the occupants of the house.

In one sense, the occupants allow us to understand who lives there and how their presence take on important meaning. An example of one variable, absence of a walkway, is "The omission of a walkway indicates a passive or avoidant stance with regard to being approached" (Leibowitz, 1999, p. 49). Leibowitz also illustrated the case of a 19 year old who was being treated for depression. The house he drew was almost bare. He showed the dramatic change of the same house, now with a door, walkway (long), chimney with smoke coming out of the chimney, a tree, and the bright sunlight. He described the impression of the house drawing at the beginning of the therapy as "The impression is of a barren, cold, empty place—inaccessible, unapproachable, and closed off—floating off in space" (p. 11).

A year later the patient's treatment showed the progress he had made in the house drawing. Leibowitz (1999) stated, "This house and its setting give a feeling of being alive, accessible, and approachable. There is a feeling of warmth" (p. 11).

The tree

The tree has not been discussed extensively, and it is sometimes ignored. Buck "brought" the test to the United States, from Germany, primarily due to the work of Koch (1952). The patient is asked to draw a tree, while holding the paper in a vertical position. It is important to treat the data as if it is an aspect of the "self." "Thus, the tree is the system that is much more a measure of the self then is the house" (Buck, 1948). The tree has come to symbolize life and growth (Hammer, 1958). It is considered that the tree is most likely one of the three drawings to convey a person's "felt image" of himself. According to Buck, the trunk represents a subject's feeling of "basic power and intense strength (ego strength)."

The branches of the tree are said to represent "the feeling to derive satisfaction from the environment" and "a reaching out to the world" (Leibowitz, 1999, p. 53).

The extensive amount of roots above ground may indicate a concern about the patient's reality functioning (Hammer, 1958). Leibowitz (1999) has described many of the details of the house, the tree, and the people, including detailed pictures, and what these details represent for the client/patient.

Torem, Gilbertson, and Light (1990) found a significant relationship between subjects' reports of physical, sexual, and verbal victimization and the number of scars, knotholes, and broken branches on the drawn trees. Torem, Gilbertson, and Light stated, "Our study examined the hypothesis that tree drawings can be useful as a diagnostic tool in a clinical setting. Our findings indicated that of all the individuals who placed a TI [traumatic indicator] on the tree, 64% reported having been abused. Thus, TI's observed on tree drawings may forewarn the clinician of previous trauma in the patient's life" (p. 904).

Note the tree of a 10-year-old boy who suffered a severe automobile accident (Figure 2.1). The tree he drew contained a broken branch and a scar at the bottom. He spoke of having a severe accident, when he was seven years old, with both physical and emotional injury (Handler, 1996, p. 265). The typical instructions for the Tree Test are to state to the client/patient, "Draw a fruit tree, but not a Christmas tree." However, it is also frequent that the clinician merely states, "Draw a tree." That direction does not include the "fruit tree." Perhaps the reason for the fruit tree instruction is that the fruit tree is sweet and nourishing. However, the simple direction that does not include the fruit tree allows both the clinician and the client/patient to make his/her choice. It is also an interesting issue to develop reasons for the patient to be cautioned not to draw a Christmas tree.

Kinetic Family Drawing (K-F-D)

The K-F-D was designed by Robert Burns (1982; Burns & Kaufman, 1970, 1972) to infuse some action into studying the family dynamics. When the call for action in the family is not present in the instructions, the result is poor and the family is usually merely drawn lined up, and with little for us to learn. The instructions to the family are "Draw a picture of your family, *doing something.*" An alternative is, "Draw everyone in your family, including you, *doing*

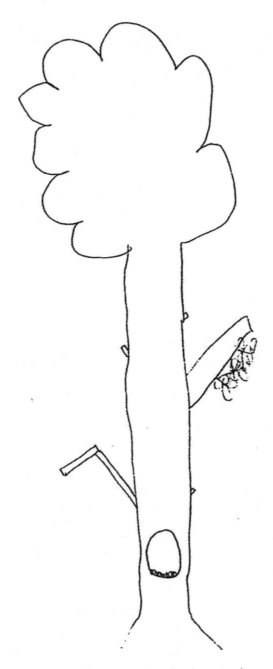

Figure 2.1 Tree drawing of 10-year-old boy in physical and emotional trauma due to an automobile accident. Note: From *Major Psychological Assessment Instruments*, 2e (p. 224), by C.S. Newmark, 1994, Austin, TX: PRO-ED. Copyright 1994 by PRO-ED, Inc. Reprinted with permission.

something." This somehow energizes the family and the family dynamics are highlighted. According to Burns the K-F-D enables the child to depict the family as a functioning, active unit, and allows the clinician to see the child's impressions of these interactions among family members. From the picture the clinician might ask what is going on in the family and might also ask the child to describe aspects of the family function.

Handler and Habenicht (1994) published a (more than 42 pages) document reviewing reliability, validity, normative findings, and cultural influences. Every study reviewed could be scored as "very good" to "excellent" for interrater reliability, found to be 87% to 95%.

We concluded that the K-F-D has not been subjected to adequate research evaluation, despite its worldwide use. We also concluded that the K-F-D still remains primarily a clinical instrument, with inadequate norms and questionable validity, despite the fact that a number of researchers have developed modified scoring systems, and despite the excellent reliability.

Omission of body parts occurred in 25% of the boys; we found that boys were more likely to omit one or more body parts, compared with girls. Therefore it is important to understand that omission of a detail or a body part in a younger boy is not necessarily a pathological sign, but instead may be due to a more typical development lag.

The review includes six pages about cultural norms. It also includes the findings from 35 unpublished doctoral dissertations. Many variables, such as gender, covary with others, such as cultural and developmental variables. Therefore, data will be needed for each age in which the K-F-D is used, across gender and across many ethnic, socioeconomic, and racial subgroups.

The review is critical of studies that emphasize single K-F-D signs and the use of a single interpretation for each of a series of signs. Instead, the authors emphasize the need for more sophisticated studies that utilize a holistic, integrative approach to interpretation. Nevertheless, despite these problems, the K-F-D is used throughout the world, probably because it generates important information about family dynamics. In addition, the authors stress the importance of research that focuses on the interpretive approach of the clinician using the K-F-D technique, rather than the K-F-D, per se.

Interpretive process

There are a number of ways in which these drawings can be interpreted. For some people they interpret piece by piece, and try to put them together. For some other clinicians the approach is a phenomenological approach. For example, Leibowitz (1999) recommends an "Impressionistic Analysis." He states, "After completion of the drawings by the patient, the therapist should react to each drawing as a whole and/or to its parts, on an impressionistic level before engaging in a structural analysis that will focus on specific interpretations associated with constituent components, e.g., the degree of shading being related to the degree of anxiety" (p. 10). Another illustration suggested by Leibowitz is the following:

> As part of the impressionistic process, the therapist can physically take the pose of the TREE, PERSONS, OR ANIMAL (or make the facial expression of to what the appearance of the HOUSE may be analogous) in order to kinesthetically emphasize with what the patient may have been experiencing, consciously or unconsciously, as he or she drew.
>
> (Leibowitz, 1999, p. 10)

Several other interpretive methods are in the literature and should be reviewed. The very creative work of Tharinger and Stark (1990) and Tharinger and Roberts (in press) will be included for description in this volume. In addition, the work of Handler and Riethmiller (1998) will be briefly described, as will the pioneer work of Koppitz (1968, 1984). Handler wrote:

> Concerning the use of individual variables, I have come to see this method is counterproductive to an experiential approach in clinical application, and to validate research. I have also come to believe that the usefulness of drawing techniques seems to be limited by the interpreter's ability to make experiential judgments about the drawings, and depends less on objective evaluations of the content of the drawings themselves, or on the stylistic variables often measured (e.g., shading, erasure, line pressure, etc.).
>
> (1998, pp. 268–269)

Handler continued, "We believe that attention to one's own reactions to the client are more useful than a detached cataloguing of observable behavior. Indeed, empathic attunement to the [client] through the use of such theoretical concepts as, 'loss of distance' [move into the drawing]; 'regression in the service of the ego' and a number of other aspects of psychodynamics to gain a better understanding of the client" (p. 268).

Just as we have described the use of discrete variables, we did several studies concerning the accuracy of experiential process of D-A-P interpretation, namely the variables of empathy, intuition, and cognitive flexibility. Burley and Handler (1997) found that those who were more accurate in D-A-P interpretation, were found to have higher scores on the Hogan Empathy Scale, the Intuition Scale of the Myers-Briggs test, and the Remote Associates Test, a measure of cognitive flexibility.

Scribner and Handler (1987) found that affiliative interpreters were more accurate in their interpretations compared with others, who were less affiliative. Also, interpreters who were unconsciously affiliative were significantly more accurate, compared with those who were only consciously affiliative. The poor interpreters were found to emphasize power, dominance, order, and precision, while the good interpreters saw themselves as responsible and cooperative in their relationships. There is an extensive chapter that would help learn experiential material. It is titled "Teaching and Learning the Administration and Interpretation of Graphic Techniques" by Leonard Handler and Robert Riethmiller, in the book called *Teaching and Learning Personality Assessment* (1998).

The review of K-F-D studies may be found in reading the summary by Handler and Habenicht (1994). It is critical of studies that emphasize single K-F-D signs and the use of a single interpretation for each of a series of signs. Instead, the authors emphasize the need for more sophisticated studies that utilize a holistic, integrative approach to interpretation.

References

Buck, J. (1948). The H-T-P technique, a qualitative and quantitative scoring manual. *Journal of Clinical Psychology, 4,* 317–396.

Buck, J. (1992). *House- Tree-Person projective drawing technique: Manual and interpretive guide.* Revised by W.W. Warren. Los Angeles: Western Psychological Services.

Burley, T. & Handler, L. (1997). Personality factors in the accurate interpretation of projective tests: The House-Tree-Person. In E. Hammer (Ed.), *Advances in projective drawing interpretation* (pp. 359–377). Springfield: Thomas.

Burns, R. (1982). *Self growth in families: Kinetic Family Drawings (K-F-D) research and application.* New York: Brunner/Mazel.

Burns, R. & Kaufman, S. (1970). *Kinetic family drawings (K-F-D); an introduction to understanding children through kinetic drawing.* New York: Brunner/Mazel.

Burns, R. & Kaufman, S. (1972). *Actions, styles and symbols in Kinetic Family Drawings (K-F-D): An interpretive manual.* New York: Brunner/ Mazel.

Cheever, J. (1954). *The Wapshot chronicle* (pp. 122–123). New York: HarperCollins.

Fischer, C. (1985/1994). *Individualizing psychological assessment* (Originally published by Brooks Cole). Mahwah: Erlbaum.

Hammer, E. (1958). *The clinical application of projective drawings.* Springfield: Thomas.

Handler, L., (1996). The clinical use of drawings. In C.S. Newmark (Ed.), *Major psychological assessment instruments* (2nd ed., p. 257). Needham Heights, MA: Allyn and Bacon.

Handler, L. & Habenicht, D. (1994). The Kinetic Family Drawing technique: A review of the literature. *Journal of Personality Assessment, 63,* 440–464.

Handler, L & Riethmiller, R. (1998). Teaching and learning the administration and interpretation of graphic techniques. In H. Handler and M. Hilsenroth, (Eds.), *Teaching and Learning Personality Assessment* (pp. 267–294). Mahwah: Erlbaum.

Jolles, I. (1971). *A catalogue for the qualitative interpretation of the House-Tree-Person (H-T-P).* Los Angeles: Western Psychological Services.

Koch, C. (1952). *The Tree Test.* New York: Grune & Stratton.

Koppitz, E. (1968). *Psychological evaluation of children's human figure drawings.* New York: Grune & Stratton.

Koppitz, E. (1984). *Psychological evaluation of children's middle school pupils.* New York: Grune & Stratton.

Leibowitz, M. (1999). *Interpreting projective drawings.* New York: Routledge, Taylor & Francis.

Scribner, C. & Handler, L. (1987). The interpreter's personality in Draw-A-Person interpretation: A study of interpersonal style. *Journal of Personality Assessment, 51,* 112–122.

Tharinger, D. & Roberts, G. (in press). *Human figure drawings in Therapeutic Assessment with children: Process, product, context, and systematic impact.*

Tharinger, D. & Stark, K. (1990). A qualitative versus quantitative approach to evaluating the Draw-A-Person and Kinetic Family Drawing: Study of mood and anxiety disorder children. *Psychological Assessment, 2,* 365–375.

Torem, M., Gilbertson, A., & Light, V. (1990). Indications of physical, sexual, and verbal victimization in projective tree drawings. *Journal of Clinical Psychology, 46,* 900–906.

3

HUMAN FIGURE DRAWINGS IN THERAPEUTIC ASSESSMENT WITH CHILDREN

Process, Product, Context, and Systemic impact

Deborah J. Tharinger and Gabrielle Roberts

The use of Human Figure Drawings (HFDs) in psychological assessment with children is common and has a long, rich, if somewhat controversial history (Riethmiller & Handler, 1997). However, regardless of one's position of interpreting HFDs from a psychological perspective, most would agree that drawing is a natural medium to use with young children and those in middle childhood. For these children, drawing is a part of their general repertoire in their everyday world. They are often asked in elementary school to illustrate stories they have written and produce art with human figures and background. Hence, children are less resistant or surprised when asked to produce and talk about their drawings than, say, adolescents or adults. Thus, HFDs have the potential to tell us much about children's perceptions of their lives and concerns, if we have the template to approach them.

In psychological assessment, HFDs are considered to be "projective" tasks, also referred to as performance-based personality instruments. The projective hypothesis accepts that individuals construct, interpret, and represent their world based on their prior experiences. Thus, each child has a developed lens through which they see and depict their experience. The process and the scenarios produced through drawings and the narratives provided from answering questions/constructing stories about the drawings are interpreted as a reflection of the child's present state of mind, past experiences, and likely current concerns. These depictions may be in awareness (consciously influenced), somewhat out of awareness, very out of awareness (unconsciously influenced), or some combination within the same set of drawing and narratives. The process and production of HFD material are seen as highly personal, idiographic, and as we will argue, likely influenced by and reflective of the quality of the relationship established between the child and the assessor.

In this chapter, we describe how we have come to use HFDs in Therapeutic Assessment (TA) with children. We do this by summarizing and illustrating six purposes they can serve. But first, we briefly introduce TA and then discuss principles for interpreting projectives and HFDs. TA is a method of psychological assessment that is collaborative and guided by consumers' questions of interest (Finn & Tonsager, 1997). TA uses collaborative psychological assessment as the centerpiece of a potent short-term intervention. For information on the development, research evidence, and illustration of TA with children, as well as the Therapeutic Assessment Project (TAP), see Hamilton et al., 2009; Tharinger et al., 2009; Tharinger, Krumholz, Austin, & Matson, 2012; Tharinger, Matson & Christopher, 2011. The goal of TA with children is to enhance parents' understanding and empathy for their child, as well as the child's sense of being accurately understood, and to increase the child's and parents' motivation and commitment to work for positive systemic change.

HFDs are one of the assessment techniques used in TA that have the potential to contribute to these goals. Although HFDs have typically been included in TAs with children conducted by Finn and his associates (Finn, Personal Communication, 2006), what we present in this chapter is a further development, resulting from the Finn and Tharinger collaboration on TAP. In TAP, we provide comprehensive TAs to children and their families and examine their effectiveness through mixed research methodologies. Families are referred to TAP by a local outpatient community mental health center, where they are on a waiting list for mental health services. The children range in age from 7 to 11. The TAs are provided by teams of two advanced graduate students, studying to become child psychologists (referred to at the Assessment Team), and supervised by licensed psychologists proficient in TA.

A comprehensive TA with children typically includes 8 to 10 sessions over a two to three month time frame. A unique aspect, in addition to gathering assessment questions from all parties involved, providing a family intervention session, and designing specific child and parent feedback, involves the parents observing all or portions of the child's testing sessions. This can occur with parents in the corner of the assessor's office, observing behind a one-way mirror, or watching by video extension in an adjacent room. This process is thought to facilitate new parental awareness, as well as help parents learn ways to enhance positive interactions with their child. The opportunity to observe and discuss reactions serves to foster trust between parents and the assessor(s), educate parents about psychological tests and other assessment procedures, demystify psychological assessment, and facilitate parents' curiosity about their child and the assessment process. This process also allows for modeling of psychological mindedness (i.e., "looking below the surface"), gives parents a chance to "discover" answers to their questions about their child, helps parents think about contextual influences on their child's behavior, and helps "shift" the story the parents have about their child.

Principles for interpreting human figure drawings

We examine general principles for interpreting the process and products of psychological assessment before reviewing approaches and issues specific to HFDs. In psychological assessment that includes objective and projective data, the interpretive task is to make sense of complex information that includes the child's overt behavior, reporting of conscious experiences and perceptions about self and other, portrayal of unconscious or less conscious dynamics and concerns, and the interpersonal relationship with the assessor (Fowler, 1998; Smith, 1998). As assessment data are usually rich, complex, and often inconsistent, theoretically based interpretations serve an organizing function. Higher-order conceptual constructs often are needed to help "explain" the apparent inconsistencies. Thus, data needs to be examined from multiple theoretical and empirical perspectives and the assessor's clinical experience. The integrative tasks are to look for meaningful patterns that capture the complexity in the child's thoughts, emotion, behavior, and interpersonal functioning; to understand how the child developed to this point in time; and to figure out what influences help to maintain behavior that is not healthy for the child or the system (typically the family, but also possibly the school). The goal for the assessor is to provide a coherent individualized portrait of the child in context that leads to enhanced understanding and motivation for change for the child.

Within collaborative and particularly Therapeutic Assessment, additional principles guide the interpretation of assessment data, including projective data and HFDs. First, data is obtained in the present moment in the context of the child's interpersonal relationship with the assessor, and must be interpreted in that light. In addition, data gathered likely is influenced by the child's perception of the relationship the assessor has established with the child's parents, so this needs to be taken into account. Furthermore, if the child's parents are observing, the child may consciously or unconsciously be communicating to the parents. And finally, the assessor is *a* if not *the* central tool in the assessment. The assessor's experience, affect, and counter-transference reactions are essential pieces of information. These must be understood to illuminate potentially important case dynamics and to contain bias in interpretation and communication of the findings.

Scoring and interpreting HFDs

The principles described above are the foundation for interpreting and integrating the information obtained through HFD methods. In addition, specific scoring and interpretative methods have been developed. HFDs typically are informally examined for developmental quality and guides have been developed to suggest what features to expect at certain ages (particularly with the Draw-A-Person—DAP). Children's HFDs are also typically "scored" to provide insight into emotional health or pathology (e.g., DAP, see Koppitz, 1968) and expression of themes in the family (e.g., Kinetic Family Drawing (KFD) see Reynolds, 1978). Typically single signs are interpreted and possibly summed to look at specific meaning and level of severity. Concerns have been noted about this approach (Handler & Riethmiller, 1998), including rote universal interpretation, especially about specific signs (e.g., shading equated with anxiety; small size equated with poor self-esteem). Also, possible farfetched interpretation (e.g., hands behind the back indicate anxiety about masturbation) and over use or exclusive use of psychoanalytic constructs in interpretation (perhaps the cigar is just a cigar) is a problem and can be alienating. In addition, not taking into account motor or neurological impairment when making interpretations (e.g., the influence of impulsiveness in the drawings produced by children with serious ADHD or poorly developed drawings by children with fine motor impairment) can result in inappropriate interpretations. Research on validity of interpretation of individual signs on HFDs, typically the DAP, has been disappointing (Tharinger & Stark, 1990).

In assessment practice, it often is the gestalt of an HFD that is clinically evaluated to derive a sense of the overall degree of a child's disturbance or distortion in relation to the self, family, and the world. Research looking at more holistic scoring of DAPs and KFDs has shown support for the validity of general impressionistic ways of scoring and interpreting in contrast to single sign scoring/interpretation. Tharinger and Stark (1990) developed an integrated, holistic scoring approach for the DAP, with boys and girls aged 9 to 12, that examined four distinct characteristics of an individual's psychological functioning. The first, *inhumanness* of the drawing, pertains to a figure that is "animalistic, grotesque, or monstrous, or, if clearly human is missing essential body parts either because they were absent or disconnected." The second characteristic, *lack of agency*, refers to a "sense of powerlessness," as though the figure drawn "would be unable to affect any change in his or her world." Third, the notion of a *lack of well-being*, describes "negative facial expressions of the individual, such as an angry, scared, or sad face." Finally, the fourth characteristic, the presence of a *hollow*, vacant, or stilted sense pertains to a figure who is "capable of interacting . . . but is somehow frozen and unable to move or use the power that may well be available to him or her."

With these four characteristics in mind, the assessor is to think of him or herself *as* the depicted figure and assign a score for the drawing that reflects an overall sense of the pathology or lack thereof, using a scale of 1 to 5 (with a score of 1 reflecting an absence of psychopathology and a score of 5 reflecting severe psychopathology). Further, Tharinger and Stark note, "it is not a matter of rating a drawing a 5 on each of the four characteristics that results in a score of 5 on the drawing. Rather, it is an integrative combination of the four characteristics that results in the overall rating of the drawing" (p. 211).

Tharinger and Stark (1990) also developed a similar holistic approach to evaluating KFDs with the same group of children. Four characteristics were discerned: *accessibility* of family members to each other; the degree of *engagement* of family members, including over and underengaged; *inappropriate* underlying family structure; and *inhumanness* of the family figures. As with the DAP system, these four characteristics are evaluated in an integrated manner to assign a ranking from 1 to 5. Tharinger and Stark obtained excellent interrater reliability for using the integrated scoring systems on the DAP and KFD, distinguished drawings of children with mood disorders from those in a control group, and found significant relationships between scores on the DAP and self-reported self-concept, as well as on the KFD and self-reported family functioning. Scoring systems using the sum of individual signs did not differentiate groups or relate to self-report measures. Overall, the results indicated that scoring methods that take in account the overall presentation of the child's and the family's psychological functioning in DAPs and KFDs have clinical utility. However, holistic scoring and interpretation also has its limitations, as will be discussed and illustrated later in this chapter. Suffice it to say that in clinical practice, holistic interpretation also needs to be informed by accompanying narrative, the child's life story, and the context of the assessment.

HFDs in therapeutic assessment with children: Process and illustration

Utilizing the principles presented earlier for interpreting projective and HFDs and being informed by the holistic scoring systems discussed above, we now describe six uses of HFDs that we have discerned from the first 10 TA cases from the TAP. The sample consisted of seven boys and three girls, with a mean age of nine, ranging from 8 to 11. The case illustrations are from this sample.

1. Building and fostering the therapeutic relationship

When HFDs are requested in the first session the child has with the assessor, the contribution to the development of the relationship is likely to be more pronounced than in cases where HFDs are requested later in the timing of the assessment. In TA, designed to be relationship-based and collaborative, the semistructured nature of the request to draw and the idiographic approach to asking questions of the drawings are deemed a benefit to early relationship formation. The assessor uses this early session to attend carefully to the child's comfort level, cues, methods of expression, and questions. The assessor uses empathy, compassion, patience, flexibility, and sensitivity, and is open to listening to associated stories a child may tell following a drawing production. The goal is to establish a safe base for the child to allow him or her to share their self and concerns, both in and out of awareness, with the assessor.

2. Observing and experiencing the child's personality and relationship capacity

HFDs, although seemingly simple, are actually complex, relatively unstructured tasks. They demand cognitive, motor, and language production; decisions about the task demands, such as erasing or using single or multiple sheets of paper; and possible frustration due to the open time frame and the absence of right or wrong answers. Thus, the production of drawings and resulting narratives provide a unique opportunity to observe and experience the child's personality and relationship capacity. Assessors are trained to observe in the categories customary in temperament/personality research (i.e., extraverted/positive emotionality; neuroticism/negative emotionality; consciousness; agreeableness). Other features; such as the child's persistence, energy level, talkativeness, motivation, need to please, and tendency to disengage or become disorganized offer useful, early information about the child's personality.

The process of producing HFDs also allows for an initial evaluation of the child's relationship capacity with the assessor. There is the opportunity to take into account and respond to the child's voice quality, intonation, eye contact, facial expressions, reciprocity, and affect. The assessor may obtain a glimpse of the child's attachment style. The assessor is trained to be alert to and aware of all counter-transference reactions, such as feeling very protective, irritated, exhausted, or kindly. These experiences are central to understanding the child and interpreting the data that will be forthcoming throughout the TA.

3. Gaining initial impressions of how the child perceives and experiences self, family, and world through the drawings

The actual drawing productions, e.g., the person(s) from the DAP, are a lasting record of the child's solution to the request to draw. In starting to make sense of the child's drawings, it is useful for the assessor to actually imagine being, for example, the person in the drawing to gain a sense of the affect and environment that the child is depicting. The posture, positioning, mood, expression, action, etc., can thus be experienced in this way. This method is consistent with the perspective of TA that psychological tests and procedures are primarily "empathy magnifiers" that help assessors "get in clients' shoes" (Finn & Tonsager, 1997). Furthermore, it is essential to take into account the developmental appropriateness of the drawing, as well as any fine motor impairment the child may have that affect the quality and integration of the drawing.

Assessors may either immediately, through extensive experience, or through subsequently consulting scoring systems and norms, be aware of the developmental quality of the child's drawings and note individual signs that may have interpretative value (although there is little research supporting such a singular approach). It can also be revealing to contrast the developmental quality across the different drawings and, if notable differences are found, to consider that developmental regression may be the product of overwhelming emotion or disorganized cognition associated with the child's experience that is surfacing in relation to a particular drawing. Furthermore, it is useful to contrast the portrayal in the drawings with how the child is being experienced in the session, e.g., a child who is presenting with withdrawn and anxious behavior in the session drawing a bold, aggressive person. These seeming inconsistencies are the basis for more complex and theoretically based interpretations introduced earlier. Assessors may find it useful to take a holistic approach to scoring and interpretation, such as that earlier described by Tharinger and Stark (1990), to gain an overall impression of the degree of health or pathology depicted in the person and family drawings.

4. Gaining further impressions through child's verbal narrative

The child's description of his or her drawings, along with responses to questions and the extended inquiry of telling a story from a drawing are further lasting records. These narratives typically provide much information about the child, both in terms of content interpretation as well as congruence or incongruence between the actual drawing and the narrative. This inconsistency offers the opportunity to understand some of the conflicts a child may be experiencing. The narrative also offers an opportunity to see how the child chooses to expand or limit what is revealed, which will enhance or curtail interpretation.

5. Interpreting meaning and level of awareness of drawings and narrative in context

It is essential when interpreting children's HFDs to take an idiographic, holistic approach that takes into account the child's relationship with the assessor, the child's personality and relationship capacity, the drawings and narratives, *and* what is known about the child's current family structure, life situation, history, and current concerns. This integration is the foundation for comprehensive analysis and interpretation, as will be illustrated below. It also may be helpful to utilize one or more of the HFDs in the feedback session with the parents to concretely demonstrate a key finding or to use the drawing and narrative as a metaphor to motivate the change process.

6. Enhancing parents' understanding and empathy for their child

Our last use of HFDs likely is unique to TA, as it involves the parents having observed the process and products of the HFD session with their child, discussing their questions and observations with an assessor, and providing comments and reactions. It is our experience that parents are very engaged, curious, and tend to provide rich commentary and background. The parents also observe the assessor being empathic, compassionate, patient, flexible, and sensitive to their child, which may transfer to new ideas about more caring parenting. Alternatively, if the parents maintain a strong scapegoating stance toward their child while observing, they may demonstrate the depth of their negative attitude and possible resistance to taking in alternate views and interpretations. This latter scenario may assist the assessors in planning how much empathy they need to provide the parents before the parents can develop empathy for their child. We now provide illustrations of these six uses of HFDs in TA using three case studies. Hopefully the case studies will demonstrate how the six uses work together to optimize the potential of using HFDs in psychological assessment.

Case illustrations

Case 1: Kathy

Kathy was 11 years old and in the fifth grade when assessed. She and her parents came to the TAP with a variety of concerns. They had questions about Kathy's trouble relating to peers. Kathy's parents were also concerned about her difficulty falling asleep at night. They had a hunch that perhaps her worries were preventing her from sleeping, and they wondered what it was she worried about. Complicating matters, Kathy's parents had extremely different parenting styles and, as a result, were inconsistent with Kathy as a parenting team. They represented two extremes on the parenting continuum; with Kathy's mother as the permissive, highly sensitive parent, and her father as the disciplinarian, lacking some sensitivity and waiting for Kathy to pull herself into maturity by her emotional and intellectual bootstraps. What the Assessment Team discovered through the TA, however, was that despite Kathy's noble efforts to hold herself up, her bootstraps, or pink shoelaces as it were, were somewhat frayed and far too heavy for her alone to hold. We got our first glimpse of this in Kathy's initial session with Jane (the assessor) in which Kathy was asked to complete some HFDs.

Building and fostering the therapeutic relationship. Jane was able to interact with Kathy during the production of the drawings, and for brief periods of time before and after the drawings were completed. As Kathy drew, Jane began the relationship building process. Immediately, Jane was able to relate to Kathy by mirroring her affect. Her tone and mood was calm, but upbeat, similar to Kathy's. She adopted some of Kathy's vocabulary, and when Kathy answered a question, Jane repeated her answer back to her, demonstrating to Kathy that she was listening and interested in what she had to say. When they talked, Jane leaned in and got a little closer. That put Jane at eye level with Kathy. At the same time, Jane didn't crowd or rush Kathy. When Jane didn't understand Kathy, she apologized for making her repeat herself.

Observing and experiencing the child's personality and relationship capacity. Kathy also demonstrated an interest and willingness to form a meaningful relationship with Jane. Kathy was a highly verbal child who readily told Jane about her troubles. She gave Jane eye contact when they spoke and, unlike many children her age, demonstrated a genuine interest in Jane and what she had to say. Kathy seemed to try very hard to show Jane that she was quite grown up. Throughout the drawings, Kathy was calm, friendly, and seemed eager to impress Jane. Kathy's relational style with Jane and her reported problems with peers suggests that perhaps Kathy could relate well to adults but lacked appropriate relational skills for interacting with those her own age.

As Kathy began to draw, she expressed the worry that her drawings would not be good enough. Jane adopted an especially calm, easygoing demeanor, gave Kathy a warm smile, and reassured her that it didn't matter how good the drawing was. Furthermore, when Kathy wished to prematurely discontinue a drawing, Jane showed acceptance and understanding, permitting her to stop. When Kathy took a particularly long time on one of her drawings Jane quietly observed, providing Kathy with the patience and assurance that she needed. By working at Kathy's pace and respecting her desire not to complete one of the drawings, Jane communicated to Kathy that she and Jane were, in fact, collaborators in this process, and that her needs superceded Jane's agenda.

Gaining initial impressions of how the child perceives and experiences self, family, and world through the drawings and narrative.

DRAW-A-PERSON: KATHY

K: *It's a teenager.* **J:** *A teenager. How old is she?* **K:** *15.* **J:** *So tell me about this person. Is this a girl or a woman?* **K:** *It's a teenager.* **J:** *A teenager. How old is she?* **K:** *15.* **J:** *Who is she?* **K:** *Just another person in the . . . uh . . . it's kind of like about, she's the main character in this and her friend dared her to go on the ride and she said it'd be a blast.* **J:** *Uh huh. Her friend went on the ride?* **K:** *Her friend went on with her and this is when she came off.* **J:** *Oh okay. So how is she feeling right now?* **K:** *Freaked.* **J:** *Why is she feeling freaked?* **K:** *Because of the ride. It was like a really fast roller coaster. You know, it was scary.* **J:** *Tell me about the sign behind her.* **K:** *It's when she's getting off the ride.* **J:** *Oh, I see.* **K:** *And this is like the front (points out) and the roller coaster goes around here (shows).* **J:** *Uh huh. Hmm. Okay. She's feeling freaked. She just got off the roller coaster. This is the sign behind her. What is she thinking right now?* **K:** *"I should've never taken it. Taken the dare."* **J:** *Okay. She's thinking, "I should've never done that," huh?* **K:** *(laughs)* **J:** *Okay. What's she gonna do right now?* **K:** *She's gonna try to hide it.* **J:** *But she's really freaked.* **K:** *Yeah.* **J:** *Um hmm. Okay. But she's gonna try and hide it, you said?* **K:** *Yeah.* **J:** *What does she need the most? What does she need right now?* **K:** *Time.*

Figure 3.1

Figure 3.2

When using the Tharinger/Stark Holistic scoring method, Kathy's drawing of a girl received a score of 4. The drawing projected a sense of extreme anxiety and sadness. Kathy's description of the drawing further depicted the lack of well-being for this character. The girl in her drawing most certainly exhibited a lack of agency, having already begun her walk on the "Path of No Return." Accordingly, the character seemed to be somewhat helpless in the face of her circumstances.

KINETIC FAMILY DRAWING: KATHY

J: *Draw me a picture of your family with you all doing something.* **J:** *This is your family?* **K:** *Uh huh.* **J:** *Tell me who everybody is.* **K:** *I'm sleeping, my mom's on the computer, and my dad's playing basketball. He used to play on a team but he hurt his leg . . . and so he can't do that anymore.* **J:** *He still plays now?* **K:** *Yeah, he plays at* *the rec center with me.* **J:** *Oh cool, so you play basketball too.* **K:** *Yeah, not really in a league but, yeah, he used to be in a league.* **J:** *And your mom is on the computer?* **K:** *Uh huh.* **J:** *And you're sleeping?* **K:** *I oversleep. It's what I do on the weekends, I oversleep.* **J:** *Okay. So how is everybody feeling in the picture?* **K:** *Just doing what they do on normal weekends. Just a normal day. Normal Saturday.* **J:** *Okay. So how's your dad feeling?* **K:** *Glad he can play basketball. I think it's his favorite sport. And that he wants me to come along. Cause we go, like, together a lot.* **J:** *Okay. Your dad wants you to go along with him? What is your mom feeling?* **K:** *Just, uh, maybe she could be, well, sometimes we get curious about something and we look it up on the internet, so that's what she's doing.* **J:** *Oh, okay. She's looking something up on the internet?* **K:** *Yeah. We do that sometimes. We figure out something but then we're curious about it, like a certain topic.* **J:** *Yeah. Okay. What's she thinking about?* **K:** *About the subject that's on the computer and wondering.* **J:** *What's gonna happen next?* **K:** *Well, my mom usually cleans the cat box and feeds them every day. And I just get ready. My dad, he's the latest at getting ready.* **J:** *What are you guys getting ready for?* **K:** *Well, we're not really getting ready for anything; it's just a free Saturday.* **J:** *So, where is all of this taking place?* **K:** *At my house. Except my dad is at the rec center.* **J:** *Oh, okay, but you and your mom are at home.* **K:** *Uh huh.*

When using the Tharinger/Stark holistic scoring method, Kathy's Kinetic Family Drawing received a score of 2.5. The compartmentalization of the family members in the drawing suggested separation and perhaps reflected isolation of family members from one another. Moreover, the lack of engagement of family members with each other may have further illustrated a lack of communication in the family. At the same time, each person in the family was portrayed doing something that he or she enjoyed and thus the picture may have reflected a fairly normal family weekend day.

Interpreting meaning and level of awareness of drawings and narrative in context. When we examined Kathy's drawings in light of the family's presenting concerns and what we learned about the family through the TA, we were able to identify ways in which Kathy used the drawings to communicate her thoughts and feelings. The assessment revealed that Kathy was a perfectionist and, accordingly, placed on herself lofty demands and high expectations. For her first drawing, Kathy was asked to draw a picture of a whole person (Draw-A-Person) and she chose to draw a male figure. For this drawing she only completed the head of the figure and asserted that she was not good at drawing bodies. Her resistance to completing the body for fear that it would not be adequate likely reflected Kathy's perfectionism. Kathy was so worried about not doing a good job for Jane that she opted not to try to draw a body at all. Her willingness and ability to draw a body on her second drawing (DAP: Female, pictured above) could have reflected a relatively greater level of confidence for drawing same-sex figures, or perhaps anxiety about male bodies, but may have also spoken to her growing comfort level with Jane as the session progressed.

Results of the TA also suggested that Kathy was suffering from a low-grade chronic depression and low self-esteem. When completing the Thematic Apperception Test, Kathy told a disproportionate number of sad stories, often involving characters trying to cope with sad feelings. Kathy also expressed the belief that her past has ruined her future. In her drawing of a female, it appeared as though Kathy offered Jane and her parents (who were watching behind the mirror) a window into those feelings and beliefs. The expression on the girls' face was one of absolute terror, and she had just walked through a doorway entitled "The Path of No Return." Kathy may have been conveying her sense that her present and future life was already doomed by her past. The look on the girl's face may have reflected the fear and sadness Kathy had with respect to her life and herself. Kathy said that the girl was going to try to "hide" her emotion, but clearly, from the picture, she was unable to do so. This also fit with other test findings from the TA that suggested that Kathy tried to manage her emotions and kept them bottled up, but then became overwhelmed, resulting in her emotions at times spilling over in ways she couldn't manage.

Kathy's Kinetic Family Drawing also provided the assessors with some sound initial hypotheses about Kathy's perception of her family. We learned through the assessment that there was marital conflict and it appeared that it was being diverted onto Kathy. Kathy's father saw her as needing more discipline, while her mother saw her as needing more love and nurturing. As Kathy's drawing suggested, more communication was needed in their parenting of Kathy. The TA revealed that Kathy was an extraordinarily sensitive child, and thus it was no surprise that she was so tuned into the emotional isolation and lack of communication in her family.

Enhancing parents' understanding and empathy for their child. Kathy's drawing of a girl was an extremely useful tool in the assessment in that it very directly provided the assessors with the sense that Kathy saw herself as a worried or unhappy child. When watching Kathy completed this drawing, her parents focused not on the content of the drawing, but on Kathy's perfectionism while drawing. Kathy's mother correctly predicted that Kathy would take a long time on the drawing and erase a lot. Her father talked about Kathy's perfectionism with her schoolwork. Kathy's parents were either not attuned to the visible cry for help in her drawing or were emotionally unable to acknowledge Kathy's anxiety and sadness at the time. Although they didn't show it on the surface, the drawing may have begun to lay groundwork for Kathy's parents to gain a deeper understanding of their daughter. For example, at feedback the assessors observed a shift in Kathy's father's understanding of his daughter from "bad" to "sad." Kathy's drawing of a scared and worried girl (who she likened to herself during the questioning) may have begun to foster his new understanding early on in the TA.

Case 2: David

David was 10 years old and in the fifth grade when assessed. He lived with his mother and eight-year-old sister. David's father lived a great distance away, and though David didn't see him often, they spoke on the phone quite frequently. In contrast, his mother's boyfriend (James) had become a daily part of David's life and planned to move into her home, along with his two children, shortly following the beginning of the assessment. David's mother described David as a highly sensitive child. David's mother was concerned that David was depressed and "stressed." She wondered which of these two conditions he most suffered from, and what the origins of his sadness and worry were. She expressed her belief that she and her son were very alike, thus she believed that David's ways of reacting to difficult circumstances mimicked her own. She admitted that she had a difficult time coping with anger and wondered how best to help him cope with his anger. David's mom also wondered if she sheltered him too much. David's questions were quite similar. He asked about where his stress and worries came from, how to cope with them, and also what to do when he is mad at himself.

Building and fostering the therapeutic relationship. As in the session with Kathy, Jane began to connect with David by tuning in to his personality and responding to his emotions. Jane maintained eye contact with David and repeatedly used his name while talking with him. By smiling and speaking in a calm tone, Jane was able to convey a sense of safety and warmth.

Observing and experiencing the child's personality and relationship capacity. Upon first meeting David, it was clear that he was a unique child. He appeared far more verbal and intellectual than other boys his age, using big words and offering in-depth descriptions. David easily talked to Jane, and was able to tell her about his worries. He revealed that he not only worried about his life (e.g., his school performance), but he also worried about the health and happiness of his parents as well as even bigger things, such as natural disasters. Given the adult-like manner in which David spoke, the assessors hypothesized that he may have had a difficult time relating to most other children his age. It was also obvious that David was a tense child. Despite this, David was a friendly and warm child. He smiled and laughed with Jane and liked to make jokes (though often they were obscure references to things, like websites, with which Jane was not familiar).

Jane and David chatted a bit while David completed his drawings. Jane asked him questions about himself as he worked. He responded well to this and opened up to Jane by telling her about his interests. When David made a comment about how his art teacher criticized the way he held his pencil, Jane took the opportunity to relate to him *about* drawing *while* he was drawing. She demonstrated acceptance for the way he held his pencil by not criticizing him as his teacher did, and by asking him about what his art teacher says and how that makes him feel. David seemed to pick up on Jane's cue that it was okay to chat during his drawings, because on the second drawing he initiated the conversation. Talking seemed to be a way for David to alleviate some of his anxiety (or just to cope with a new or potentially uncomfortable situation).

Gaining initial impressions of how the child perceives and experiences self, family, and world through the drawings and narrative.

DRAW-A-PERSON: DAVID

J: Is this a boy or a girl? **D:** A boy. **J:** A boy. How old is he? **D:** Uh, I would say he's in high school. **J:** In high school? **D:** Yeah. **J:** Okay. Can you tell me a little bit about him? Like how's he feeling? **D:** Basically he's a typical, normal kid. **J:** Oh yeah, a typical normal kid? **D:** Yeah.

J: So what is a typical normal kid? **D:** Um, he's usually a person who likes football, who just basically hangs up pictures of like football players and such. And basically—the sort of person who is just sort of carefree. **J:** Oh, okay. He's kinda carefree. **D:** Yeah. **J:** Okay .So how's he feeling right now? **D:** He's basically content with what's going on. **J:** Feeling content. What's he thinking about? **D:** Well, I didn't think about that one. He's probably just thinking about what's for dinner, hoping that it's not like tuna casserole. **J:** So he really is like a typical high school kid, huh? **D:** Yeah.

When using the Tharinger/Stark Holistic scoring method, David's drawing of a boy was given a score of 2.5. While the picture didn't elicit acute concern across any of the scoring domains, there were some potentially worrisome aspects of the drawing. David indicated that it was a drawing of a "typical, normal kid" who liked football, yet the boy in the picture did not look like the high school jock that David was reportedly depicting. Furthermore, the boy in the picture appeared to have a sad, or at least introspective, facial expression; more closely resembling David than a kid with no worries. This incongruence between the drawing and the description may have reflected a discomfort David had with telling Jane about who he really drew (as it was so early in the assessment), or it may have been that David was truly not in touch with who a typical, normal kid was, reflecting his difficulty relating to peers.

KINETIC FAMILY DRAWING: DAVID

J: Okay. So now tell me about who is in the picture. Tell me who this is here. **D:** My dad. **J:** Okay, and who is this? **D:** Me. **J:** That's you. Okay. And who is that? **D:** I made her a little too small but that's my sister. **J:** That's okay. That's your sister. You wish you'd drawn her a little bit bigger. **D:** Way too small. **J:** And who is that? **D:** Mom. **J:** Now tell me about what's going on in the picture, what are you guys doing? **D:** Basically, eating at Thanksgiving dinner. **J:** You are eating at

Figure 3.3

Figure 3.4

Thanksgiving? **D:** Yeah. **J:** Okay. So this is your dad, this is you; this is your sister, and your mom. **D:** Yep. **J:** And it's Thanksgiving so this is the turkey here? **D:** Yep. **J:** Okay. How's everyone feeling? How's your dad feeling? **D:** My dad—all of us are probably feeling pretty hungry. **J:** Pretty hungry. What about, so you're all feeling hungry of course. I always feel hungry before Thanksgiving too. **D:** Knowing how long the turkey takes. **J:** But what about feelings, like emotions like happy, sad, mad, that kind of stuff? **D:** Like probably pretty happy because we're able to eat. **J:** Oh okay. So is everyone happy or are some people feeling happy and some people feeling different things? **D:** Mom's probably feeling pretty weary because she had to carve up everything, even though she did get a little help. **J:** Oh. Who did she get help from. **D:** Dad would probably be watching football. **J:** Oh, okay, so you and your sister would be helping your mom? **D:** Yeah, cutting up the carrots and peeling potatoes. **J:** That's what you would be doing, and your sister, and you [your] dad would be watching football? **D:** Yeah probably. **J:** Probably. And so your mom is feeling pretty weary did you say because— **D:** Yeah, because of cooking everything. **J:** Okay. Anything else about this picture? What are people thinking about? **D:** Food! **J:** (laughs) They are thinking about the food? **D:** Yeah. **J:** Okay. Now, what's gonna happen after this? **D:** Pumpkin pie! **J:** Pumpkin pie? **D:** Hopefully. **J:** Is this kinda like what your family is like most of the time? **D:** No, usually we don't cook.

When using the Tharinger/Stark Holistic scoring method, David's KFD received a score of 2. The drawing was fairly straightforward, but, like the DAP, included some details that may have been significant with respect to David and his family. The absence of the children's faces in the picture may have suggested their relative unimportance in the family, suggesting that the children's needs were overpowered by the needs of the adults. Similarly, the omission of eyes or a mouth on David's father's profile may have reflected his relative absence in David's life. Moreover, although everyone was sitting at the table, the scene seemed somewhat void of engagement among family members. With only the backs of the children's heads and profiles of the parents visible, the picture had a slightly vacant feel to it.

Interpreting meaning and level of awareness of drawings and narrative in context. Neither the boy in David's DAP nor the family in his KFD resembled David or his family life. Instead, though the characters and scenes may have in some ways reflected his life, they appeared to more strongly project his ideal self and his ideal family. In his DAP for example, David depicted a "typical, normal kid" who was interested in football and worried about nothing more than "what's for dinner." David on the other hand, was not a typical kid, and he was constantly worried about himself and the world around him.

Similarly, the family scene portrayed in David's KFD suggested that he desired a family life that he did not have and for which he was hungry. David included his father in his drawing and made no mention of James (his mom's boyfriend). When Jane asked him if that was what his family was like most of the time, David said, "No, usually we don't cook," suggesting that it would otherwise be an accurate depiction of his family. By contrast, David almost never sat at a dinner table with his father, yet frequently ate dinner with James; his mother's soon-to-be live-in boyfriend. David did not mention James at all throughout the entire TA. This omission in the family drawing and his inclusion of his father suggested that David longed for what he may have considered to be a "normal, typical" family life. Whereas Kathy's drawings seemed to provide a direct window into her thoughts and feelings, the insight provided by David's drawings and descriptions came from how starkly they differed from his actual life. David had not yet integrated the changes in his family structure.

Enhancing parents' understanding and empathy for their child. While observing David from behind the mirror, his mother was able to recognize that David's KFD was a likely reflection of the carefree, "normal" kid he wished to be or to become. Interestingly, with respect to the KFD, she did not comment on his choice to include his father in the picture. Moreover, she carried a lot of guilt surrounding what she perceived to be her parenting faults with David. For these reasons, it may have been too difficult at that time for her to consciously acknowledge that with his KFD David may have been suggesting that his ideal family included his father.

Case 3: Chad

In this final case illustration, we provide a more concise analysis. Chad was 11 years old when assessed and the eldest of five siblings (one biological brother, one half sister, and two half brothers). He lived with his mother and his stepfather. Chad's father left when he was young and Chad had very little contact with him. The family experienced poverty; they lived in government subsidized housing and often lacked gas money and money to pay for utilities.

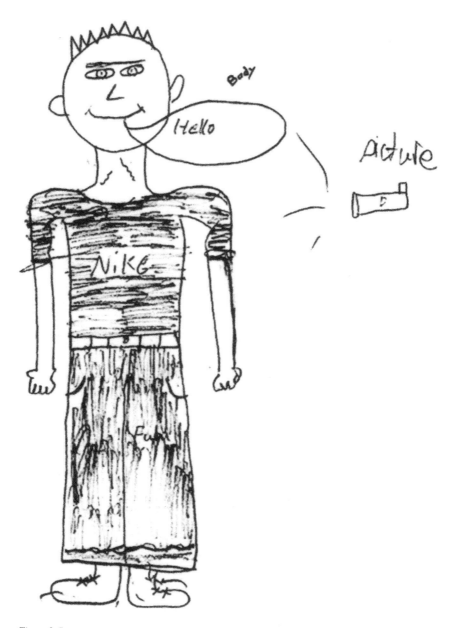

Figure 3.5

Concerns and questions for the assessment focused on Chad's acting-out behavior. In addition, Chad felt rejected by his father and stepfather and felt he was "in the way" of his mother. When we met Chad, he had was running away from home often. Chad was also getting into trouble at school for behaving

Figure 3.6

aggressively with teachers and students. Chad's mother sought to figure out "what to do about" her son. She wanted to know "what was wrong with him" and what she should do. She felt too overwhelmed to parent him and desired to send him to a residential treatment program. It appeared to the assessors as if Chad had in many ways been on his own since he was very young. He seemed to have learned not to count on his family to help him navigate through life and was therefore figuring it out on his own, often on the streets.

DRAW-A-PERSON AND KINETIC FAMILY DRAWING: CHAD

Chad's drawings were striking in that they so concretely exemplify his coping mechanism and, at the same time, his stark inability to cope. Chad's DAP of an 11-year-old boy was likely autobiographical. The drawing resembled the boy that Chad had learned to be on the outside, and perhaps the person he wished to be on the inside. The boy was tough. He had spiked hair and broad shoulders, not to mention name-brand clothing, which may have represented financial strength. Like the boy, Chad had created a tough exterior for himself. He fought, made his own rules and, in many ways, fended for himself. Yet on the inside, Chad appeared to be quite paralyzed.

When asked to draw a picture of his family, Chad did not want to complete the task and expressed confusion to the assessor regarding what family to draw. When the assessor told him to draw whomever he considered to be his family, Chad began to draw his friend Teddy. It was immediately apparent that Chad's drawing ability regressed developmentally from the DAP where he was able to draw any person he wanted, to the KFD, where he was asked to draw his family. Furthermore, after partially completing the drawing of Teddy, Chad stopped and told the examiner that this drawing was too difficult to finish. When queried as to whom else he would have included in the picture, Chad indicated that it would have been other members of Teddy's family. The contrast between these two drawings appeared to depict that between Chad's self-made rock-hard exterior and his decimated, needy, and painful inner state.

Summary and discussion

From start to finish, HFDs stand to contribute a wealth of information to psychological assessment with children. When used in TA, a collaborative method of assessment guided by questions from the client(s), we have identified six uses for HFDs: (1) establishing and fostering the relationship between the child and the assessor; (2) observing and experiencing the child's personality and relationship capacity; (3) gaining initial impressions of how the child perceives and experiences self, family, and world through his or her drawings; (4) gaining further impressions through the child's verbal narrative elaboration of the drawings; (5) interpreting the meaning and level of awareness of the child's drawings and narrative in light of his or her current family structure, life situation, history, and current concerns ; and (6) enhancing parents' understanding and empathy for their child by providing an opportunity for the parents to experience and discuss their child's process and products with the HFD methods.

HFDs inform the assessment the instant that the child is given the instruction to draw. In this moment, characteristics of the child's personality begin to emerge through the child's interpretation of, planning (or lack thereof), and approach to the task. The assessor learns about the child and his or her relational capacity throughout the drawing process and uses the drawings and subsequent inquiry as a forum to further the relationship building process. In this context, the assessor not only experiences the child's interpersonal skills, but also senses what it feels like to spend time with the child. In examining both the overt rhythm of their interactions and his or her own counter-transference reactions to the child, the assessor develops a sense for how the child's parents and teachers may experience the child. For example, the assessor working with Chad acknowledged first being taken aback and frustrated when Chad struggled so intensely when asked to draw his family, as he had readily depicted himself when asked to produce a DAP. However, the assessor in the subsequent moments reported developing an enhanced empathy for the level at which Chad experienced his family dysfunction and felt a new connection with him.

Concurrently in TA as practiced in TAP, the child's parents observe the child from behind a one-way mirror and, with the guidance of another assessor, begin their deeper exploration into their assumptions about their child and the motivations for his or her behavior. Comments offered by the parents to the accompanying assessor also inform the assessment by helping the assessor to understand the parents' view of their child and the nature of the family system. The assessor asks questions of the parents about their child throughout the observing sessions, thereby modeling the curiosity about the child that the assessor wishes to develop in the parents. When applicable, the assessor begins to lay the groundwork for change by presenting, or "being curious about," possible alternative explanations for the child's behavior in the sessions. This behind-the-mirror observation provides a unique opportunity for the parents to observe their child while someone else interacts with their child.

Useful information also is gleaned from the drawings produced by the child and the inquiry that follows. Drawings typically solicited in TA include the DAP, HFD, KFD, and perhaps an imaginary animal. The scores assigned to these drawings are intended to be indicative of the emotional health of the child and characteristics of the child's environment and family system. The decision on how to score the drawings, however, remains a controversial one. The validity of scoring methods that involve the interpretation and summing of single, specific aspects of the drawing has not been well supported (Tharinger & Stark, 1990). Alternately, the integrated, holistic scoring approach for the DAP and KFD developed by Tharinger and Stark has demonstrated empirical validity. By this method, the assessor follows a set of guidelines to assess different characteristics of the drawing and uses the scores assigned to those aspects to inform the overall score assigned to the drawing; which represents an integration (not simply a summing) of the scores and is interpreted in terms of depicted degree of health or pathology. However, interpretations of a drawing alone are not recommended, as the narrative and context are necessary to obtain a fuller and often more complex understanding. The child's explanation of the drawing or accompanying story that follows likely provides further insight into the child and his or her worldview. The child is prompted by the assessor to answer questions about the drawing and perhaps to tell a story about it. As is the nature of TA, the type of information obtained from the inquiry is quite idiographic. The case studies presented earlier demonstrate that sometimes the information lies in exactly what is there, and at other times, what is important is what is not there. The interpretation of the drawing and the child's description is greatly enhanced when conceptualized in the context of what is known about the child and his or her family, historically and currently. For example, in her KFD Kathy depicted that her family members are somewhat cut off from one another. In the context of what was learned about the family throughout the assessment, this drawing is consistent with the notion that Kathy's family would benefit from increased communication among family members. Similarly, her DAP of the young terrified girl is consistent with other assessment findings that suggested she was depressed and had a low self-esteem. Clearly, Kathy interpreted the request to draw as an opportunity for her to directly convey to the assessor and her family how she felt. David, on the other hand, took the opposite approach. He used the drawings not to directly communicate how he experienced his life, but rather to explain how he wished his life to be. The depictions both in his DAP of a boy and his KFD appeared, in context, to be idealizations of himself and his life. Furthermore, David's drawings offered insight through the incongruence between his DAP (of a rather introverted and atypical child) and the corresponding narrative, which described a popular jock.

On the other hand, the information most compelling from Chad's HFDs was the contrast between the two drawings, and his inability to complete the KFD. Taken in context, Chad had experienced such an extreme amount of trauma in his life that his process and products in the drawing task appeared to reveal the success and failure of his coping mechanisms. His DAP of a tough boy who could take care of himself seemed to be a direct depiction of how he copes in life. Conversely, Chad refused to complete the KFD and the developmental quality of that which he did draw was astonishingly less than that of his DAP. Taken out of context, one might infer that his inability to complete the KFD was merely a demonstration of the oppositional defiant behavior that his mother and teachers complained about. When considered in the context of his family and history, however, it seemed as though Chad's inability to draw his family provided a wealth of insight into the depth of his trauma and the difficulty he experiences despite the tough exterior he learned to develop. Chad's scenario explicates the emotional difference between the request to draw "a person" or "a boy" and the instruction to draw "your family." Drawing "a boy" is a more open-ended request by which the child can depict whomever he chooses and can portray himself if he so chooses without saying it is himself. Hence, Chad was able to depict the characterization of himself that he had invented. By contrast, the request to draw "your family" was such a difficult proposition for Chad that he was unable to complete it and the person he did draw was not a family member.

Valuable information thus lies in the process, products, context, and systemic impact of HFDs in TA. As drawing is a familiar medium for young children, they are often able to convey thoughts or feelings that they cannot or do not feel comfortable vocalizing. Thus, although they are just one piece of the puzzle, HFDs have the potential to contribute multiple types and levels of information to an assessment. In closing, we hope that the rich nature of using HFDs in TA with children was apparent through the six uses proposed and illustration. We further hope that assessment professionals will be encouraged to expand their thinking about HFDs in psychological assessment, as well as to incorporate methods from TA into their assessment practices with children.

References

Finn, S. E., & Tonsager, M. E. (1997). Information-gathering and therapeutic models of assessment: Complementary paradigms. *Psychological Assessment, 9*, 374–385.

Fowler, J. C. (1998). The trouble with learning personality assessment. In L. Handler & M. J. Hilsenroth (Eds.), *Teaching and learning personality assessment*. Mahwah: Lawrence Erlbaum.

Hamilton, A. M., Fowler, J. L., Hersh, B., Austin, C. A., Finn, S. E., Tharinger, D. J., Parton, V. T., Stahl, K., & Arora, P. (2009). Why won't my parents help me? Therapeutic Assessment of a child and his family. *Journal of Personality Assessment, 91*, 108–120.

Handler, L., & Riethmiller, R. J. (1998). Teaching and learning the administration and interpretation of graphic techniques. In L. Handler & M. J. Hilsenroth, (Eds.), *Teaching and learning personality assessment*. Mahwah: Lawrence Erlbaum.

Koppitz, E. M. (1968). *Psychological evaluation of children's human figure drawings*. New York: Grune & Stratton.

Reynolds, C. R. (1978). A quick scoring guide to the interpretation of children's Kinetic Family Drawings (KFD). *Psychology in the Schools, 15*, 489–492.

Riethmiller, R. J., & Handler, L. (1997). The great figure drawing controversy: The integration of research and clinical practice. *Journal of Personality Assessment, 69*, 488–496.

Smith, B. L. (1998). The impossible takes a little longer: The role of theory in teaching psychological assessment. In L. Handler & M. J. Hilsenroth (Eds.), *Teaching and learning personality assessment*. Mahwah: Lawrence Erlbaum.

Tharinger, D. J., Finn, S. E., Gentry, L. B., Hamilton, A. M., Fowler, J. L., Matson, M., Krumholz, L., & Walkowiak, J. (2009). Therapeutic Assessment with children: A pilot study of treatment acceptability and outcome. *Journal of Personality Assessment, 91*, 238–244.

Tharinger, D. J., Krumholz, L., Austin, C., & Matson, M. (2011). The development and model of Therapeutic Assessment with children: Application to school-based assessment. In M.

A. Bray & T. J. Kehle (Eds.), *Oxford press handbook of school psychology*, (pp. 224–245). New York: Oxford University Press.

Tharinger, D. J., Matson, M., & Christopher, G. (2011). Play, creative expression, and playfulness in Therapeutic Assessment with children. In S. W. Russ & L. N. Niec (Eds.), *An evidence-based approach to play in intervention and prevention: Integrating developmental and clinical science* (pp. 109–145). New York/London: Guilford.

Tharinger, D., & Stark, K. (1990). A qualitative versus quantitative approach to evaluating the Draw-A-Person and Kinetic Family Drawing: A study of mood- and anxiety-disorder children. *Psychological Assessment: Journal of Consulting and Clinical Psychology, 2*, 365–375.

4

DRAW-A-PERSON SCREENING PROCEDURE FOR EMOTIONAL DISTURBANCE VALIDITY EVIDENCE

Achilles N. Bardos and Maria Doropoulou

Perhaps very few tools and techniques enjoy the controversy that surrounds the use of human figure drawings (HFD) in the psychological assessment literature. With a history of about 100 years the use of human figure drawings in personality assessment has indeed been controversial and conflicting. Comprehensive reviews of the literature concluded that the hypotheses posed by Machover (1949) in regard to the connection of specific signs in the drawings and psychopathology lacked empirical support (Kahill, 1984), while Koppitz's (1968) scoring system of emotional indicators on children's drawings failed the test of diagnostic utility in empirical evaluations (Mortensen, 1984). In 1991, we developed the Draw A Person: Screening Procedure for Emotional Disturbance (DAP:SPED; Naglieri, McNeish, & Bardos, 1991) in an effort to address a number of criticisms about the use of the HFD technique in psychological evaluations. First, we wanted to address the need for a refined set of scoring rules to increase objectivity in scoring and improve reliability, a serious concern noted in the literature in regards to the DAP procedures (Anastasi, 1988). We addressed this by creating scoring criteria that were objective and easy to score across three drawings of a man, woman, and self and by providing an overall score based on the evaluation of the three drawings. Scoring criteria were selected after a thorough review of the literature in regards to specific items connected to emotional disturbance, yet we selected the final set of items following specific statistical criteria in terms of the frequency of their occurrence in the general population. The general population reference group was operationalized with a nationally representative sample of 2,260 students ages 6 to 17 years old. Next, we wanted to demonstrate that the approach we were proposing could empirically demonstrate its ability to differentiate between normal and clinical populations. We offered such evidence in a series of studies we presented in the technical manual. In one study with a sample of 81 students identified and receiving services in an Ohio school under the "severe behavior handicapped" label we found the clinical sample to perform significantly higher when compared to a control sample. The participants in the study were also matched on a general nonverbal ability test and found no significant correlations between their overall IQ and DAP:SPED total scores. In another study with 49 adolescents who attended a residential psychiatric facility in New York the DAP:SPED significantly differentiated between the two groups as it did with another group of special education children in a Board of Cooperative Education Services (BOCES) setting in a western New York region. Finally, the fourth validity study, involved students who were receiving services at a day school program of the Devereux Foundation, and once again the DAP:SPED Total score significantly differentiated and identified students who were in need of a further psychological evaluation based on their performance on the DAP:SPED Total score.

Scorer reliability of human figure drawings has been in the forefront of the criticism for HFD tests. Palmer, Farrar, Nouriman Ghahary, Panella, and De-Graw (2000) reported interrater reliabilities with a median value of .52. Thomas and Jolley (1998) further suggested that there is relatively little evidence regarding the interrater reliabilities of clinician's interpretations of human figure drawings as many interpretations are not derived directly from the HFD scores. Reliability studies were conducted with the DAP:SPED. Internal consistency reliability indices were determined using the Cronbach's alpha and were in the mid 70s across males and females, substantially higher than the reliability values in the .20s reported by Anastasi (1988) for this kind of measures. In addition, interrater and intrarater reliability studies were performed. McNeish (1989), in a pilot version of the DAP:SPED reported reliability coefficients ranging from .91 (interrater) to .94 (intrarater). Similar interrater (.84) and intrarater (.83) values were reported using the final version of the DAP:SPED scoring system using a sample of 54 participants. Finally the stability of the DAP:SPED was examined by administering the scale two times over a one-week interval to a sample of 67 students who were attending a school for children with emotional difficulties and learning disabilities. The mean T-scores of 54.6 ($SD = 9.8$) and retest score of 52.9 ($SD = 8.4$) did not differ significantly. This evidence suggests that when an objective scoring system like in the DAP:SPED is applied, the decisions reached by the scores can be reliable.

It has been twenty years since Bardos (1993) responded to the critics of the Draw A Person: Screening Procedure for Emotional Disturbance (DAP:SPED; Naglieri, McNeish, & Bardos, 1991) two years after the publication of the DAP:SPED. Recognizing that there were a number of published approaches for the evaluation of human figure drawings, Bardos (1993) suggested that reviewers and critics of human figure drawings scoring systems should offer an independent evaluation of each scoring and interpretation technique and not group all HFD scoring systems and approaches into one. It is unclear why this approach is followed for HFD as we not do such "joint/group" evaluations for behavior ratings scales, other personality inventories, intelligence, or achievement tests.

Prior to presenting some of the validity evidence accumulated for the DAP:SPED during the last 20 years, we will present some specifics on the administration of the DAP:SPED, briefly demonstrate the scoring with one drawing and offer some recommendations of how this information can be used and reported in a psychological evaluation.

Administering the DAP:SPED

Administration of the DAP:SPED is simple and can be performed in a group or individual setting. The student is presented with the DAP:SPED record form, a multipage document that includes a section where the participant draws a picture of a man, woman, and self. Each of these pages is followed by a page that includes the administration directions and scoring criteria. The paper is presented folded to the client so the scoring criteria and directions are not visible. Holding the technical manual or another copy of a record form the examiner reads the following:

> I'd like you to draw some pictures for me. First I'd like you to draw a picture of a man. Make the very best picture you can. Take your time and work very carefully, and I'll tell you when to stop. Remember; be sure to draw the whole man. Please begin.
>
> (Naglieri, McNeish, & Bardos, 1991, p. 21)

The client proceeds with the drawing of a man's figure and continues in the same manner with the drawings of a woman and self. The directions are repeated each time for all three drawings. Scoring is taking place at the end of the session, once all three drawings are completed. Although not a DAP:SPED requirement or part of the test, upon completion of the drawings a brief follow-up interview with the child can take place. In this interview the examiner might ask the child to identify the person depicted, feelings, behaviors about the person depicted, and the relationship with child.

Scoring the DAP:SPED drawings

The DAP:SPED is comprised of 55 scoring criteria/items that are applied for each of the three (Man, Woman, Self) drawings separately. Upon completion of the scoring for each item, the raw scores from the three drawings are summed and a DAP:SPED Total score (T-score values with a mean of 50 and $SD = 10$) is derived using the separate gender specific norms. There are two types of DAP:SPED items. The first nine items address the physical dimensions of the drawings while the remaining items are referred to as content specific items. The measurement items were derived after a detailed measurement of all 6,000 plus drawings. All figure measurements were conducted in millimeters.

SELF

Figure 4.1 Drawing of "self" by a 9-year-old female.

For example, we obtained data on the height of each drawing in millimeters to set the criterion and determine if a figure is tall or short, the position of the drawing on the paper, (top, bottom, right, left) etc., and whether the drawing was slanted. Measuring the drawings in millimeters is not required by the DAP:SPED user, as the information obtained from these measurements were translated into 10 scoring templates/overlays. There are three sets of templates for each of the three age normative groups of 6–8, 9–12, and 13–17 years old. A template common for all ages is used to determine if a drawing is slanted

45

(right or left). When scoring, the user lays these templates on the top of each drawing and makes a dichotomous decision. When the criterion is met a score of 1 is marked. When the criterion is not met, the score is marked as 0. The greater the number of points earned translates to a higher value of a DAP:SPED Total score.

The drawing of self by a nine-year-old female is presented in Figure 4.1 to illustrate the scoring system.

A total of nine points were earned for this drawing. If we hypothesize that five more points were earned for this girl's drawing of a Man and Woman, this would result in an overall total raw score of 19. A raw score of 19 corresponds to a DAP:SPED Total score of 70. A score > 65 suggests that further evaluation is strongly indicated.

A brief description of the criteria and the points earned across the 55 items is described in Tables 4.1 and 4.2. A separate scoring template with detailed directions and sample drawings as needed is included in the DAP:SPED technical manual.

Table 4.1 Scoring a drawing and a brief description of the dap:sped measurement items

Item #	Item brief description (for a detailed description of each criterion, the user is referred to the DAP:SPED technical manual pages 27–29)	Score
1. Tall Figure	Using the proper age template, the user determines if the height of the drawing exceeds the average dimensions of figures drawn by children in the 9–12 age group. In this case the drawing earns a score of 1.	1
2. Short Figure	Because of score earned above, the score here is 0.	0
3. Big Figure	Using the proper age template the user determines if the size of the drawing exceeds the dimensions (height and width) of the figures drawn by children in the 9–12 age group. In this case the drawing earns a score of 1.	1
4. Little Figure	Because of score earned in #3 above, the score here is 0.	0
5. Top Placement	Using the proper age template the user determines if the drawing is placed high enough to earn a point, which is not the case here.	0
6. Bottom Placement	Similarly, it earns a score of 0 for this item.	0
7. Left Placement	Using the proper age template the user determines if the drawing is placed towards the right or left side of the page, which is not the case for item 7, earning a score of 0.	0
8. Right Placement	Similarly, it earns a score of 0 for this item.	0
9. Slanting Figure	The drawing is not slanted (a template is available).	0

Table 4.2 Scoring a drawing and a brief description of the dap:sped content items

Item #		Score
1. Legs Together	The drawing earns a score if the legs are drawn together with no visible space between them.	0
2. Baseline Drawn	A score is earned if a ground line, grass, is present.	1
3. Lettering-Numbering	This score is earned if letters or words appear anywhere on the page other than the figure (i.e., Me).	1
4. Rotated Page	If the child rotated the page to draw the figure.	0
5. Left/right Facing Figure	A score is earned if the entire figure or the head is in right or left facing position.	0
6. Figure Facing Away	A score is earned if the figure's head is facing away.	0
7. Failed Integration	The three criteria for this particular item relate to the proper attachment of body parts, i.e., head, arms, etc.	0
8. Transparencies	If a body part is showing through clothing.	0
9. Restart	If a drawing was abandoned and a new one was included.	0
10. Head Omitted	If this body part is absent.	0
11. Hair Omitted	If this body part is absent.	0
12. Eyes Omitted	If this body part is absent.	0
13. Nose Omitted	If this body part is absent.	0
14. Mouth Omitted	If this body part is absent.	0
15. Torso Omitted	If this body part is absent.	0
16. Arms Omitted	If this body part is absent.	0
17. Fingers Omitted	If this body part is absent.	0
18. Legs Omitted	If this body part is absent.	0
19. Feet Omitted	If this body part is absent.	0
20. Crotch Erasure	If you erasure is apparent in the area of the figure's crotch.	0
21. Crotch Shading	If this body part is present, or as described.	0
22. Hand Shading	If this body part is present, or as described.	0
23. Legs Together	The drawing earns a score if the legs are drawn together with no visible space between them.	0
24. Baseline Drawn	A score is earned if a ground line, grass, is present.	1
25. Lettering-Numbering	This score is earned if letters or words appear anywhere on the page other than the figure (i.e., Me).	1
26. Rotated Page	If the child rotated the page to draw the figure.	0
27. Left/right Facing Figure	A score is earned if the entire figure or the head is in right or left facing position.	0

(Continued)

Table 4.2 (Continued)

Item #		Score
28. Figure Facing Away	A score is earned if the figure's head is facing away.	0
29. Failed Integration	The three criteria for this particular item relate to the proper attachment of body parts, i.e., head, arms, etc.	0
30. Transparencies	If a body part is showing through clothing.	0
31. Restart	If a drawing was abandoned and a new one was included.	0
32. Head Omitted	If this body part is absent.	0
33. Hair Omitted	If this body part is absent.	0
34. Eyes Omitted	If this body part is absent.	0
35. Nose Omitted	If this body part is absent.	0
36. Mouth Omitted	If this body part is absent.	0
37. Torso Omitted	If this body part is absent.	0
38. Arms Omitted	If this body part is absent.	0
39. Fingers Omitted	If this body part is absent.	0
40. Legs Omitted	If this body part is absent.	0
41. Feet Omitted	If this body part is absent.	0
42. Crotch Erasure	If you erasure is apparent in the area of the figure's crotch.	0
43. Crotch Shading	If this body part is present, or as described.	0
44. Hand Shading	If this body part is present, or as described.	0

Reporting the DAP:SPED scores and performance in a psychological report

Findings of the DAP:SPED evaluation can be presented in a psychological report as follows:

> Julie's emotional status was assessed using several measures, including the drawing of human figures. On the Draw A Person: Screening Procedure for Emotional Disturbance (DAP:SPED), she earned a T-score of 64 (90% confidence range is 58–70) which is ranked at the 92nd meaning and suggests that her drawings included more signs of possible emotional difficulties than about 92% of children the same age in the general population. This performance suggested that further evaluation of her emotional well-being was strongly indicated.

If additional data on the drawings become available through a follow-up interview with the child, they can be presented as well. However, a clear distinction is recommended in the reporting as one piece of evidence is based on an objective scoring system while others are based on a clinical interpretation.

Learning the DAP:SPED scoring system

The procedures and sample drawings used for the training of the DAP:SPED standardization sample examiners are presented in a separate chapter on the DAP:SPED technical manual. It is recommended that in order to be considered a "trained," competent examiner/user, these samples be completed by future users of the DAP:SPED procedure in order to maintain reliable scoring outcomes.

Validity evidence of the DAP:SPED

In the next few paragraphs we will present the findings of some research studies for the DAP:SPED reported in the literature for a period of about 20 years. The validity evidence is organized according to the proposed uses of the DAP:SPED.

The DAP:SPED as a screening tool for the identification of emotional difficulties

The main validity claim for the DAP:SPED, as the test name implies, is its use and function as a measure to identify children with emotional and behavior difficulties. A number of studies have been conducted to establish the validity evidence of the DAP:SPED as a screening tool. Brief summaries of these studies are discussed below.

In a study with 54 children diagnosed with an emotional disorder, Naglieri and Pfeiffer (1992) reported the mean DAP:SPED scores to be significantly higher than those of a control group of children in regular education. Seventy-eight percent of the control group and 48% of the clinical group were identified correctly using the proposed by the DAP:SPED cut-off T-score of 55. Twenty-two percent of the control group was identified as false positive and 52% of clinical group was identified as false negative. About 26% fewer errors were made on the basis of the DAP:SPED scores alone relative to what it would be expected by chance alone (Naglieri & Pfeiffer, 1992).

Similarly, McNeish & Naglieri (1993), administered the DAP:SPED to 81 regular education and 81 students in special education with serious emotional disturbance between the ages of 7 and 13. There were significant differences between the mean T-scores earned by special education students ($M = 55.3$, $SD = 10.6$) in comparison to the regular education sample ($M = 49.5$, $SD = 8.6$). The study reported that, using the T = 55 as a recommended cut-off score for further evaluation, 59% of the special education students were correctly identified in their respective groups, and 68% of the general education students were correctly identified as not needing further evaluation. The authors reported that use of the DAP:SPED alone would result in an 18% of the children classified correctly beyond a level that would have been expected by chance alone.

A sample of 126 students, 63 of whom were diagnosed and receiving special education services under the Severe Emotional Disturbance category in Colorado and a matched regular education sample, were administered the DAP:SPED as well as two rating scales, the Devereux School Form (Naglieri, Lebuffe, & Pfeiffer, 1993) and the Millon Adolescent Clinical Inventory (MACI; Millon, Millon, Davis, & Grossman, 1993). The clinical sample performed significantly different across all three measures (Dwors, 1996, see discussion below on incremental validity).

Wrightson and Saklofske (2000) administered the DAP:SPED to a sample of 77 secondary school students from an urban Canadian school district. They examined its ability to discriminate between three groups of students. These were mainstream students, students who attend an alternative school for children with special social, emotional, and academic needs, and students with severe behavioral problems who have had multiple suspensions or expulsions from school. Although no differences were found between the two special education groups, statistically significant differences were found between the regular mainstream group and both the alternate education and behavior groups. Surprisingly, although the authors reported statistically significant differences between the regular education ($M = 44.8$; $SD = 8.2$) and both the alternate special education placement group 54.4 ($SD = 8.4$) and the group with the behavior issues 57.30 ($SD = 13.5$), findings which were consistent with all other similar studies, they contradicted their findings stating that the DAP:SPED may have limited utility in the identification of adolescents with behavior problems. This remains a puzzling interpretation! The study also examined the DAP:SPED's concurrent validity with other behavioral measures, the Teacher Report Form of the Child Behavior Checklist (CBCL) and the Devereux Behavior Rating Scale—School Form (DBRSSF). Significant but low positive correlations were obtained between the DAP:SPED total score and the subscale and total scores of the other measures. This finding is consistent with reports by Bardos (1995) who also reported low and non-significant correlation between the DAP:SPED and the Devereux Behavior Rating scales for a sample of 5–12 years old children but statistically significant correlations for the 13–18 years old group.

The relationship between the DAP:SPED and its relationship to internalizing and externalizing behaviors utilizing a shortened version of the Child Behavior Checklist (SAC) and a measure of psychological adjustment (Child and Adolescent Adjustment Profile—CAAP) was administered to a sample of 68 children who were receiving clinical services through outpatient or residential treatment centers (Matto, 2002). Using the DAP:SPED as predictor of externalizing behaviors and after controlling for CAAP's Hostility, the DAP:SPED was not found to be a significant predictor well and beyond of what the CAAP's Hostility scale was offering. However, after controlling for the CAAP Withdrawal, the

DAP:SPED accounted for an additional 10.8% of total variance, indicating that the DAP:SPED scores were related to higher internalized behavior difficulties. The author concluded that in addition to the parent data the DAP:SPED offers significant clinical data for triangulation purposes that have the potential to improve the clinical decision making process.

In another study, Matto, Naglieri, and Clausen (2005) examined the performance and relationship between the DAP:SPED and a strength-based emotional and behavior based assessments for a group of 9 to 14-year-old students. A sample of 91 students in regular education and a sample of 18 with a diagnosis of emotional disturbance were administered the DAP:SPED and the Behavior and Emotional Rating Scale (BERS-2; Epstein & Sharma, 1998), a strength-based, standardized, norm-referenced tool that assesses a child's strengths across five subscales: Interpersonal Strengths, Family Involvement, Intrapersonal Strengths, School Functioning, and Affective Strengths. Statistically significant differences were found between the DAP:SPED total score for the special education group ($M = 56.1$; $SD = 10.9$) and the regular education sample ($M = 50.02$; $SD = 8.38$). The Interpersonal (a measure of emotional control and affect management) and Intrapersonal (a measure of a child's broad sense of self) strengths were used in the study and found to correlate significantly with the DAP:SPED (.36 and .34), respectively, for ratings completed by the parents and students themselves (.27) for the Intrapersonal scale.

In summary, the DAP:SPED was developed to serve as an easy to administer and score procedure to identify children with emotional difficulties. As a tool it offers a means of collecting data by allowing the child to express their inner world through the drawings of human figures, "presenting" with drawing the adults he/she relates to and the perception of themselves. It is perhaps the supportive evidence accumulated over the years that lead some researchers and reviewers to conclude that "there is some evidence that the DAP:SPED can be used to screen for mental disorders among children" (Garb, Wood, Lilienfeld, & Nezworski, 2002, p. 459).

Incremental validity of the DAP:SPED in psychological evaluations

Incremental validity refers to the degree/amount of predictive validity a tool is able to add in an evaluation over and above the information offered by other already administered tools. In the Dwors (1996) study described earlier with a matched sample of special of special and regular education children the correlations between the DAP:SPED and the Millon Adolescent Clinical Inventory and Devereux School Form were low and nonsignificant. However when a discriminating analysis was performed to test the differential diagnosis strength of the tools, utilizing all variables by the three measures (MACI, Devereux, and DAP:SPED), the Devereux Depression and Interpersonal scales, the DAP:SPED, followed by the MACI Personality Patterns Unruly and Inhibited

51

scales contributed the greatest amount in correctly classifying the students in their two respective groups of regular and special education. In a follow up stepwise discriminating analysis, once again the Devereux Depression and Interpersonal scales contributed the most in the correct classification of the students followed by the DAP:SPED and MACI Conforming scale score. When Jackknife classification analyses were performed, once with only the Devereux and DAP:SPED and an additional with only the Devereux and MACI, the overall classification accuracy was almost identical with 89.7% and 88.1 % values, respectively. When the Devereux, DAP:SPED, and MACI were used alone as criterion variables, the overall correct classification reached were 88.9%, 64.3%, and 61.9%. These finding suggest that use of either of the two over and above the administration of the Devereux will result in similar classification accuracy. However, given the cost and resource requirements of the DAP:SPED and MACI, respectively, one might consider this issue as it might have significant resource and financial implications in a school setting.

In the Matto et.al. (2005) study—described earlier—the incremental predictive validity of the DAP:SPED with the Interpersonal and Interpersonal Strength based measures also demonstrated that the DAP:SPED accounted for 7 % of the variance in these measures after controlling for age, gender, and race. When controlling for gender and the student report of Intrapersonal Strength, the DAP:SPED accounted for an additional 5% of variation suggesting that "the DAP:SPED remains a significant predictor in variance accounted for even after the effects of the student–report measure are partialled out" (Matto et al., 2005, p. 44). Reporting on the relationship between the Interpersonal and Intrapersonal measures and special education placement, the authors concluded that "the DAP:SPED appears to be a strong measure in capturing the interpersonal dimension" of a youth's emotional and behavior functioning.

Calculating the value of DAP:SPED incremental validity, however, might not be as simple of a matter. Perhaps the quantitative value of the score offered by the DAP:SPED alone might not capture the value seen by 39% of clinical psychologist who reported "always or frequently" using human figure drawings in their evaluations and 80% of them who use it "at least occasionally" (Watkins, Campbell, Nieberding, & Hallmark, 1995).

Performance of race and ethnic groups

"Projective techniques may be biased against North American minority groups and individuals who live outside North America (Lilienfeld et al., 2000). The use and interpretation of human figure drawings across ethnic and cultural groups has been addressed in the literature with Handler and Habernicht (1994) reporting significant differences across ethnic groups and an recommendation that caution should be exercised when using and interpreting human figure drawings with minority and non-Americans. A small number of studies have been completed relevant to this issue, addressing the performance of minority and cultural groups on the DAP:SPED. The studies reported below do not address issues of bias per se, as we believe the concept of bias requires a data driven comprehensive examination, and it is our belief that the term "bias" is used and referred to too loosely by researchers and practitioners.

Naglieri et al. (1991) performed an analysis of race and ethnic difference between male and female, Black and White students across the three age groups of the DAP:SPED standardization sample and found minor to no statistically significant differences. Similarly, no significant differences were found between Hispanic and non-Hispanic students for the 6–8 and 9–12 age groups, with significant differences noted for the 13–17 year old age group. Hispanic students earned a higher score on the DAP:SPED ($M = 53.36$, $SD = 10$) than the non-Hispanic students ($M = 49.61$, $SD = 9.68$). To examine the performance of different race and ethnic populations, Matto and Naglieri (2005) acquired two matched on gender, grade, and school classroom samples of 394 children and adolescents between the ages of 6 through 17 years of age from DAP:SPED nationally representative sample. No significant differences were found for the size of figures and the presence of shading on drawings by Black and White children. A statistically significant difference but with a small effect size (.25) was found between Black–White pairs on the figure omissions composite. Similarly, no statistically significant differences were found between the DAP:SPED total T-scores among the sample pairs (Black and White youth or Hispanic and White youth), which lends support to the hypothesis that the DAP:SPED yields similar scores across these ethnic and racial groups.

The construct of perception of time has been discussed as a cultural variable to consider when working with various ethnic and cultural groups. Since the DAP:SPED requires the completion of the three drawings within a five-minute time limit a study was conducted (Helm-Yost, 1993) with Navajo children. One of the study's goals was to examine whether a timed or untimed administration is a confounding variable when calculating the overall DAP:SPED: T-score. The study examined the performance of 40 male and female reservation Navajo children who attended public schools, 20 of them previously identified with an emotional disability. DAP:SPED: T-scores alone accurately identified 6 of the 12 subjects. Of the six participants, four performed within the "indicated further evaluation" DAP:SPED classification recommendation, and the remaining with the further evaluation is "strongly indicated". In addition, using comparison groups of typically developed and children with emotional difficulties, the DAP:SPED was administered with the timed standardization procedures and comparison groups were administered the test in untimed conditions. There were no differences (main effect of time) reported between the two administrations, suggesting that the DAP:SPED scores of Navajo children were not influenced by whether the DAP:SPED was administered in a timed or untimed conditions for both the typical as well as the group identified with emotional difficulties.

In a study conducted in Greece, Politikos (1997) used the same steps and statistical procedures that were applied for the development of the DAP:SPED in the United States. An item analysis was performed for 93 "candidate" items/signs for the final DAP:SPED scoring system, for each of the three drawings of 240 students, ages 8 to 11 years old. The students were attending two private schools in Athens, Greece. Of the 240 subjects, 52.5% were male and 47.5% were female and attended third (36%), fourth (33%), and fifth (31%) grades. Similar to the U.S. sample, there were significant gender differences with males scoring higher than females on the overall DAP:SPED Total raw score. This however was observed only on the Woman and Self drawings, while there were no gender differences present on the Man drawing. In order to determine if the DAP:SPED Greek data and the U.S. norms are similar, for potential use of the DAP:SPED with Greek children, item frequencies were examined and compared to determine if the items in the Greek children's drawings shared the same statistical properties as the ones in the U.S. sample. As with the U.S. sample, the rule of items occurring with less than 16% frequency for both the content and measurement features was applied. Only 50 out of the 55 DAP:SPED items appeared infrequently in Greek children's drawings. Although this indicates an overall agreement between indicators of emotional disturbance for the U.S. and Greek samples, interestingly enough, none of the DAP:SPED measurement items appeared significant for the Greek population. These findings offer support to Handler and Habernicht (1994) suggestion of cultural differences in human figure drawings and suggest that a new standardization sample and scoring specific to Greek children's drawings must be developed along with supported validation studies. No other studies outside the United States and Canada are known that have utilized the DAP:SPED scoring system thus this remains an area that deserves further exploration.

Performance of other special groups and settings

Drawings of sexually abused children

There are numerous articles, studies, and opinions regarding human figure drawings and their use in psychological evaluations of sexually abused children. In a study that investigated the impact of rater knowledge on sexually abused and nonabused girls' scores on the DAP:SPED, Human Figure drawings of 20 sexually abused and 20 nonsexually abused girls were randomly assigned and scored in conditions where the examiners were either aware or not of the child's abuse history. Three examiners independently rated the drawings. "Results revealed no significant effect for girls' abuse status or the case description given to raters, thereby suggesting that the DAP:SPED is sufficiently objective to withstand the confounding influence of varying case descriptions" (Bruening, Wagner, & Johnson, 1997).

Students with hearing impairments

In a statewide study in Colorado with children receiving services due to hearing impairments, McCall, Benyamin, and Bardos (2012) reported that from a total of 305 children identified and receiving special education services, mostly with learning issues, only six of them were receiving services for emotional difficulties. When scoring these children's drawings with the DAP:SPED screening criteria 74 students earned a DAP:SPED score that would classify them in the "further evaluation" recommended category, while 45 earned a DAP:SPED score of 65 and above, in the "strongly recommended" for further evaluation category. This data suggest that perhaps children who are deaf might not receive comprehensive special education services that address their emotional needs as well. However the findings reported in the literature with the DAP:SPED and the performance of hearing impaired children were not consistent. In a study with 39 hearing impaired children (Briccetti, 1994) the DAP:SPED did not discriminate between emotionally disturbed and a control group and the DAP:SPED misclassified students according to emotional functioning as measured by a behavior rating scale completed by the students' teachers. Although this study ignored previous findings that behavior rating scales have shown low correlations with human figure drawings, the findings point to conflicting evidence. One could safely conclude that the verdict is still out for the DAP:SPED with this clinical population.

DAP:SPED: Looking forward

Twenty years ago we wanted to develop a scoring procedure for human figure drawings using an actuarial approach to address issues of objectivity in the scoring and interpretation. We utilized a nationally standardized sample with drawings of over 2,000 children to establish a database of how typically developed children draw and supported the toll with additional validity studies. Although the evidence of the DAP:SPED has been supportive, the test can benefit from a new standardization sample. For some difficult to comprehend reasons, publishers of many frequently used personality assessment inventories resist in obtaining recent standardization data when compared to practices with intelligence and achievement tests.

In conclusion, the validity studies presented in this brief review offer support for the DAP:SPED intended use and claims presented in its technical manual. That is, the DAP:SPED can function as a screening measure of emotional difficulties and contribute to personality assessment evaluations. Like with any other tool, the DAP:SPED should not be used alone to identify or diagnose emotional difficulties or disorders. Practitioners who choose to use the DAP:SPED must read the technical manual and complete the "Learning the scoring" relevant chapter. Additional training materials can also be found at www.AchillesBardos.com.

References

Anastasi, A. (1988). *Psychological testing* (6th ed.). New York: MacMillan.

Bardos, A. N. (1993). Human Figure Drawings: Abusing the abused. *School Psychology Quarterly, 8,* 177–181.

Bardos, A. N. (January, 1995). *Screening for emotional disturbance using a new Draw A Person scoring system.* Paper presented at the Assessment 95th conference, Tuscon, AZ.

Briccetti, K. (1994). Emotional indicators of deaf children on the Draw-A-Person test. *American Annals of the Deaf, 139,* 500–505.

Bruening, C. C., Wagner, W. G., & Johnson, J. T. (1997). Impact of rater knowledge on sexually abused and non-abused girls' scores on the Draw-A-Person: Screening Procedure for Emotional Disturbance (DAP:SPED). *Journal of Personality Assessment, 68,* 665–677.

Dwors, J. (1996). *Differences in normal and seriously emotional disturbed students on the Devereux Behavior Rating Scale-School Form, DAP:SPED and the Millon Adolescent Clinical Inventory.* Unpublished doctoral dissertation, University of Northern Colorado, Greeley, Colorado.

Epstein, M. H., & Sharma, J. (1998). Behavioral and emotional rating scale: A strength-based approach to assessment. Austin, TX: PRO-ED.

Garb, H. N., Wood, J. M., Lilienfeld, S. O., & Nezworski, M. T. (2002). Effective use of projective techniques in clinical practice: Let the data help with selection and interpretation. *Professional Psychology: Research & Practice, 33,* 454–463.

Handler, L. & Habenicht, D. (1994). The Kinetic Family Drawing Test: A review of the literature. *Journal of Personality Assessment, 62* (3), 440–464.

Helm-Yost, D. (1993). *The differentiation ability of the DAP:SPED with Navajo children when considering the variable of time.* Doctoral dissertation, Northern Arizona University.

Kahill, S. (1984). Human Figure Drawings in adults: An update of the empirical evidence, 1967–1982. *Canadian Psychology, 25,* 269–292.

Koppitz, E. M. (1968). *Psychological evaluation of children's human figure drawings.* New York: Grune & Stratton.

Lilienfeld, S. O., Wood, J. M., & Garb, H. N (2000). The scientific status of projective techniques. *Psychological Science in the Public Interest, 1* (2), 27–66.

McCall, C., Benyamin, N. & Bardos, A. (November 2012). Effectiveness of the Draw A Person: screening procedure for emotional disturbance in children with hearing impairments. Poster presented at the Colorado Society for School Psychologists Annual conference, Beaver Creek, Colorado.

Machover, K. (1949). *Personality projection in the drawing of a human figure.* Springfield: Charles C. Thomas.

Matto, H. C. (2002). Investigating the validity of the Draw-A-Person: Screening Procedure for Emotional Disturbance: A measurement validation study with high-risk youth. *Psychological Assessment, 14,* 221–225.

Matto, H., & Naglieri, J. A. (2005). Race and ethnic differences and human figure drawings: Clinical utility of the DAP:SPED. *Journal of Clinical Child and Adolescent Psychology, 34,* 706–711.

Matto, H., Naglieri, J. A, & Clausen, C. (2005). Validity of the Draw-A-Person: Screening Procedure for Emotional Disturbance (DAP:SPED) in strengths-based assessment. *Research on Social Work Practice, 15,* 41–46.

McNeish, T. J. (1989). *Reliability and validity of a human figure drawing screening measure to identify emotional or behavior disorders in children.* Unpublished doctoral dissertation, Ohio State University, Columbus, Ohio.

McNeish, T. J., & Naglieri, J. A. (1993). Identification of individuals with serious emotional disturbance using the Draw a Person: Screening Procedure for Emotional Disturbance. *Journal of Special Education, 27,* 115–121.

Millon, T., Millon, C. R., Davis, R., & Grossman, S. (1993). *The Millon Adolescent Clinical Inventory (MACI).* Minneapolis: Pearson.

Mortensen, K.V. (1984). *Children's human figure drawings: Development, sex differences and relation to psychological theories.* Dansk: Psykologisk Forlag.

Naglieri, J. A., Lebuffe, P., & Pfeiffer, S. (1993). *Devereux Behavior Rating scale- School form manual.* San Antonio, TX: The Psychological Corporation.

Naglieri, J. A., McNeish, T., & Bardos, A. N. *Draw A Person: Screening Procedure for Emotional Disturbance.* Austin, TX: Pro-Ed, Inc.

Naglieri, J. A., & Pfeiffer, S. I. (1992). Performance of disruptive behaviors disordered and normal samples on the Draw A Person: Screening Procedure for Emotional Disturbance. *Psychological Assessment, 4,* 156–159.

Palmer, L., Farrar, A.N., Nouriman Ghahary, M.V., Panella, M., & DeGraw, D. (2000). An investigation of the clinical use of the House-Tree-Person projective drawings in the psychological evaluation of child sexual abuse. *Child Maltreatment, 5* (2), 169–175.

Politikos, N. (1997). *A cross validation of the Draw A Person: Quantitative Scoring System and the Draw A Person: Screening Procedure For Emotional Disturbance.* Unpublished doctoral dissertation; University of Northern Colorado, Greeley, Colorado.

Thomas, G. V., & Jolley, R. P. (1998). Drawing conclusions: A re-examination of empirical and conceptual bases for psychological evaluations of children from their drawings. *British Journal of Clinical Psychology, 37,* 127–139.

Watkins, C. E., Campbell, V. L.; Nieberding, R., & Hallmark, R. (1995) Contemporary practice of psychological assessment by clinical psychologists. *Professional Psychology: Research and Practice, 26,* 54–60.

Wrightson, L., & Saklofske, D. H. (2000). Validity and reliability of the Draw a Person: Screening Procedure for Emotional Disturbance with adolescent students. *Canadian Journal of School Psychology, 16,* 95–102.

5

SEXUALLY AND PHYSICALLY ABUSED CHILDREN

Antoinette D. Thomas and Deborah Engram

Human figure drawing and emotional distress

Human figure drawing (HFD) has been used as a measure of projected self, based on one's body image since Machover's work in 1949. Subjects do not only project on drawing their present self (Hammer, 1958) but also threat perceived in others (Falk, 1981) among other projections. Family drawings release additional feelings in the context of family interpersonal relationships (Burns & Kaufman, 1972; Di Leo, 1983).

Sexually and physically abused children are likely to express their emotional distress in their figure drawings. Blain, Bergner, Lewis, and Goldstein (1981) assert that figure drawings are most appropriate means of detection in child abuse. However, the focus has been shifted from detection to understanding and guiding psychotherapy (Piperno, Di Biasi, & Levi, 2007).

Drawings serve as disguised, unobtrusive measures because they do not rely on conscious report. Abused children are not likely to report ill treatment; they are verbally unsophisticated and may repress or suppress their feelings. Drawings seem to be an answer to the need for non-physical indicators of abuse. Physical signs are not always present or observable and, even when observed, they are open to multiple interpretations. Furthermore, abusing parents do not seek immediate medical attention. Internal feelings, experiences, and thoughts are revealed in drawings because they are not obscured by psychological defenses such as self-blaming (Timberlake, 1979).

Meta-analysis

Meta-analysis of 12 studies (West, 1998) of sexually abused and nonabused children indicated that projective techniques, including Draw-A-Person (DAP, Harris, 1963), can discriminate abused/distressed from non–abused/non-distressed children quite well. Sexually abused children drew more anxiety signs derived from Koppitz (1968) Emotional Indicators than nonabused children (Hibbard & Hartman, 1990). Physically abused children expressed their feelings of inadequacy and insecurity in their figure drawings (Hammer, 1968; Hjorth & Harway, 1981).

An empirical study

Thomas and Engram's (1986) study included 20 children (10 sexually and 10 physically abused). These children constituted all complete files of abuse cases referred to a rural public health clinic in Alberta, Canada during one calendar year. All studied material was derived from the clinic's archives, preserving children and families' anonymity. The clinic also served an Indian reserve. One child was eliminated to avoid the confounding effect of mental retardation on results (Wysocki & Wysocki, 1973). The definitions of both types of abuse followed those accepted by social and mental health agencies. Abusive acts occurred within one year prior to testing. All tests were previously individually administered and scored by the second author. This clinical psychologist also provided children's brief history and spontaneous comments they made on their drawings.

Each child was individually administered an intelligence test, one very young child in each abusive group was given the Wechsler Preschool and Primary Scale of Intelligence (WPPSI, Wechsler, 1963), otherwise the Wechsler Intelligence Scale for Children-Revised (WISC-R, Wechsler, 1974), was administered. Only self-presentation of Draw-A-Person test (Harris, 1963) was administered and the cognitive/developmental aspect scored.

"Draw-A-Family" test (Hulse, 1952) was chosen because the instructions do not specify self-inclusion, as does the Kinetic Family Drawings (Burns & Kaufman, 1972). Self-exclusion is considered an important emotional element (Di Leo, 1973, 1983). The DAP preceded Family Drawings. An honors psychology student performed statistical analyses.

Of the 20 children, 9 were Cree Indians (three males, six females) and 11 were White Canadians six males, five females). Males and females were unevenly presented in the two abusive categories, as commonly found in national statistics. Survivors of sexual abuse were two males and eight females, while those exposed to physical abuse were seven males and three females. Three sexually abused children were also physically abused or neglected. Physically abused children were not sexually abused. Children's upper age limit was determined by the Goodenough-Harris test norms. They ranged from 4 to 15 with an average child age of nine years ($SD = 2.9$). According to Piagetian stages, three groups were formed for statistical manipulation: up to 7 years, 8–11 years and 12–15 years.

Single human figures

Cognitive impairments

Analysis of variance (ANOVA, Graziano & Raulin, 1993), examined age groups by sex by race by abusive category by cognitive scores ($3 \times 2 \times 2 \times 2 \times 2$).

A clean main effect ($F = 7.43, p < .02$) indicated that Full Scale intelligence scores (WISC-R or equivalent) were significantly higher than the DAP cognitive scores.

Emotional distress, or other forms of psychopathology, may be reflected on drawing performance, as concluded by reviewers of research on the DAP (Abell, Von Briesen, & Watz, 1996). Abell et al. warned against using the DAP as a measure of cognitive ability on clinical populations, since the Goodenough-Harris was originally validated within normal school children. Abell et al. found the mean standard score for the DAP to be significantly lower than the mean Full IQ on the WISC-R in a large outpatient mental health sample of children 5 to 15 years of age. Similar results were obtained from another study on a large sample of adolescent boys 14 to 15 years old at a residential treatment center (Abell, Horkheimer, & Horkheimer, 1998).

The magnitude of mean scores differences in the present study exceeded those reported in both the above-mentioned studies (13.9 points versus 10 and 5 points, respectively, Table 5.1). Culbertson (1987) also reported statistically significant lower scores on the DAP than the WISC-R in a physically abused group of children as compared to matching learning disabled and emotionally disturbed groups.

Similar results were found upon the use of another method of analysis of variance (F test) between scores on the WISC-R (or equivalent) and the DAP. Differences were statistically significant for: (a) whole sample ($F = 12.87, p = .001$), (b) sexually abused group ($F = 5.35, p < .05$) and (c) physically abused group ($F = 5.56, p < .05$).

As groups, children under investigation showed intellectual inhibition when they drew human figures. That is, the pain and humiliation they had experienced as persons and were inflicted upon them by others have distorted their former integrated perceptions of humans. Therefore, they drew poor figures, in terms of details, proportion, and perspective, all of which lead to low scores on

Table 5.1 Rounded summary statistics on the wisc-r or equivalent and the draw-a-person test for physically and sexually abused children

	Physically Abused (n = 10)	Sexually Abused (n = 10)	Total Group (N = 20)
Wechsler IQ			
M	95.5	94.6	95.1
SD	12.7	13.9	13.0
DAP			
M	83.5	79.0	81.2
SD	9.9	12.8	11.3
(DAP minus IQ)			
M	−12.0	−15.7	−13.9
SD	12.2	13.8	12.8

the DAP. In examining these results, however, one should take into consideration small sample size and unequal cell sizes.

No statistically significant differences were found for sex, race, and category of abuse or age groups. Similarly, no interaction between variables was statistically significant. In addition, there were no statistically significant variations within variables (Multivariate Analysis of Variance [MANOVA]). That is, compared to one's intellectual potential as assessed by a formal IQ test (Wechsler tests), a child's intellectual potential was meaningfully reduced in a task involving human context which reflected own body image as well as other human images, when such a child was exposed to sexual or physical abuse.

Distress characteristics

Drawings' *global quality* was primarily considered. That is, the general impression given by a drawing which involves clusters of drawing characteristics, rather than individual signs in drawing literature.

However, considering Emotional Indicators (EI, Koppitz, 1968) identified in a list of drawing signs derived from Machover, Hammer as well as her own clinical work. These signs differentiated between children with and without emotional problems, were found in up to 15% of HFDs at a given age from five to twelve, and were not related to age or maturation. Combinations of her well-known Emotional Indicators were supported by her research results and have been subject to controversial results when taken separately.

In the sexually abused group, two Emotional Indicators were found. **Absence of hands and fingers** (three cases) pointing to difficulties in reaching out for others to communicate with and **one or both hands shorter than waist**, which implied similar connotation (seven cases). Two Emotional Indicators were found in the physically abused group. **Absence of feet** two cases) reflecting feelings of immobility as well as **presence of teeth** (five cases) symbolizing aggression, either one are own or as perceived in others.

The number of various Emotional Indicators was considered. In the sexually abused group, one EI was found in five cases, and three to six were noticed in three cases. In the physically abused group, one EI was found in three cases, and two to four were seen in six cases.

Identified drawing characteristics: Eyes

Interesting characteristics were observed in single figures' eyes (House-Tree-Person [HTP]: Self). According to children's verbal comments within the *sexually* abused group, those who seem to consider the experience as an initiation into an adult-like life—regardless of their feelings toward abusers—drew **large cosmetic eyes with eyelashes** (four cases). Such eyes symbolized both cosmetic adult women's eyes and readiness for more visual stimuli.

While those who reported excessive emotional distress drew **dots, dashes, or hollow eyes** (five cases). Symbolic inference is lack of interest in perceiving the environment (Burns & Kaufman, 1972). Yates, Beutler, and Crago (1985) found that female incest victims tended to either over or under represent secondary sexual characteristics in figure drawings.

These two opposing characteristics balance each other therefore cancel statistical significance in groups.

Eyes drawn as **dots, dashes, or hollow eyes** (eyes without pupils) were also found in 8 out of 10 single figures drawn by *physically* abused children. Hollow eyes was statistically and significantly discriminative of physically abused children (Culbertson, 1987).

Illustrations

SEXUALLY ABUSED CHILDREN

1. Large cosmetic eyes

In single figure drawing (Figure 5.1), the significance of large opened eyes with eyelashes were supported by cosmetic lips and incomplete erasing of the upper body in an attempt to draw full breasts, as noted by the examiner. In reality, the subject had a skinny underdeveloped body, which may have added to her fantasy of being a woman, prematurely imposed by the abusive act. The subject identified her single figure drawing as "a 15 year old girl; me." Adding a year to her age, provided yet another corroborative element. Incomplete erasing and redrawing of the lower body also reflected preoccupation and conflict concerning this area. Global impression could be "unhappiness."

Family drawing consisted of only one person; her abusive father portrayed as a muscular male in his underwear, which he was not in reality according to therapist's notes. This figure clearly illustrated his perceived physical overpower. The inappropriate clothes are not common in children's drawings of their families. Being the sole figure also reflected the magnitude of his presence in the perception of her family. His wide-open eyes, similar to eyes in self-presentation in single figure, are projections identified in this study of "seeing too much" as an early inappropriate introduction to sexuality. The subject commented on her family drawing "I chose not to think of my mother as family, I certainly am not going to do anything with him." Such was her verbal rational for the exclusion of the maternal figure as well as self-presentation in family drawing. It was also an attempted denial of a conflictuous reality.

2. Hollow eyes

Hollow eyes in self-presentation reflected blocking of visual input, as chosen by a 10-year-old boy (Figure 5.2).

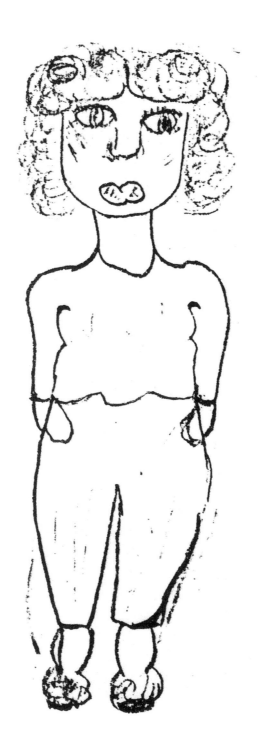

Figure 5.1

Figure 5.2

Poor erasing and redrawing appeared in the genital area reflecting emotional difficulties associated with this body part. Similar performance in the head reflected troubled thoughts and memories.

In family drawing, all family members, parents, sibling, and self-presentation were drawn facing a TV set with their backs to the viewer. This presentation is a strong indication of a withdrawal desire (Hammer, 1964).

An uncle sexually assaulted him while he was in the shower. He told the examiner that he did not enjoy the experience, was very stressed, and could not accept it. He developed asthma attacks whenever an adult male entered the house.

3. Dashes for eyes

Self-presentation of an 11-year-old girl had dashes for eyes and mouth, single lined arms and legs, club feet, omission of nose, neck, and waist, as well as messy hair (Figure 5.3). It is a dramatic portray of the child's pain and depression. The figure's developmental level is much lower than chronological age. Eyes in family drawing, were done in dashes, depicting painful and avoided visual input.

Figure 5.3

Several men had sexually abused her and she suffered from a venereal decease, as appeared in social workers' investigations. She was also neglect victim; the parents had abandoned their seven children without money, food, or proper shelter. Children's hair had lice. In her family drawing, parents were excluded. She drew her six younger siblings sleeping on the floor covered with one blanket or sheet. This was their state when the social services had intervened. On the right part of the page— with a separating line—she drew herself carrying her baby brother. The matter was brought to officials' attention when she was found stealing milk to feed the baby.

PHYSICALLY ABUSED CHILDREN

1a. Dots for eyes

A five-year, eight-month old boy had set fire under his bed several times; including two major ones. As a matching punishment, his mother burned his hand across the four fingers. The examiner saw burn traces at the time of drawings, three weeks after. Parents believed in harsh body punishment as an effective rearing practice.

Body distortion appeared in self-presentation (Figure 5.4). The mouth exceeded face boundaries and a gap existed between upper and lower parts of the face, which the child identified as such, when questioned by the examiner. An "S" letter was drawn on the right arm, interpreted by the child as

Figure 5.4

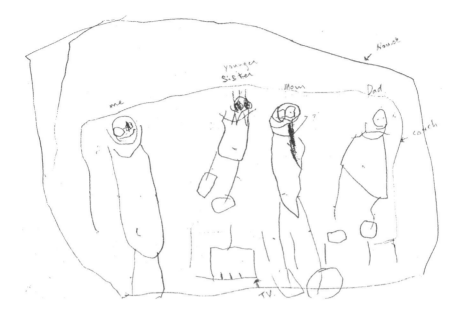

Figure 5.5

"superman" sign, identifying in fantasy with a powerful figure. The slanted figure is an Emotional Indicator reflecting feelings of personal imbalance within the environment (Koppitz, 1968). Such an EI is embedded in a general morbid context and not considered separately. He spontaneously drew another single figure as self-presentation on another sheet. Fire coming out from the mouth symbolized his imaginary power associated with setting fires.

In Figure 5.5, he drew distorted bodies of all family members including self-presentation. All figures also lacked arms symbolizing serious lack of communication within the family. The child was cognitively able to draw arms, which he did in his two single drawings.

1b. Dark dots for eyes

This eight-year-old boy suffered from enuresis and encopresis, which are presented by dark shading below waist in self-presentation and two figures in family drawing (Figure 5.6). He commented on the single figure drawing "a boy who likes to pretend he's an animal." This statement reflected his dissatisfaction with his life, on account of documented physical abuse by his father. It is interesting to notice that the dog in family drawing is the only creature without sharp teeth, tears, or black shading.

He excluded himself, his mother, and brother from the family drawing. But he added a crying baby, a passer-by, and a dog. The child drew an adult figure in the upper left corner, whom he identified as "father." Then he drew another

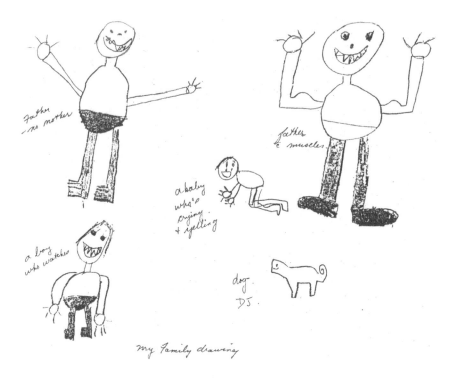

Father
- no mother

a baby
who's
crying
+ yelling

father
& muscles

a boy
who watches

dog.
DS.

my family drawing

Figure 5.6

paternal figure in the upper right corner. This presentation suggested perceived "double" presence of the paternal punitive figure within the family context. Muscles in the paternal figure's arms—unsupported by reality—reflected perceived physical overpower. Aggression, symbolized by sharp teeth in three figures—except those of the added baby and dog—reflected perceived aggression in the paternal figure as well as others.

Self-exclusion was found in family drawings of children who did not feel that they belonged to their families and were not appreciated by their families. These children also felt inadequate (Di Leo, 1973, 1983). This profile would have been lost, had the Kinetic Family Drawing (K-F-D) been administered in lieu of Hulse's instructions that do not request self-presentation.

2. Hollow eyes
Family drawing done by a 14-year-old boy consisted only of the maternal figure behind an ironing board, seen in Figure 5.7.

The head in the maternal figure was drawn at a different vertical axis from the lower body. No upper body below the face, considered as body distortion. The figure's legs were drawn apart at the skirt edges, as found in younger children's drawings. Legs were stiff, similar in shape to ironing

Figure 5.7

board legs. This reflected regression to a much younger age, atypical at his age group.

Yet, the adolescent was able to draw a whole body in self-presentation. Hollow eyes are found in both self and mother drawings. His mother got him to cook, do a lot of house chores, and often prevented him from going out.

Burns and Kaufman (1972) reported that ironing boards were produced by adolescent boys with a great deal of conflict and ambivalence toward maternal figure. Mother's missing arms and hands, which symbolize means of communication with others, support this interpretation. Self-exclusion depicted lack of belonging to the maternal figure, as being members of a family.

Parents were separated, he lived with his mother, and his father had visitation rights. He was the physically and verbally abusive parent, who hit him because he found him "stupid." No wonder the youngster excluded him too from the family drawing.

He labelled the single figure "a rock star," a role model for a better life. The figure's vacant eyes symbolized the desire to cut off visual input, commonly noticed in this group. The long neck symbolized difficulty in maintaining mental control over body impulses (Buck, 1966), which could be aggression as suggested by sharp teeth.

Touching on drawings reliability

Projective drawings critics question their reliability on account of differences between two or more drawings' qualities within a short time span. Subjects do not only employ their cognitive and developmental levels in their human figures drawings. They are mostly influenced by their feelings toward drawn characters, as demonstrated in the following examples.

The child's mother tried several times to get rid of her, when two to five months old, by leaving her on the streets of a large city, 60 miles away from home. The child was brought back by social services. At a later age, her mother got married to the child's sexual abuser. Mother and stepfather were alcoholics. She was badly beaten and given overdose of sleeping pills when she was brought to social services' attention. At the time of evaluation she lived in a good foster home.

Asked to draw a family, the 10-year-old girl excluded herself from all three drawn figures, each done on a separate sheet. She started drawing an adult female figure as her mother, but changed it to her therapist (Figure 5.8). She said, "my mom is not happy but you are." Well-drawn details, such as head and body details, pattern and flower on the dress, high-heeled shoes, and socks suggested positive and feminine perception of the female therapist. In addition, global quality of this figure was much higher than all other figures. It is interesting to notice that this specific person, the therapist, who cared for her, did not hinder her cognitive capacity; the figure had relatively higher drawing quality than her age level. Yet at the same setting, her cognitive capacity was hindered in an attempt to draw the abusive stepfather, in Figure 5.9. The face had no features and the half-drawn body circumference stopped at the genital area. This paralyzed attempt to draw the abuser is in sharp contrast with her drawn therapist's figure. She verbally expressed hatred toward the stepfather, who was in prison at evaluation time.

A similar paralyzed attempt to draw the paternal figure—her mother's companion who assaulted her—in an attempt to draw her family. The 12-year-old girl spent a whole hour to produce half the peripheral line of the figure. The tremendous pain associated with this figure was implied. She lived with her biological mother, who had a number of male companions. The child was sexually abused by several of them. Her biological father was unknown. She referred to the single figure she drew earlier saying, "this is me, this is my only family." The figure's hollow eyes show need for visual blockage.

Task refusal

One child in the *sexually* abused group as well as three children in the *physically* abused group refused to draw their families. It may reflect intolerance to stress elicited by pondering on family relationships, in complete task refusal. Refusal to draw one's family was only found in children who come from broken homes (Di Leo, 1983).

Figure 5.8

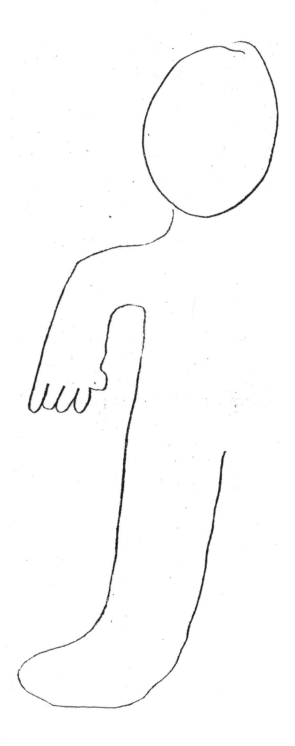

Figure 5.9

Overview

Figure drawings can play a significant role as an integral part of detection procedures in sexual and physical abuse (Blain et al., 1981). Both the quantitative-cognitive and the qualitative-emotional aspects of human figure drawings could be helpful in the detection process. However, figure drawings such as the Kinetic Family Drawings (Burns and Kaufman, 1972) could not be used as an indicator of physical or sexual abuse (Piperno et al., 2007). Yet, they are helpful in psychotherapy and rehabilitation.

On the quantitative-cognitive level, sexually and physically abused children were likely to render much lower performance on the Draw-A-Person test than the Wechsler tests of intelligence. Sattler (1982) reported that the DAP tended to provide lower IQs than the Wechsler tests. However, the magnitude of discrepancies would have warranted mention had they reached a volume such as found in this study.

There were no statistically significant differences between White Canadians and Cree Indians. Matto and Naglieri (2005) reported similar findings. No statistically significant differences were found between White and each of Black and Hispanic groups, 6–17 years old, on DAP: SPED total T-scores. The DAP: SPED stands for Screening Procedure for Emotional Disturbance (Naglieri, McNaish, & Bardos, 1991).

On the qualitative-emotional level, several clues shed light on some sexually and physically abused children's feelings about themselves and their families. Mainly, the global drawing quality, viewers' associated impressions, combinations of single and family drawing characteristics, supported by verbal comments made by children as well as case material in children's files.

None of the investigated children, in either category, drew his or her family members including self-presentation, showing neutral or happy affect. The only drawn family including self-presentation was a foster family of a sexually abused girl. It must have been very painful for these children to feel alienation and lack of appreciation by their families. This probably portrayed the fact that their families did not protect them from the assault or it had occurred within the family. Piperno et al. (2007) reported similar results, based on qualitative and quantitative variables such as the quality of drawings and children's perception of their family members and their perception of themselves within their families. While control group children drew themselves near or between parents. Matched physically and sexually groups were likely to exclude their primary caregiver from family drawings.

In their single figures, *sexually* abused children drew *two opposed eye styles.* Some made "very small eyes as dots, dashes or hollow eyes," so that the drawn person seemed unable to see or visual input was reduced to a minimal, symbolizing shrinked visual interest. Others drew "large, opened eyes with lashes" in female drawings, expressing visual curiosity. Corroborate material suggested that these subjects perceived the experience as an early initiation to sexuality, regardless of their feelings toward the abuser. These opposed styles are instructive in qualitative analysis but would cancel each other in quantitative manipulation. Yates, Beutler, and Crago's (1985) research results support associated inferences. Incest victims tended to either over or under-represent sexual characteristics in their drawings, though eyes are not secondary sexual characteristics, such as full hips and breasts.

Self-exclusion, reflecting feelings of rejection, was common. One or both parental figures were excluded, drawn on separate paper or replaced by a pet. When parental figures were present, their affect was concealed in a "back to the viewer" presentation or emotional conflict appeared as one parent frowned while the other smiled. Task refusal clearly reflected nonbelonging and inability to momentarily relive interpersonal relationships within the family. A child referred to her single figure drawing as "me, I am my only family."

In some cases when the paternal figure was the abuser, two different family drawing profiles were noted. Failure to complete the peripheral lines of his figure reflected a paralyzed effect, which consumed the traumatic affect. This family profile corresponded with "dots for eyes" in the single figure drawing. The other family drawing profile also focused on the paternal figure. When the paternal figure was completed; it had large eyes and appeared in underwear. This family profile corresponded with "large opened eyes with lashes" in the single figure drawing.

In their single figure drawing, *physically* abused children seemed to avoid painful visual input reflected in tiny eyes as dots, dashes, or vacant eyes, which occurred in most cases.

In family drawing where parents were present, pain was reflected in distorted figures. Pain was also symbolized in burning objects such as an ironing board or wieners on a grill. Some physically abused children may reveal a fantasy of replacing hurting parental figures by a loving relative or adding a non-existing paternal figure. Giving the figure unrealistic physical strength and representing him twice to the exclusion of weak figures such as self and maternal figures expresses overemphasis of the punitive paternal figure's power.

All family members, including self-presentation, were excluded from some family drawings. Own family was replaced by a playground or a grill, reflected avoidance of dealing with punitive parental figures. Such avoidance was even more dramatic in task refusal by other children. Inferences based on these drawing characteristics are consistent with findings about physically abused child's poor interpersonal relationships (e.g. Hjorth & Harway, 1981).

The fact that drawing characteristics present in one figure while absent in another was often taken as lack of reliability of human figure drawings. A comprehensive understanding interprets this fact as having different thoughts and feelings about certain persons in one's life when drawing each figure. A case study provides a clear example. It does not take a figure-drawing expert to notice the striking difference in quality between figures done in the same setting. The 11-year-old sexually abused girl's drawing of her female therapist whose empathy and care have been experienced, was by far superior, qualitatively and quantitatively, compared to the abusive paternal single figure. Poorly drawn figures may not always reflect a cognitive level, especially in family drawings. The emotional impact which the figure represents may very well prevent the employment of higher potential quality characteristics in the ability to draw.

Cree Indian children did not differ from White children living within a close geographical vicinity in Alberta, Canada, in their performance on the Goodenough-Harris test, the Wechsler tests, or in the discrepancy between scores on these tests. Impairments in cognitive function and the expression of emotional well-being, which followed abusive experiences, were similarly manifested in test performance of both cultural groups. In addition, family drawings' profiles did not yield apparent differences pertaining to differences in culture between these two groups. Rather, children from both cultural backgrounds were more concerned with the expression of their feelings about themselves and their families than projecting cultural characteristics on their drawings.

References

Abell, C. S., Horkheimer, R., & Horkheimer, E. N (1998). Intellectual evaluations of adolescents via human figure drawings: An empirical comparison of two methods. *Journal of Clinical Psychology, 54,* 811–815.

Abell, C. S., Von Briesen, P. D., & Watz, S. (1996). Intellectual evaluations of children using human figure drawings: An empirical investigation of two methods. *Journal of Clinical Psychology, 52,* 67–74.

Blain, G. H., Bergner, R. M., Lewis, M. L., & Goldstein, M. A. (1981). The use of objectively scorable House-Tree-Person indicators to establish child abuse. *Journal of Clinical Psychology, 37,* 667–673.

Buck, J. N. (1966). *The House-Tree-Person technique, revised manual.* Beverly Hills, CA: Western Psychological Services.

Burns, R. C., & Kaufman, S. H. (1972). *Actions, styles and symbols in Kinetic Family Drawing (KFD): An interpretative manual.* New York: Brunner/Mazel.

Culbertson, F. M. (1987). Graphic characteristics on the Draw-A-Person test for identification of physical abuse. *Journal of Art Therapy, 4,* 30–33.

Di Leo, J. H. (1973). *Children's drawings as diagnostic aids.* New York: Brunner/Mazel.

Di Leo, J. H. (1983). *Interpreting children's drawings.* New York: Brunner/Mazel.

Falk, J. D. (1981). Understanding children's art: An analysis of literature. *Journal of Personality Assessment, 45,* 465–472.

Graziano, A. M., & Raulin, M. L. (1993). *Research methods: A process of inquiry* (2nd ed.). New York: Harper Collins College.

Hammer, E. F. (1958/1967). *The clinical application of projective drawings.* Springfield: Charles C. Thomas.

Hammer, E. F. (1964). *The H-T-P clinical research manual* (3rd ed.). Beverly Hills, CA: Western Psychological Services.

Hammer, E. (1968). Projective drawings. In A. Rabin (Ed.), *Projective techniques in personality assessment* (pp. 366–393). New York: Springer.

Harris, D. (1963). *Goodenough-Harris Drawing Test: Manual.* New York: Harcourt, Brace & World.

Hibbard, R. A., & Hartman, G. L. (1990). Emotional indicators in human figure drawings of sexually victimized and non-abused children. *Journal of Clinical Psychology, 46,* 211–219.

Hjorth, C. W., & Harway, M. (1981). The body-image of physically abused and normal adolescents. *Journal of Clinical Psychology, 37,* 863–866.

Hulse, W. C. (1952). Child conflict expressed through family drawings. *Journal of Projective Techniques, 16,* 66–79.

Koppitz, E. M. (1968). *Psychological evaluation of children's human figure drawings.* New York: Grune & Stratton.

Machover, K. (1949). *Personality projection in the drawing of the human figure.* Springfield: Charles C. Thomas.

Matto, H. C., & Naglieri, J. A. (2005). Race and ethnic differences and Human Figure Drawings: Clinical utility of DAP: SPED. *Journal of Clinical Child and Adolescent Psychology, 34,* 706–711.

Naglieri, J. A., McNaish, T. J., & Bardos, A. N. (1991). *Draw A Person: Screening Procedure for Emotional Disturbance.* Austin, TX: ProEd.

Piperno, F., Di Biasi, S., & Levi, G. (2007). Evaluating family drawings of physically and sexually abused children. *European Child & Adolescent Psychiatry, 16,* 389–397.

Sattler, J. M. (1982). *Assessment of children's intelligence and special abilities* (2nd ed.). Boston: Allyn & Bacon.

Thomas, A. D., & Engram, D. (1986, July). Canadian-Cree Indian comparisons. In F. Culbertson (chair), *Cross-cultural studies of abused children: Psychometric properties of the Draw-A-Person test.* Symposium conducted at the convention of the International Council of Psychologists, Tel-Aviv, Israel.

Timberlake, E. M. (1979). Aggression and depression among abused and non-abused children in foster care. *Children and Youth Services Review, 1,* 279–291.

Wechsler, D. (1963). *The Wechsler Pre-school and Primary Scale of Intelligence Manual.* New York: The Psychological Corporation.

Wechsler, D. (1974). *The Wechsler Intelligence Scale for Children-Revised manual.* New York: The Psychological Corporation.

West, M. M. (1998). Meta analysis of studies assessing the efficacy of projective techniques in discriminating child sexual abuse. *Child Abuse and Neglect, 22,* 1151–1166.

Wysocki, B. A., & Wysocki, A. C. (1973). The body image of normal and retarded children. *Journal of Clinical Psychology, 29,* 7–10.

Yates, A., Beutler, L. E., & Crago, M. (1985). Drawings of child victims of incest. *Child Abuse & Neglect, 9,* 183–189.

6

ANOREXIC HOUSE-TREE-PERSON DRAWINGS

Profile and reliability

Antoinette D. Thomas, John W. Getz, Justin D. Smith,
and Elaine Rivas

Introduction

The distorted view of one's body image is a hallmark of anorexia nervosa. Body image and self-concept are central attributes. The criteria for anorexia nervosa includes, "disturbance in the perception of the shape or size of his or her body" (American Psychiatric Association, 2000, p. 583). The centrality of this attribute suggests body size estimation would be a worthwhile approach to assessing body image disturbance in anorexia nervosa (Skrzypek, Wehmeier, & Remschmidt, 2001). The current study used a blind identification procedure to identify characteristics of figure drawings produced by anorexic patients. A reliability study was then performed using the identified characteristics to determine the potential utility of figure drawings to assess anorexia nervosa.

Skrzypek et al. (2001), based on findings of a review article, suggest that anorexic patients' body image disturbance is not due to any perceptual deficit but is based on cognitive-evaluative dissatisfaction. Thus, body image estimation is related to the individual's attitude toward his/her body. Anorexics' body dissatisfaction is often manifested in their irrational worries about fatness, resulting in the relentless pursuit of thinness (Halmi, 1994; Harper-Giuffre & Mackenzie, 1992). Anorexic patients process non-self-images similarly to control subjects, but their processing of self-images is quite discrepant. Neurobiological research results show increases and decreases in assessed body dimensions, as well as specific brain regions for such disturbance (Kaye, 2008; Sachdev, Mondraty, Wen, & Guilford, 2008; Skrzypek et al., 2001). A study of neurobiological differences in the processing of self-images found that anorexic patients do not appear to engage the attentional system or the insula (the central lobe of the cerebrum) (Sachdev et al., 2008). This recent sophisticated research shows that anorexic patients process body images differently than those unaffected by the disorder.

However, disturbance in the processing of body images does not fully explain the manifestation of anorexia nervosa. Despite recent speculation, it is doubtful that cultural pressures for thinness in industrial countries solely cause anorexia nervosa either, since anorexia affects less than 1% of the general population (Kaye, 2008). Other characteristics are certainly at work with anorexic patients, contributing to the development and maintenance of this disorder, such as: (a) Negative body image leads to feelings of inadequacy (Kerr, Skok, & McLaughlin, 1991), suggesting self-worth becomes equated with body appearance; (b) low self-esteem, the main predictor of the anorexic behavior, indicates the importance of psychological aspects (Kerr et al., 1991); (c) anorexic patients desire to be in a prepubertal state and find comfort in prepubertal appearance suggesting that the psychological meaning of thinness and starvation behavior might be a fear of maturation; and (d) anorexic patients have more sexual inhibitions and are less sexually active than normal and bulimic subjects (Haimes & Katz, 1988). Additionally, non-clinical personality characteristics of anorexic patients, as compared to normal and bulimic subjects, include timidity, general restraint, and refrain from absorption in sensory experiences (Pryor & Wiederman, 1996).

Self-image and self-concept in figure drawings

The House-Tree-Person (H-T-P, Buck, 1948) is a widely used projective drawing technique for subjects 15 years old and above. The Tree and Person are considered self-representations. The drawing of a Person tends to elicit an accurate self-portrait or an ideal self-portrait, that is, the closer-to-conscious view of oneself and its interaction with the environment. The drawing of a Tree is said to reflect relatively deeper and more unconscious feelings about oneself and its interaction with the environment (Hammer, 1997). Within figure drawing literature, global ratings of body image acquired satisfactory reliability (e.g., Riethmiller & Handler, 1997). Skrzypek et al. (2001) suggest that body size estimation remains an appropriate approach to assessing body image disturbance in anorexia nervosa. Anorexic patients are likely to project their body image and self-concept on their drawings (Swenson, 1968) suggesting that the H-T-P task could be used to assess the disorder.

Significant associations between scores on various aspects of figure drawings and other measures of body image and self-concept were found in all studies reviewed by Swenson (1968) using adult populations. For example, the size of college students' person drawings was similar to themselves (Swenson, 1968), and global ratings of immature figures were significantly associated with low self-concept scores (Swenson, 1968).

Female subjects over 14 years of age are expected to draw mature figures. Secondary sexual differentiation in figure drawings by females varied around puberty and in late adolescence. In a non-psychiatric sample, post-menarche subjects evidenced greater secondary sexual differentiation than premenarche girls of the same age (Rierdan & Koff, 1980b). Considering menarche as a primarily integrative experience with other aspects of their self and body perceptions, late adolescents drew less emphasized secondary sexual features than early adolescents, but their figures depicted mature female bodies unlike premenarche girls (Rierdan & Koff, 1980a). Robins, Blatt, and Ford (1991) found that after a course of intensive psychotherapy, figure drawings improved significantly in terms of patients producing more mature, higher quality figures, which the authors believe reflected the development of a stable, realistic, and essentially positive self-identity.

Study 1: Blind identification and development of drawing characteristics

Forty H-T-P sets were used in the blind identification task. This set was equally derived from a pool of subjects from four diagnostic groups: anxiety, insomnia, depression, and anorexia, using DSM-IV-TR criteria. Each subject formed discrete psychiatric diagnoses in their respective classification. No subjects were dually diagnosed.

The first author adhered to a strict blind procedure in examining the 40 sets of drawings, provided by the second author who was all patients' psychotherapist, without preselected criteria. Blind scoring in research contributes to drawing validity (Waehler, 1997). Only patient's initials identified H-T-P sets. Information usually used in blind research, such as age and sex of subjects, as well as drawn figures, was concealed. Complying with previous recommendations, no preselected list of signs (Riethmiller & Handler, 1997) or automatic sign count (Waehler, 1997) were employed. Six anorexic H-T-P sets were correctly sorted out of the examined 40 cases. Of the correctly identified anorexic subjects, all were female, five were late adolescents, and one was 30 years old. Correctly and blindly sorted anorexic H-T-Ps; were reexamined to identify a general "'anorexic profile."

An anorexic drawing profile

An overall profile of a latency figure emerged in all cases. Late adolescents and adult women drew prepubertal, innocent-looking girls, as evidenced by a lack of indications of a mature female body. The figure could be identifiable as female by a hairdo or a dress without which the figure would be of indiscriminate sex. Body internal details, such as clothes details were very few. Figures tended to be small or of low quality (i.e., disproportionate) when oversized. Trunks were thin and possibly narrower than the heads. Facial features and head contour were mostly similar to children's drawings. Lastly, female subjects drew same sex figures, suggesting positive gender identity.

Many of the characteristics included in the anorexic drawing profile are consistent with previous research findings: Figures lacked secondary sexual features, such as breasts and full hips, incompatible with subjects' life cycle (Rierdan & Koff, 1980a). The body or dress had few or no internal details, suggesting emotional immaturity (Riethmiller & Handler, 1997). Tendency toward small figure sizes reflected social withdrawal (Halmi, 1994; Harper-Giuffre & MacKenzie, 1992). Tube-like trunks which could be narrower than heads might reflect their striving for thinness. Their figure drawings also depicted latency age general appearance, such as childish hairdo and dress style. In addition, facial features and head shape resembled those drawn by children. The "latency girl" figure clearly portrayed the anorexic desire to be in a prepubertal state and appearance (Haimes & Katz, 1988; Johnson, 1982; Kerr et al., 1991). Physically immature figures, stripped from secondary sexual features, reflected anorexics' inhibited sexuality (Haimes & Katz, 1988; Kerr et al., 1991) as well as their non-clinical personality characteristics of timidity, restraint, and avoidance of sensory experiences (Pryor & Wiederman, 1996).

Anorexic women produced same sex Person drawings. Swenson (1968) concluded that the sex of the first drawn figure sufficiently supported relatedness to body image or self-concept, though insufficient as a diagnostic sign in individual cases. It is suggested that anorexic women value their gender as perceived in latency. The anorexic woman readily endorses her female gender, but seems to dwell in a time machine that brings her back to her latency phase, never to outgrow this period.

Low self-esteem has emerged as one of the risk factors and predictors of the tendency toward the anorexic behavior (Grant & Fodor, 1986; Kerr et al., 1991). The global unrealistic, regressed human figure drawn by anorexic patients seems to reflect their low self-esteem and dissatisfaction with their actual bodies. However, the confidently drawn, relatively higher quality Trees, suggested the existence of a better self-concept. The Tree reflects a less conscious self-portrait of more basic and deeper layers of personality than the Person, which represents interaction with the environment (Buck, 1966).

The anorexic drawing profile includes several interrelated drawing indices, complying with the principle of "aggregation of variables" (Riethmiller & Handler, 1997) and recommended by them for obtaining better construct validity than depending on one or very few drawing signs. Clinicians may find this profile helpful in understanding their patients and probably use the assumed underlying self-concept in their interventions. The anorexic drawing profile led to the identification of Person and Tree drawing characteristics believed to be markers of the presence of anorexia that could be used for identification of the disorder in the H–T–P. Tree drawing characteristics are based on evaluative dimensions identified by Buck (1966).

Identified drawing characteristics

Person:

1. Absence of mature female body features (breasts, full hips, or narrower waist than full hips) not merely narrower waist than lower part of dress as in children drawings.
2. Estimated figure age is prepubertal.
3. Body has three or fewer details (one neckline, belt, lines for sleeves, pants or dress, skirt pleats, decoration, or other clothes details).
4. Suggested female figure; hairdo or dress needed to determine gender.
5. Childish head (full circle), facial features (dots or circles for eyes, one dimensional mouth, vertical nose line not longer than horizontal line), childish body parts (grape fingers, clubfeet) or no facial features.
6. Thin body (same width or narrower than head).
7. Rather small figure size (4 inches or less) or poor quality oversize (8 inches or more).

Tree:

1. Better line quality than Person, steadier lines.
2. Better details, proportion and/or perspective than Person.

Illustrations

Figure drawings norms for late adolescents and adults include: body wider than head, a woman's body shows breasts, full hips and/or narrow waist, especially when the figure has a unisex garment, details of clothes, upper arms and thighs wider than forearms and lower thighs, arms drawn close to the body or engaged in an action, oval face, well-shaped eyes with pupils, two-dimensional nose with vertical line longer than the horizontal, two-dimensional mouth, hands, and shaped feet or shoes.

Case 1

All anorexic patients' drawing characteristics were displayed in Figures 6.1 and 6.2, drawn by a 16-year-old female. The innocent-looking little girl had a log-like thin body similar to a Tree trunk. It lacked secondary sexual characteristics, such as full hips and breasts as well as clothes details. Hairdo and flared skirt suggested figure's gender. Childish drawing characteristics were: body narrower than head, stick-like arms extended far away from body, round face and eyes, one-dimensional mouth, tiny fingers protruding from forearm, and club feet pointing to opposed directions. The figure was placed at the lower third of the vertical page axis, probably suggesting withdrawal tendency within the environment.

The Tree's closed trunk and implied foliage gave the drawing a relatively higher quality than that of the Person.

Figure 6.1

Figure 6.2

Case 2

Similarly, all anorexic patients' drawing characteristics were found in Figures 6.3 and 6.4, done by a 17-year-old female. The 11-inch long figure of low graphic quality presented an Emotional Indicator (EI, Koppitz, 1968), suggesting compensation for inadequacy feelings. The body had no secondary sexual characteristics, such as full hips and breasts. The prepuberty figure was identified as a female only by a hairdo. The only garment details were sleeves end lines and shirt end line. However, neck and pants' lower limits were missing; pants flew into undifferentiated shoes or feet. Several childish drawing characteristics were noticed: round face, oval nose, no shoulders, arms curved upward as neck extension and away from body; hair merged only from top of head, club feet pointing to opposed directions, asymmetric size and shape of eyes; fingers protrude from forearms; some grape fingers others defected in placement, number, or relative length. The Person had an innocent, rather scared glance and general appearance. In addition, the redrawn lines without erasing the extraneous ones suggested disinterest in the human figure and underestimation of its aesthetic appearance. The long

Figure 6.3

Figure 6.4

neck in the absence of shoulders may suggest difficult and forced control of mind over body.

Open Tree trunk at the lower end reflected insufficient boundaries between self and environment. Otherwise, firm well-controlled lines and general Tree quality, in terms of details and proportion, were relatively much better than those found in the Person.

Case 3

This case also met all above-mentioned characteristics. Tiny body in Figure 6.5 was as wide as face. The 1-inch figure was identifiable as a female by a peripheral dress shape and a hairdo. No secondary sexual characteristics, such as full hips and breasts. The figure suggested a pre-puberty age. Dress had no inner details and face had no facial features; round head, while body in profile. Dress style, clubfeet, as well as Person's general appearance gave the impression of a child's production, not that of a 19 year old. Flowers, watered by the Person, had intricate details with water well done drops. This stands in contrast with lack of facial features in the Person, suggesting concealed emotions from the therapist. Tiny figure as well as the space which all three units occupied—less than one fourth of the page—reflected withdrawal tendencies.

The Tree was very well done and obviously superior to the Person.

Figure 6.5

Case 4

Figures 6.6 and 6.7 also met all our characteristics. A rather small Person, drawn by this 17-year-old female, had a skinny body with no secondary sexual characteristics, other than a slight waist indication. The dress had no internal details. The body was narrower than the head. It depicted a cute female child, on account of hairdo and peripheral dress shape, wearing a party crown. Childish drawing features—which also included some perceptual errors—were: a dot for nose, one dimensional conventional smile mouth, fingers protruding from forearms, feet in opposing directions, forearms wider than upper arms, and stick-like legs. Emphasis on the headpiece may suggest infantile satisfaction in fantasy.

The small Tree trunk was opened at both ends, suggesting poor boundaries within the environment. However, the Tree was still better than the Person on account of steady lines, implied foliage, and general qualities. Both tiny units may reflect withdrawal tendencies and inadequacy feelings.

Case 5

With the exception of the third and the seventh identified characteristics (no internal dress details and a rather small or oversize body), other anorexic drawing characteristics appeared in Figures 6.8 and 6.9, drawn by a 30-year-old female patient. Notice the partly erased stick person underneath the drawn figure. Low human body value embedded in the stick figure was surmounted by a relatively higher one, though still incompatible with age level drawings of a human figure. The body was very thin and much narrower than the head.

Figure 6.6

Figure 6.7

Figure 6.8

Figure 6.9

Body contour consisted of short broken lines. The figure's age seemed prepubertal in the absence of mature feminine features. Childish hairstyle, eyes, and lips determined the Person's gender. Childish drawing features were also: perfectly round head and its oversize compared to body, facial features and neck relatively smaller than expected for head size, feet in opposed directions, and relatively narrower left thigh at its joint with body than lower thigh part.

Tree lines were firm, well controlled, and not broken as those of the Person. The general quality of the Tree was higher than the Person, in terms of perspective and proportion.

Note: All patients ignored Test instructions to draw each unit (House, Tree, and Person) on a separate page.

Study 2: The reliability study: Methods and procedures

Interrater reliability task

The forth author did preliminary work and discussed with the third author the appropriate method. The third author chose the two raters, organized and conducted the task, conducted the data analysis, and wrote the Method and Results sections.

Two psychology graduate student raters were trained on the nine criteria described above using a set of 10 randomly selected sample drawing sets.

Interrater reliability was established using a different set of 10 Tree and Person drawings. Female adolescents and young adults in an intensive residential treatment center produced both the sample drawings and the 10 drawing sets used in the interrater reliability task.

Experimental identification task

The experimental task consisted of employing the above coding criteria to a set of 40 House and Tree sets in an attempt to identify anorexic-produced drawings. The two raters were asked to review the 40 sets of drawings and then provide their level of confidence, on a 1–5 Likert-type scale, that an anorexic client produced the drawing. The scale was defined as 1 = Highly Unlikely, 2 = Somewhat Unlikely, 3 = Neutral, 4 = Somewhat Likely, 5 = Highly Likely. They were also asked to track their ratings of the nine criteria for later interrater reliability estimates. The researchers categorized each drawing set based on the raters' level of confidence that the drawing was produced by an anorexic. In an effort to maintain the most conservative estimates, "Highly Likely" was chosen as the selection criterion. Those cases rated as "Highly Likely" were then placed in one of two categories, either Correctly Identified as Anorexic or Incorrectly Identified as Anorexic. The remainders of the drawings receiving a confidence rating of 4 or less were deemed to not be produced by an anorexic and were placed in either of the two remaining categories: Correctly Identified as Non-Anorexic or Incorrectly Identified as Non-Anorexic (i.e., failure to detect the desired target).

Data analysis

Interrater reliability was calculated using Cohen's Kappa Coefficient to determine adequate agreement on the nine criteria prior to the experimental identification task. Cohen's Kappa (Cohen, 1960) establishes the level of agreement when only two raters are involved and controls for the hypothetical probability of chance agreement making it a more robust measure of agreement than simple percentage.

The experimental task of identifying anorexic-produced drawings was completed by the two raters and a Kappa Coefficient was used to calculate the level of agreement between the raters on the categorical placement of each drawing in the four categories: Correctly Identified as Anorexic, Incorrectly Identified as Anorexic, Correctly Identified as Nonanorexic, or Incorrectly Identified as Nonanorexic. Kappa Coefficient takes into account the expected agreement due to chance alone. In addition, Kappa Coefficient was again used to determine interrater reliability on the nine criteria in the experimental task to determine if adequate agreement had been maintained following the training period and initial reliability estimate.

Interrater reliability task

Following training, the raters' agreement on the 10 drawing sets resulted in $\kappa = .46$. Landis and Koch (1977) suggest a moderate level of agreement based on this kappa value, which was determined to be sufficient to proceed with the experimental identification task. Additional training and clarification was conducted in an effort to increase agreement in the experimental identification task. Initial training, the interrater reliability task, and the supplemental clarification of criteria were completed in about 45 minutes.

Experimental identification task

After determining the accuracy of the drawing identifications, Kappa coefficients were calculated for each of the four categories (Correctly Identified as Anorexic, Incorrectly Identified as Anorexic, Correctly Identified as Nonanorexic, Incorrectly Identified as Nonanorexic), resulting in Substantial (.61–.80) to Almost Perfect (.81–1.00) Agreement (Landis & Koch, 1977). The overall Cohen's Kappa Coefficient for the experimental identification task resulted in Almost Perfect Agreement, $\kappa = .83$, $SE = .11$, $z = 7.5$, $p < .01$. Results of the experimental identification task are provided in Table 6.1.

The ratings of the nine identified characteristics of the anorexic profile were then examined to determine if satisfactory interrater reliability was achieved in the experimental identification task and identify any problematic criteria. Overall, the interrater reliability of the experimental task resulted in Substantial Agreement, $\kappa = .67$. The seven criteria pertaining to the Person Drawing were satisfactory, ranging from $\kappa = .40$ to $\kappa = .80$. The lowest agreement came from the criteria for Suggested Female Figure, while the highest was from the criterion for Childish Head. The two criteria pertaining to the Tree drawing resulted in lower agreement. Better Line Quality resulted in $\kappa = .36$ and Better Details resulted in $\kappa = .19$. These Kappa values are only Slight to Fair Agreement (Landis & Koch, 1977). The overall p-value was at the .01 level for the nine criteria. P-values for each criterion were significant at the .05 level or better, despite Slight to Fair Agreement on three criteria.

Table 6.1 H–T–P anorexia coding task results

	Correctly Identified as Anorexic		Incorrectly Identified as Anorexic		Correctly Identified as Nonanorexic		Incorrectly Identified as Nonanorexic	
Coder	1	2	1	2	1	2	1	2
Number of Cases	5	6	1	2	30	29	4	3
Coefficient Kappa	$\kappa = .80$		$\kappa = .65$		$\kappa = .94$		$\kappa = .72$	

Discussion

The z-score and resulting level of significance indicate that obtaining a kappa of .83 is highly unlikely due to chance alone. The obtained coefficient statistic is compared against a $\kappa = .25$, the expected level of agreement of two raters with four categories based purely on chance alone. A significant kappa value greater than .70 indicates that the coding criteria used to identify anorexic patients' Tree and Person drawings; produces high agreement about the identification of anorexic and nonanorexic drawings. Based on the coefficient kappa values of each of the four categories presented in Table 6.1, one can see that there is high agreement on two of the categories. Raters highly agreed on drawings identified correctly for both the anorexic-produced and nonanorexic-produced drawings. There was lower agreement on the two categories where drawings were identified as either having been produced by anorexic participants incorrectly or identified as having not been produced by anorexic participants when they in fact had been. The near perfect agreement obtained for correctly identifying drawings that were not produced by an anorexic patient suggests this coding system could be used, with some confidence, to exclude nonanorexic drawings when attempting to identify the disorder.

These findings suggest the coding system described here has satisfactory reliability that results in a high level of accurate identification. This system could aid clinicians and researchers in identifying patients with anorexia from Tree and Person drawings of the H-T-P test. Future research with this method could test the validity of this method against established anorexia nervosa assessment methods and the clinical judgment of seasoned mental health service providers and other experts familiar with Tree and Figure drawings.

References

American Psychiatric Association. (2000). *Diagnostic and statistical manual of mental disorders, Fourth Edition, Text Revision*. Washington: American Psychiatric Press.

Buck, J. N. (1966). *The House-Tree-Person technique, revised manual*. Beverly Hills: Western Psychological Services.

Buck, J. N. (1948). The H-T-P technique: A quantitative and qualitative scoring manual. Monograph supplement. *Journal of Clinical Psychology, 5*, 1–120.

Cohen, J. (1960). A coefficient of agreement for nominal scales. *Educational and Psychological Measurement, 20*, 37–46.

Halmi, K. A. (1994). Eating disorders: Anorexia nervosa, bulimia nervosa and obesity. In R. E. Hales, S. C. Yudofsky, & J. A. Talbott (Eds.), *Textbook of psychiatry* (2nd ed., pp. 857–875). Washington: American Psychiatric Press.

Hammer, E. F. (1997). *Advances in projective drawing interpretation*. Springfield: Charles C. Thomas.

Harper-Giuffre, H., & MacKenzie, K. R. (1992). *Group psychotherapy for eating disorders*. Washington: American Psychiatric Press.

Kaye, W. (2008). Neurobiology of anorexia and bulimia nervosa. *Physiology & Behavior, 94,* 121–135.

Kerr, J. K., Skok, R. L., & McLaughlin, T. F. (1991). Characteristics common to females who exhibit anorexic or bulimic behavior: A review of current literature. *Journal of Clinical Psychology, 47,* 846–853.

Landis, J. R., & Koch, G. G. (1977). The measurement of observer agreement for categorical data. *Biometrics, 33,* 159–174.

Pryor, T., & Wiedermann, M. W. (1996). Measurement of non-clinical personality characteristics of women with anorexia nervosa or bulimia nervosa. *Journal of Personality Assessment, 67,* 414–421.

Rierdan, J. & Koff, E. (1980a). Representation of the female body by early and late adolescence. *Journal of Youth and Adolescence, 9,* 339–346.

Rierdan, J. & Koff, E. (1980b). The psychological impact of menarche: Integrative versus disruptive changes. *Journal of Youth and Adolescence, 9,* 49–58.

Riethmiller, R. J. & Handler, L. (1997). Problematic methods and unwarranted conclusions in DAP research: Suggestions for improved research procedures. *Journal of Personality Assessment, 69,* 459–475.

Robins, C. E., Blatt, S. J., & Ford, R. Q. (1991). Changes in human figure drawings during intensive treatment. *Journal of Personality Assessment, 57,* 477–497.

Sachdev, P., Mondraty, N., Wen, W., & Gulliford, K. (2008). Brains of anorexia nervosa patients process self-images differently from non-self-images: An fMRI study. *Neuropsychologia, 46,* 2161–2168.

Skrzypek, S., Wehmeier, P. M., & Remschmidt, H. (2001). Body image assessment using body size estimation in recent studies on anorexia nervosa: A brief review. *European Child & Adolescent Psychiatry, 10,* 215–221.

Swensen, C. E. (1968). Empirical evaluations of human figure drawings: 1957–1966. *Psychological Bulletin, 70,* 20–44.

Waehler, C. A. (1997). Drawing bridges between science and practice. *Journal of Personality Assessment, 69,* 482–487.

7

SECTION 1: OSTEOPATHIC BODY HEALING REFLECTED ON CHILDREN'S DRAWINGS

Antoinette D. Thomas and Denyse Dufresne

Osteopathy

The term osteopathy is derived from two words; "osteom" means all living tissue and "pathos" means suffering structures. In 1874, Dr. Andrew Taylor Still, an American surgeon, established the principles of osteopathy after many years of research and practice. Medical schools in the United States have acknowledged this specialty in the graduating year.

As a science, osteopathy is rooted in anatomical and physiological interactions within all body systems, as related to natural laws such as body equilibrium and gravity line in the body. Considering the body as one functional unit and its ability to regulate itself are fundamental osteopathic principles.

Osteopathy is not to be confused with manual therapy or chiropractics. It is an older form of natural medicine, based on a precise sense of touch (palpitation), which frees restrictions in body tissues to restore mobility and normal function. Osteopathic treatment frees restricted body structures, such as bones, ligaments, tendons, and muscles. It also liberates the blood and lymphatic circulation that may be disturbed and encourages metabolic exchanges through all body systems.

Osteopathy deals with causes rather than symptoms. Patients often report significant improvement in their body ailments after a few therapeutic sessions.

An empirical study

Thomas and Dufresne (2000, 2002) assumed that perceived osteopathic improvement could be reflected in human figure drawings. That is, drawings done after therapeutic treatments would be closer to physically normal children's figure drawings than those done before treatment.

The purpose of this study was *first,* to find out to what extent can mere employment of quantitative and qualitative characteristics of children's human figure drawings identify physical improvement. That is, in absence of information about children's gender, age, associated comments, physical ailments, and desire of improvement. *Second,* to compare osteopathic parameters of improvement to psychological understanding. *Third,* to use both disciplines' backgrounds to determine whether physical improvement can be projected on and perceived in drawings within one hour after an osteopathic treatment.

The second author, a renowned child osteopath, systematically asks children to Draw-A-Person before and after each treatment session. Studied sets of Before and After drawings constitute all the drawings found in her clinical files during the past 13 years. Four cases drawn with markers or crayons and two done by severely retarded children were excluded. This small number of available cases (26 sets of drawings) was due to the fact that her clients were predominantly babies. In addition, some children refused to draw; others left the office in a hurry before doing After drawings.

The therapist gave each set of Before and After drawings a serial number. In addition, random sequence of A or B was given to Before and After drawings. Children's age, gender, physical problems, and verbal comments were concealed. The first author carried out blind sorting of the two drawings' sequence. Blindly sorted sequences, as well as drawing inferences were sent in writing to the second author, who compared them to sequences: Before and After treatment.

The two authors met to study pertinent information in children's files, such as their physical ailments, age, and gender. They discussed osteopathic versus psychological rationale employed in each set of drawings.

Four osteopathic parameters are similar to or refinements of psychological knowledge, one constitutes a new dimension.

Twenty-two children made 26 sets of Before and After therapy drawings. They fall into two groups: (a) "First Session" group consisted of nine children, two boys and seven girls, ranging in age from 5 to 10 years, with an average age of 8 years, and (B) "Subsequent Session" group which included 13 children. One of them had more than one session, thus producing 17 sets of drawings. They were nine boys and four girls, ranging in age from 6 to 12, with an average age of 9 years.

In First Session group, one third (3 out of 9 sets of drawings) were correctly and blindly sorted out. Two thirds (12 out of 17 sets of drawings) were correctly and blindly identified in Subsequent Sessions group.

Osteopathic parameters

1. Pressure on top of head and shoulders

This osteopathic parameter offers some unfamiliar rationale of improvement to Human Figure Drawing literature (HFD). Hair and elaborated hairstyles acquire scores in quantitative systems such as those of Harris (1963) and Naglieri (1988). Consequently, a baldhead obtains a lower score than a head covered with hair; particularly the well groomed. Similarly, an added hat obtains additional score for costume. In qualitative analysis, styled hair and/or a hat provide a more normal or elaborate elements in drawn figures.

Osteopathic perception, however, finds support in linguistic expressions. It is commonly said that people carry the burden of their tensions and troubles on their heads and shoulders. Translated to drawings characteristics, this can be manifested in the following three ways, to graphically show pressure on heads.

1. a. Hair glued on head. A five-year-old girl drew Figures 7.1 and 7.2. Her physical problems were meningitis, pneumonia, headaches, vertigo (dizziness and imbalance), and outward bending of ankles and knees (Before: 7.1, After: 7.2).

In osteopathic judgment, hair was too close to top of head in Before, while lightweight curls were not stuck to head in After, indicating improvement. Using psychological view of better hairstyle in After than Before led to a similar sequence.

1. b. Heavy hair shading. An 8-year-old boy had "0" score on APGAR at birth as well as oxygen loss, Attention Deficit and Hyperactivity Disorder (ADHD), and shift of cranial (head) bones associated with forward protrusion of chin. Hair was heavily shaded in Before, but much fluffier in After, making it an improvement in osteopathic perception. Considering hair to be tidier in Before than After led to an opposed evaluation sequence by the psychologist.

1.c. A hat. A nine-year-old girl walked on tiptoes and had equilibrium difficulties. A hat in Before was an added weight on hair and head, while all weight is lifted off the head in After, making it an osteopathic sign of improvement. Whereas a DAP score would find hat and hair of higher quality in Before than baldhead in After. This led to an error in blind psychological sequence evaluation.

2. Body weight equally supported on both legs and feet

While both disciplines agree upon the importance of similarity in the direction of body and feet, osteopathic position is stricter.

A 9-year old boy drew Figures 7.3 and 7.4. He fell on his head from the second floor at 18 months and was involved in a car accident at age two, coded (Before: 7.3, After:7.4).

From an osteopathic perception, the body rested on both feet in Figure 7.4 unlike Figure 7.3 (body's weight supported on the right foot). Thus showing improvement. Similarly, from a psychological perspective, the legs were more asymmetrical in Figure 7.3 than in Figure 7.4, which makes them more normally drawn.

3. Alignment of right and left body sides around body midline

This subtle osteopathic position brings to focus asymmetry between body sides as a negative characteristic in HFD literature. Osteopathic position, however, is more rigorous, even in young children's drawings. Similar criteria are used by

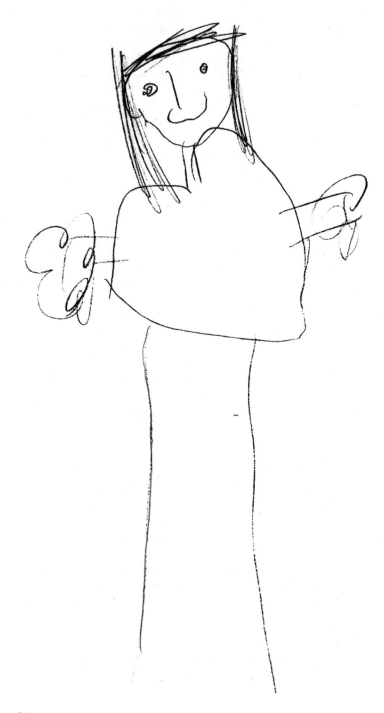

Figure 7.1

Figure 7.2

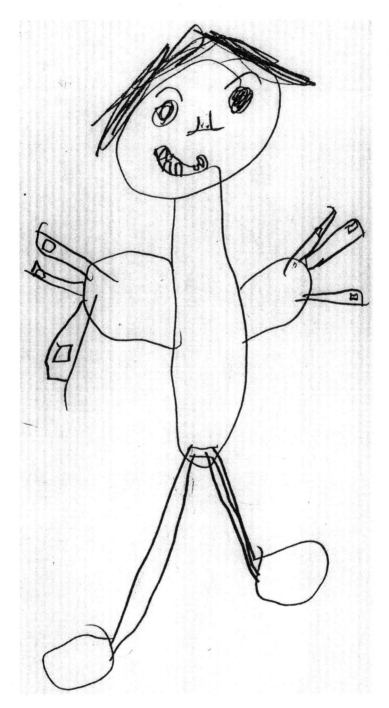

Figure 7.3

Figure 7.4

both disciplines in Set 30, previously examined in Parameter 1. a. Left shoulder in Before overlaps with face. In After, space exists between left shoulder and face. Body sides are relatively less asymmetrical.

4. Restricted versus liberated body parts

Figures 7.5 and 7.6 were drawn by an eight-year-old girl; whose problems were stomachache before meals and family communication difficulties (Before: Figure 7.6, After: Figure 7.5).

Osteopaths would notice that shoulders are lifted up like two humps, as if carrying a heavy weight in Figure 7.6, replaced by rounded shoulders in Figure 7.5; where the whole body seems more liberated than Figure 7.6. Psychologically, shoulders in Figure 7.5 would acquire a higher developmental score than Figure 7.6. In addition; thick hair covering the shin in Figure 7.6—as a perceptual deficit—is relatively lighter in Figure 7.5.

5. Counter clockwise spiral movement

This is an introduced notion to psychological drawing literature. In a normal abdomen, the cranial sacral movement (third movement after pulse rate and respiration) should be predominantly counter clock-wise (Barral & Mercier, 1988), as an important osteopathic principle.

A nine-year-old girl drew Figures 7.7 and 7.8. Her symptoms were: shifted head off shoulders, liver problem, central chain, or core-link problem (internal linkage of organs from base of head to bottom of abdomen) and toeing-in feet coded (Before: Figure 7.8, After: Figure 7.7).

Drawn trees have been considered as self-presentation on a less conscious level compared with the drawn persons (Buck, 1948; Hammer, 1997). However, drawings interpreters never evaluated the direction of spiral movement drawn on the tree trunk. A psychologist would consider both spiral drawings as psychic trauma (Hammer, 1964) regardless of their direction. Osteopaths would notice that spiral movement on tree trunk in Figure 7.8 is clockwise, but reversed in Figure 7.7. The osteopath worked on core link. This released abdominal tension related to toeing-in and led to normal counter clockwise movement in abdomen.

This notion is supported by the fact that both disciplines agree that the body in Figure 7.7 is of higher quality than in Figure 7.8. In both views, grossly asymmetrical upper body link to neck in Figure 7.8 (Before) became symmetrical in Figure 7.7 (After). Consequently body sides are equal around body midline in After. That is, a body of higher quality. Both disciplines would value the person being connected to her dog in Figure 7.7 but not in Figure 7.8. For an osteopath, even the dog's head is more liberated in Figure 7.7 than in Figure 7.8. Hair is heavier on the head in Figure 7.8 (Before) than in Figure 7.7 (After), as only evaluated by an osteopath. A psychologist would find flowers in Figure 7.7 to provide a happier mood than in Figure 7.8.

Figure 7.5

Figure 7.6

Figure 7.7

Figure 7.8

Overview

The most important result of this study is the substantial differences in children's figure drawings. Two figures drawn an hour apart were quite different in their characteristics. Such discrepancies could hardly be due to lack of reliability of figure drawings, as some projective drawings critics claim. Rather, children projected on their drawings of human figures what they felt about their bodies, when they experienced physical pain and when they were partly relieved. Employing osteopathic parameters, children expressed physical improvement as reflected on their Human Figure Drawings. Employment of psychological figure drawing characteristics led to partial success in judging improvement.

Two thirds of blind evaluations of improvement was accurate, in comparing figures drawn before and after osteopathic treatments beyond the first session. Osteopaths consider the first session to be unique, as compared to subsequent sessions, due to children's unfamiliarity with osteopathic techniques and with the therapist. They would also focus on basic ailments, which were submitted to different degrees of compensatory mechanisms.

Blind sorting of sequence of the two drawing pairs was hindered by differences between the two disciplines in employed parameters. For example, a hat and shaded hair were positively viewed by figure drawing psychologists but negatively considered by osteopaths. Added difficulties for the psychologist were absence of information about the treated physical ailments and absence of associative verbal comments made by children.

Osteopathic parameters—especially the unknown one to figure drawing literature—need further investigation. They may potentially enhance our psychological understanding of figure drawings, in cases of physical ailments.

SECTION 2: THE INFLUENCE OF OSTEOPATHIC TREATMENT ON CHILDREN'S DRAWINGS

Antoinette D. Thomas and Sonia Pinard

Would young children feel better about their bodies if they received physical treatments, which their doctors did not request? Would their body image, reflected on their Human Figure Drawings improve after a few treatment sessions? Could a psychologist blindly detect an improved set of drawings: a man, a woman, and self-presentation?

The objective of this quantitative and qualitative research was to evaluate the impact of three osteopathic treatments on the general well-being of kindergarten children. Well-being was defined as "children's physiology and/or emotions" (Rey & Rey-Debove, 1990). Treatments are supposed to improve body vitality and mobility of structures. The present study was done in partial fulfilment of Pinard's Diplomat in Osteopathy.

Hypothesis

It was hypothesized that three osteopathic treatments (manipulated variable) would improve physical lesions to promote children's physiology and/or emotions. Physical lesions are minute subnormalities in the *quality, position, mobility,* and *vitality of* tissues. Emotions, as reflected on human figure drawings, were assessed by Emotional Indicators (EI, Koppitz, 1968) as well as global quality of drawings, blindly evaluated by a psychologist.

Participating children

The sample consisted of kindergarten children in a school hosting 13 classes in a Montreal suburb. School principal and teachers' approvals were obtained to participate in the study. Three hundred letters were sent to parents, explaining the nature of the study. Those who signed consent forms for children's participation were 34 parents. They also responded to a health history questionnaire. Six children were dropped from the study due to withdrawal or disqualification.

Exclusion criteria included neurological defects or problems, receiving physical therapy, starting any medication or osteopathic treatment in the last six months, any cranium trauma, intellectual deficiency, deafness or blindness, any type of therapy in the previous six months, and older than 6 years 11 months or younger than 4 years 11 months. Inclusion criteria were: 5 years 0 months to 6 years 11 months of age and kindergarten attendance at the chosen school.

Participants were 28 children whose ages ranged from five years seven months to six years eight months ($M = 6.10$, $SD = 1.08$).

Two control devices were simultaneously employed. First research design was the Experimental Method. Investigated aspect was three osteopathic treatments followed by random assignment to Experimental and Control Groups. In lieu of the three osteopathic treatments offered to the Experimental Group—according to the "Collège d'Études Ostéopathiques" norms—Control Group did not receive any; children led normal lives during a time lapse of one month. The *second* control device was: Each subject served as his or her own control in Quasi-Experimental design (A-B-A). The first "A" was baseline measure and is referred to as Time 1, where both groups performed a drawing task. The "B" consisted of the month in which the Experimental Group received osteopathic treatments, while the Control Group led normal life. The second "A" referred to as Time 2, constituted re-administration of drawing task. Both groups made drawings under similar conditions at school.

Randomly assigned 15 children (10 boys and 5 girls) formed the Experimental Group and 13 children (8 boys and 5 girls) the Control Group. The two groups were statistically gender compatible. Demographic variables were also similar. Class teachers were given written detailed modified instructions to administer the drawing task. Children were gathered in nine small groups ranging from two to six participants.

The *quantitative* evaluation of human figures was based on Draw-A-Person test (Naglieri, 1988). It was the most recent standardized figure drawing test, which includes a man, a woman and self-presentations. The study somewhat departed from Naglieri's instructions of drawing a man first. Children were given the choice between a man or a woman for their first figure. Then, they were asked to draw the opposite gender in their second figure. In addition, time was unlimited as opposed to Naglieri's five minutes limit. Naglieri's total scores were transferred to standard scores.

Qualitative evaluation was derived from two sources. First, blind psychological evaluation of the higher global quality of all three figures in one set as compared to another set, done by the same child. Time 1 (before three osteopathic treatments) and Time 2 (after the third treatment) were not made known to the evaluator. Second, age and gender appropriate Emotional Indicators such as poor body integration (Koppitz, 1968).

Who did what?

To control for possible information contamination, research assignments were distributed between the osteopathic researcher (Pinard) and the consultant psychologist (Thomas). The researcher contacted the school and its board, wrote detailed letters to parents of all kindergarten children in the 13 classes. She displayed the purpose of the study, procedure, and inclusion and exclusion characteristics. Confidentiality of information and results were specified. She gave serial numbers to all children, randomly assigned them to each group (first 15 parents' acceptances to one group), and balanced gender. She also calculated DAP standard scores, later specified Time 1 and Time 2 sets, and sent material to a statistician.

Thomas scored Naglieri's cognitive scale and Koppitz's Emotional Indicators in both sets of three figure drawings in both groups. She blindly evaluated the global quality of randomized order of the two sets to identify sequence (Time 1 and Time 2) in all cases. She acted as a consultant for the research design and statistical manipulation.

Testing material and statistical methods

A devised grid included: (a) Naglieri (1988) scoring system (DAP), for each drawing of a man, a woman, and self-presentation, and (b) Koppitz (1968) Emotional Indicators applicable to participants' ages and gender. Health-history questionnaires covered demographic information as well as inclusion and exclusion criteria. Statistical analysis consisted of Pearson Product Moment Correlation Coefficient (r) and two-tailed t-test.

How was it done?

Written modified administration instructions were given to teachers, who were always blind as to children's groups. They administered the drawing test in group settings of two to six children each. Children were encouraged to take their time and to do their best. They were provided with a letter size paper for each drawing, a #2 pencil and an eraser. Teachers wrote, on the back of drawing sheets, children's report about who they drew: man, woman, or self. The second administration was repeated one week after the last osteopathic treatment. A maximum of one treatment a week was done, from mid-May to mid-June, according to parents' availability. All the drawings were sent for scoring and global evaluation to the psychologist.

What happened?

1. Quantitative results

There were no meaningful changes in the developmental cognitive aspect of figure drawing over a month interval, between two sets of drawings. Naglieri's standard scores evaluated children's cognitive development, t-scores between Time 1 and Time 2 were not statistically significant in both groups. In the Experimental Group ($M1 = 101.87, SD = 3.55, M2 = 102.20, SD = 4.14, r = .88, p = .001, t = -.168, p = .869$ ns). Similarly, in the Control Group ($M1 = 94.69, SD = 3.97, M2 = 94.77, SD = 4.61, r = .81, p = .001, t = -.029, p = .978$ ns).

2. A. Global quality evaluation of figure drawing

Three subgroups within the Experimental and Control groups were: (A) Correctly evaluated, the Time 2 being higher in global quality than Time 1, (B) Not evaluated, for discrepancy within global quality of one set of three Persons as compared to another set. These were three cases in the Experimental group and four cases in the Control group, and (C) Incorrectly evaluated. Subgroup (B) was excluded in both groups.

Global quality evaluation sequence was correct in two thirds of cases in both groups. In the Experimental Group, eight cases were correct and four incorrect. In the Control Group, six cases were correct and three incorrect.

2. B. Emotional indicators

Emotional Indicators (errors) were examined in *correctly* globally and blindly evaluated subgroups within Experimental and Control Groups. The total number of errors in final set of drawings (Time 2) was less than those occurring in

110

the initial set (Time1). Such improvement was statistically significant at the .01 level, within the Experimental Group's subgroup ($t = 3.78, p = .007$). The difference between the two sets of drawings was not statistically significant within the Control Group's subgroup ($t = .84, p =$ ns).

Support for global quality evaluation from emotional indicators

It is interesting to examine the total Emotional Indicators (Koppitz, 1968) or errors obtained by the four cases which were wrongly globally evaluated by the psychologist. The total Emotional Indicators is 12 in Time 1 and 25 in Time 2. That is, emotional indicators or errors were twice as many after the three osteopathic treatments than before therapy. That is, both global quality and number of errors are consistent in reflecting lower performance in Time 2 as compared to Time 1. Research design did include investigations about the presence of negative life experiences around the time when these children drew the second set of Persons in Time 2.

What is the point?

The blind evaluation of the global quality of the final set of drawings as being higher than the initial set was correct in two thirds of evaluated cases in the Experimental Group. Emotional Indicators (Koppitz, 1968), or errors, were fewer after, than before treatment, being statistically significant at the .01 level in the correctly globally and blindly subgroup of the Experimental Group. Such differences were not statistically significant within the Control Group.

These results support our hypothesis. Such statistically significant results are the *first* reported in osteopathic research. Considering the *very small* size of our sample, qualitative evaluation of human figure drawings is potentially useful.

It seems that the lack of statistically significant results, when the Experimental Group was analyzed as a whole, was due to the influence of the four wrongly globally evaluated cases. Such error was associated with qualitative errors but in the opposite direction. Twice as many total Emotional Indicators were found in Time 2 (final) than in Time 1 (initial) drawings.

The quantitative results (Naglieri, 1988) of the whole Two Groups obtained statistically significant correlation in total standard scores, between initial and final drawings. That is, there was no cognitive improvement within one month, as expected.

Illustrations

Drawing sizes were reduced and grouped in one page. The upper three human figure drawings of the D-A-P, in the two illustrations, are Time 1 (before treatment), while the lower three figure drawings are Time 2 (after three treatments), within the Experimental Group.

Case 1. *Obvious global quality improvement*

Nora was a six-years-and-two-months-old girl, whose drawings are shown in Figure 7.9. Her drawings were readily identifiable as being of higher global quality in the lower set than in the upper set. Hers is one of the eight blindly and correctly evaluated sequences in the Experimental Group. Several individual characteristics seem to work together, giving global impressions. Such characteristics are cited below. In both upper and lower sets of drawings, the left figure was a woman, middle was a man, and right figure was the child's self-presentation.

Figure 7.8 In general, all figures seem more relaxed in the lower than in the upper set. Eyes in the lower set have proportionate pupils within good sized eye circles. They are much more advanced than the filled-in dots in the upper set. Noses are two dimensional and include nostrils in the lower set, while noses in the upper set consist of a dot or a small circle. Neck-arm connections are drawn in sharp angels in five out of six in upper figures. Quite the opposite is noticed in the lower set; only one angled connection is seen. Number of fingers on hands in the lower set exceeds those in the upper set.

There is an improvement, between the two sets, in the man's right arm. In the upper figure the arm tapering is reversed; its width is narrower where it joins the body than the forearm connecting to hand/fingers. Trunks and legs are wider and better in proportion in the lower than in the upper figure. The left leg connection to hip in the upper woman's figure is tiny, wider at the ankle. Adopting an osteopathic parameter, all figures in upper set wear hats, but none does in lower set. Hats are interpreted as felt stress on figures' heads.

Case 2. *Would you agree with the incorrect sequence?*

Suzy was six years and six months old when she drew two sets of three human figures, each, in Figure 7.10. Why was blind global quality evaluation of sequence incorrect? Let us see. In upper set of drawings (Time 1) the left figure is a woman, middle is a man, and the right figure is self-presentation. Left figure in lower set (Time 2) is a girl, middle figure is a "rock" boy, and right figure is self-presentation.

The three figures in Time 1 (before therapy) seem to have higher global quality than those in Time 2 (after therapy). The three persons in the upper set seem to be smiling. All wide mouths are two dimensional. All six arms consist of two parallel lines and have equal width at their connections to body and hands. All figures have fingers protruding from forearms. All six legs are two dimensional.

In the lower set, facial expressions seem stiff. Only one mouth (boy's) is two dimensional. The girl has a one-dimensional mouth and it is missing in self-presentation (an Emotional Indicator or error, Koppitz, 1968). Self-presentation

Woman man Self

Woman man Self

Figure 7.9

woman

man

self

girl

boy (rock)

self

Figure 7.10

also misses a nose (another EI) and eyes are quite different in size. The girl's arms consist of two elongated shapes inside another two larger elongated shapes. Whether outer or inside shapes represent arms is not clear. In either case, arms are glued to the body and are too short compared to length of trunk. The boy's arms are also glued to the body, too short and done in zigzag lines. Thus, in these two figures arm-body attachments are poor. The boy has one-dimensional legs. None of the lower three figures has fingers. "Girl" is unidentifiable as a female. This figure's head is tilted; its axis is clearly off that of the body's axis. Adapting an osteopathic parameter, the curly, thick and long hair on the boy represents stress on the head.

What may be done in the future?

Drawing task would consist of only one "self-representation." It would be easier for blind global quality comparisons than comparing three figures in Time 1 to three figures in Time 2. Focus is usually mainly on self-image, rather than parental images. This would also reduce administration time. Effect of osteopathic treatments and its reflection on human figure drawings would be more evident when subjects are drawn from "one specific physical-need population" rather than a normal population. In case of children's population, their age would best be seven years and above. Eye-hand coordination would be more established than younger children. In addition, several Emotional Indicators (Koppitz, 1968) appear beyond five or six years of age, such as shading. Test administrators could be given supplementary guidelines for post-drawing inquiries, such as, asking children—in privacy—about unclear parts of drawings, (i.e., is this a tongue or a tooth?) and gently inquiring about children's emotions, (i.e., were they recently shouted at, punished or had a fight with a sibling?). Quasi-experimental design A-B-A seems most appropriate for similar research, as each subject becomes their own control in comparisons between before and after treatments. Larger samples are generally advisable, whenever possible.

References

Barral, J. P., & Mercier, P. (1988). *Visceral manipulation*. Seattle: Eastland Press.

Buck, J. N. (1948). The House-Tree-Person technique: A quantitative and qualitative scoring manual. *Clinical Psychology Monographs, 5*, 1–120.

Hammer, E. F. (1964). *The H-T-P clinical research manual* (3rd ed.). Beverly Hills: Western Psychological Services.

Hammer, E. (Ed.) (1997). *Advances in projective drawing interpretation* Springfield: Charles C. Thomas.

Harris, D. (1963). *Goodenough-Harris Drawing Test: Manual*. New York: Harcourt, Brace & World.

Koppitz, E. M. (1968). *Psychological evaluation of children's human figure drawings*. New York: Grune & Stratton.

Naglieri, J. A. (1988). *Draw A Person: A quantitative scoring system*. New York: The Psychological Corporation.

Rey, A. & Rey-Debove, J. (1990). *Le Petit Robert 1 par Paul Robert* [The small Robert 1 by Paul Robert]. Montreal: Les Dictionnaires Robert-Canada.

Thomas, A. D. & Dufresne, D. (2000). *Projective drawings: Osteopathic parameters.* Library of Congress Copyright: TXu 984–076.

Thomas, A. D., & Dufresne, D. (2002). Perceived body healing in children's drawings. In U. Gielen & A. L. Comunian (Eds.), *It's All About Relationships: Proceedings of the 58th Annual Convention of the International Council of Psychologists, July 2000, Padua, Italy.* Lengerich: Pabst.

8

THE FANTASY ANIMAL AND STORY-TELLING GAME

Leonard Handler

Stories have always had the magic associated with growth and development in our lives, but they do more than entertain us. They frequently carry symbolic messages which otherwise would be rejected. Children are typically raised on stories, as we were. The stories ranged from those of Maurice Sendak to those I made up when our children were young. They still remember those stories as they continued on into adulthood.

Given that many children and adolescents enjoy hearing and telling stories, I began asking children to "make up a story about a pet," but this approach did not yield any more than "ordinary" stories, with limited clinical material. This certainly was not what I had in mind; it produced only limited clinical material.

I decided to follow Altman, Briggs, Frankel, Fensler, and Patone (2002) who expressed what I had in mind: "For therapeutic change to occur, one must be able to conceive that something new and unexpected could occur in the interaction with the therapist that could upset the child's expectations and lead to change his or her internal object representation" (p. 11).

Note that all clients' names and identifying information have been greatly altered to protect their privacy.

Alice

One day I met Alice, a very frightened five-year-old girl. She stood rigidly silent before me, mute and terrified. I found myself finally putting a blank page in front of her, providing a pencil, and asking the child to "Draw a make-believe animal, one that no one has ever seen or heard of before." The child was surprised, but she suddenly became thoroughly engaged. She scribbled actively on the paper and placed a dot in one of the loops of her scribbles.

I asked Alice to tell me a story about the animal. She said something like, "This little fishie (pointing to the dot) is stuck inside the momma fishie and can't get out and it's drowning." The girl's mother had returned to the home after being away for almost a year. After returning, her mother kept constant connection with her daughter. There was no freedom to separate and to individuate. I then told the child a story, a therapeutic story much like this one: "The little fishie is stuck inside the mommy fish and will drown. But along came a helper fishie and made an opening, and the baby swam out, freely". Upon hearing the story, Alice immediately became active and playful. Her anxiety was gone.

During the next session the child drew the "baby fishy" being trapped again, but this time she had made an opening, allowing the "fishy" to swim in and out at will. There is something about the power and the immediacy of the assessor's story that had a therapeutic effect. The assessor can often grasp the immediate message the child was giving us, symbolically, otherwise known as externalization, in which the child's thoughts, feelings, and actions are expressed by the characters in the story, rather than by the child himself /herself.

Billy

In a recently published case study of a six-year-old boy, Billy, it became evident that he had been constantly challenging his parents' rules (Handler, 2012). He felt the need to protect *himself* from what he felt was their supposed "overwhelming power." He challenged them constantly, even for small requests of his mother and father. For example, what he wanted to wear that day, despite the fact that it appeared to be inappropriate.

I noted a similar response by Billy in his first visit, when the boy had a temper tantrum, hid under my desk, and stayed mute for most of the session. I also remained quiet during the session, but at the end of the session I reflected to Billy that we had a poor session because he didn't get his way. I suggested to him that we might have a better session, and more fun, next time.

At the next session I engaged Billy by asking him to draw a make-believe animal, one that no one had ever seen or heard of before. He was then asked to give the animal a name. Billy worked willingly and furiously on the drawing. I asked him again to give the animal a name, and he called it a Three-Headed Animal. I told Billy that I would then tell *him* a story about the animal, after I heard *his* story. I used his make believe animal drawings and mutual storytelling about them, rather than talk about his problems directly. In the first story he told, he challenged the therapist. Therefore, in turn, I developed "the king of the jungle" animal, a make-believe animal, who pressed the boy to follow adult rules and instructions of the new environment, the jungle.

Here is what the make-believe animal (me) said to Billy, firmly but gently: "You know, I am the king of the jungle. Everyone listens to me and does what I ask, (not that I tell) because I am the king of the whole jungle. I make the rules and you need to obey them and we can be friends." "You will not need all those spines (spines protruding from the make believe animal) to protect you, because I will protect you. That's what a king does." (Handler, 2012, p. 249).

I chose the case of Billy to mention because the child and I conducted most of the therapy using his drawings and our stories. Billy listened to the Lion

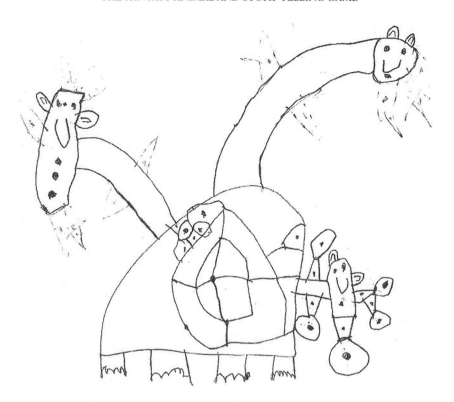

Figure 8.1 Three-headed animal. Note: reprinted, with permission, from finn, fischer, & handler (2012). *Collaborative/therapeutic assessment: a casebook and guide.* Hoboken, nj: john wiley & sons, p. 248.

throughout the therapy process, although he often tested the limits of the Lion. For example, in first drawing he indicated that the Lion was afraid of the three-headed animal. He smiled smugly, and then added that the three-headed animal was better because *he* had spines. When I pressured Billy about the spines he revealed that the spines were *only* to protect *him* from bad animals. Billy was telling me he needed to manage the adults in his life, especially his parents. Billy's attitude was reflected in his home, where he resisted their input and desires, simple as they might be.

I felt a need to establish the Lion (me) as a benign but authoritative figure in his life (the lion) and he need not use the spines to protect him because the Lion would protect him. Billy recognized that he could rely on the Lion's protection and cooperation, because he wanted to hear what the Lion said. He added ears to the heads, in order to "hear him."

At one point I told Billy that the Lion was very, very, very good at protecting everyone in the jungle, especially three-headed animals, so he could put away the spines

119

and let him do the job. I added that the Lion said to Billy that he, the Lion, would teach the three-headed animal to take his turn when he was more grown up.

The Lion and each of the five drawings, over a number of sessions, reflected Billy's attempts to cooperate, despite some further reluctance. He was unsure the protection was safe and secure. This reluctance is reflected in the drawing done during a rainstorm, where he drew a "Lightning Animal." Billy revealed that the "Lightning Animal" thought that it was so powerful, it could knock down *anything* or *anybody*. Note the worried look of the make-believe animal, and the agitation lines drawn within the figure.

Billy felt the "Lightning Animal" was strong and dangerous, until he accepted the reassurance by the Lion, who affirmed, "Sun, sun, sun, on the Lightning Animal, with all your power and make him go away, when I growl." The Lion shouted this with all his power, and very soon the lightning disappeared. Billy changed his mind as he sang the new title, "Now my name is 'Let the Lion Do it All.'" Since the worried stance was significantly reduced towards the end of the therapy sessions, he was more able to affiliate and collaborate with his parents and with me. Five of the complex drawings and their associated stories are now available (Finn, Fischer, & Handler, 2012, pp. 243–267).

Throughout the drawing and story-telling sessions, Billy tried to hide his fear, but began to rely on the Lion and did not attempt to hide his fear by powerful resistance with authority figures. On one occasion, when we were having a therapy session, during a violent storm, I could see that he was frightened. The Lightning Animal had a very worried face. In the work of Finn, Fischer, and Handler ("Lightning Animal," pp. 256–257) it was pretty clear that he needed support. He seemed to fear annihilation, with no way to defend himself. The Lion (me) said to Billy, "I can tame *any* animal, no matter how strong or how dangerous they are. I have special ways to tame them and to make them safe, even with very, very, very dangerous ones" (Handler, 2012, pp. 22–57).

At this point Billy showed surprise and interest. He listened to what I said about the powers of the Lion, making the animal safe. Billy said it was not possible to establish safety, alone, because the job was too great, or perhaps impossible. Given a few theatrics, I made a demand to the sun to make the lightning go away and for the sun to then shine: "Sun, sun, shine on the Lightning Animal with all your power and make the lightning go away, when I growl. And the Lion growled and the sun shone very, very, very brightly on the Lightning Animal and it dried up all the Lightning, and very, very soon the lightning disappeared" (Handler, 2012, p. 257). A happy Billy left the session, smiling and singing, "Now my name is 'Let the Lion do it all.'" Billy now had less to worry about, and he demonstrated it by his singing.

The authors of each chapter in the book (Finn, Fischer, & Handler, 2012) were asked to discuss the factors in each case that led to success. Although I cited nine such factors, there is room here for only two others (Handler, 2012, p. 264). The first, "Establish a playful, non-threatening relationship that facilitates a spontaneous relationship between the child and the clinician" was the

Figure 8.2 Lightning animal. Note: reprinted, with permission, from finn, fischer, & handler (2012). *Collaborative/therapeutic assessment: a casebook and guide.* Hoboken, nj: john wiley & sons, p. 256.

first factor. The use of drawings throughout the case highlights my observation that figure drawings, properly used, can be an excellent vehicle in the use of drawings in assessment. But as much more important is an excellent way to treat many problem patients. In addition, the combination of drawing and story-telling; is a powerful way to attend to the client's emotional needs, in treatment. In addition, a dramatic change in mood can be seen with the child, adolescent, or adult.

The use of alliteration, the active repetition of a key word or two, somehow seems to drive home to the client that the clinician is emphatic about how strongly he or she believes the interpretation to be. When Lisa, to be discussed later in this study, was asked what would happen to them if their father died, Lisa's father said, "Oh children, *I* am strong and healthy and I will be alive for many, many years and take care of you." I continued with the story I was telling, "They climbed on their dad and kissed and hugged him." At this point Lisa corrected me, saying that it should be "hugged and kissed" rather than the more correct, "kissed and hugged." This correction seemed to illustrate that she was carefully listening to my story.

Annie

Another child, Annie, was a six-year-old blonde, originally from Boston, who lived with her mother, a drug addict, until she was four, when she came to live with her grandmother on a permanent basis. Annie was exposed to drug parties, and was consistently neglected and left alone for hours at a time. She was frightened by the chaos in her home and could not understand the reactions of the crowds of people who came to her home for drug parties. Often there was not enough food to eat and Annie was not well groomed.

Annie's grandmother was troubled by the child's behavior. She was enuretic and was afraid to be alone in any room. She clung to her grandmother and followed her from room to room. Annie also had many frightening dreams. She also had difficulty in school; she shouted out whenever she wanted to and was too hyperactive to focus on school work. She was very hyperactive in my office; she jumped from one activity to another, investigating every corner of the room and asking questions about the decorations. As soon as I started to answer her question, she moved away, changed the subject, and asked a different question.

After one or two sessions like this, I began to help Annie focus on one thing at a time. For example, when she asked about an object I put it in her hands and we "studied" it together. She came to like this type of interaction and gradually was able to focus for longer times. I felt that if Annie could be less agitated and more focused, she would soon develop the ability to soothe herself and to delay gratification.

Gradually, over several months, Annie became more settled, but she still clung to her many stuffed animals and dolls she would bring to the sessions. Gradually she settled down and we were able to talk, draw, or play a few games without interruption. A turning point came when Annie asked if I wanted to take care of the three dolls she brought to her session. She lectured me about the kind of care and feeding they would need. I placed them carefully on a large chair at the corner of the room, a chair no one else ever used. I covered them with blankets and tucked them in. Each time she came for her session she checked on her "babies" and was reassured that they were being well cared for.

Finally, during the next session, she asked to draw and I suggested the make-believe animal drawing. She drew what she called a funny-looking tiger-raccoon and told the following story:

Annie: Along came a spider and the raccoon ate it. The tiger ate the spider and there it was, in his stomach. It [the bad object, probably represented by the mother] was in his stomach and he couldn't get it out. Now what to do! "I know what to do" the raccoon said, "I'm going to eat another spider, and a fourth spider, and then a sixth spider. They could never get eaten again, never could get out again"!

Dr. H: Did it [the spider] want to get out?

Annie:　It wanted to get eaten, but it didn't want to get eaten. It was crying. It wanted to get out, but it couldn't.

Dr. H:　Why?

Then I told my story: Once upon a time there was a spider and he was very, very, very nice. But it was lonely and it said, "Oh, I'm so lonely! I'm afraid to be out here alone. Maybe a raccoon can come and eat me and I can be safe inside the raccoon-tiger. So the raccoon-tiger ate the spider".

Annie:　Lots of them!

Dr. H:　And all of a sudden the spiders want to come out! "OK" said the raccoon-spider, and he went "cough, cough, cough" and out came the spiders! But soon they got scared and lonely again. "Oh", they said, "we wish we could be back again".

Annie:　(agitated) No, no, no, no!

Dr. H:　"Oh please, please, please", said the spiders. "Maybe, maybe, maybe", said one smart spider. "Maybe you'll let us come in and go out again when we want to".

Annie:　(with a very surprised look on her face, as if it was a new idea to her) What happened!? They got eaten and when they wanted to come out, they did?

Dr. H:　Yes, they got eaten and when they wanted to come out, so they did.

Annie:　(filled with excitement) They *did!*

Dr. H:　So they liked it in there.

Annie:　(interrupting) And they liked it [being] out.

Dr. H:　Yes, and they liked it out. But what they liked best of all is that they could come in and out whenever they wanted to.

At this point Annie was alive with joy. She reached over, took the drawing, and added large tears of joy all around the pictures she had drawn, and added "The end" at the top. Annie, like Alice, now allows herself to grow and develop, illustrating the normal separation and individuation process described by Mahler (1975). Originally Annie was ambivalent about whether she could begin to develop separateness, but she seemed to like the idea that she could also be connected. Previously, the only way she could conceptualize herself being psychologically secure was to be part of someone else (grandmother). The idea of being a separate self was novel to her.

Lisa

There are several case studies published using the Make Believe Animal Drawing and Story-Telling. The case of Lisa (Handler, 2007, pp. 68–69) is about a girl whose mother died due to cancer. Her mother had promised Lisa she would never leave the child. But now Lisa was suffering from the loss. It seemed, to the father that the child had worked through her loss, but she was really suffering badly. She drew a picture of a boy, next to a fox, shouting "Help, help!" She continued, "the fox lived in the woods . . . his mom died. One day *I* (patient/client) was in the forest . . . His dad, he went to get food one day and a hyena came and killed him, so we went to a cave and lived happily ever after" (Handler, 2007, pp. 68–69). My story focused on the reality of the loss and the strength of the father, reinforcing his ability to take care of and protect her. Note the use of the phrase, "One day *I* was in the forest," suggesting that she was now personalized in telling her story.

Then it was my turn to respond therapeutically to her story: "Once upon a time there was a fox in the woods and his mom died and the dad was with them. The kids were all sad and they were scared, too. 'What will happen if you died, too?' they asked their dad. 'Oh children' he said, 'I am strong and healthy and I will be alive for many, many years and I will always be with you and take care of you.' The children started to smile and then they laughed and all of them laughed together and the dad made dinner for everyone to eat. They climbed on their dad and kissed and hugged him." At this point Lisa interrupted and said, "You forgot to say, 'Don't worry, I will always be with you.' Then she got sick and had to die" (Handler, 2007, p. 69). Then I ended with, "If you close your eyes and see a picture of your mother, she can *always* be with you in your mind (p. 69). So the kids all closed their eyes and got pictures of their mama in their minds, and they said, 'Hi mom, I'm so, so, so glad to see you'. And they were happy."

Following the previous story Lisa soon became better connected, more cooperative, and quite friendly. She asked me to repeat the story again, which is a good sign that the story had important meaning for her. In this way she was able to tell me how hurt she was. Her sadness had not been resolved in continued sessions, and her father continued to belief that she had resolved her feelings of anger at the promised loss. She was arrogant and demanding of me in therapy sessions, but settled down for some time.

I asked her again to draw a make believe animal and Lisa drew a picture of a boy, next to a fox, shouting "Help, help" and used the term "booga booga," as if she used that expression to get rid of the fox. In her story Lisa placed the fox as living in the woods. It was described as having a short tail and no whiskers. As she continued to tell her story, "His mom died. One day *I* was in the forest; *I* saw it." Lisa then focused on how her father went to the woods and was killed by a hyena. Her reaction to the feared animal was to go "into the woods" and live in a cave "happily." In one sense the child was denying her feelings of loss. I told my story in a way that could be able to facilitate expression of her openness, to help in resolving the loss of her mother, and fear that she could lose her father as well.

More detail about this case is presented in the details of the case study by Handler (2007, pp. 68–70).

Toobers and Zots© is an award-winning creative construction toy, with bendable Toobers (long, polystyrene tubular forms) and Zots, smaller interesting shapes that fit on the tubers. These parts can be used to construct nearly an infinite variety of objects, from animals, to humans, to musical instruments, and much, much more. Children usually approach these multishape, multicolored foam pieces with great interest.

Although most children quickly become involved in manipulating the pieces, some are reluctant to approach or embrace them. Most of the time, when I ask the child to "make something, anything you like" they actively manipulate the various pieces, although some children limit their involvement at first and merely examine the pieces. Ordinarily, these children embrace the toy when they feel more at ease. Their reluctance to become involved is sometimes related to my open-ended request to make "anything." Some children ask for specific directions or they ask me to choose what they should make, while others just jump in and regale me with the many different objects they make.

Some children make up a game with the Toobers and Zots©, asking me to guess what they have constructed and then it is their turn to guess what I have made. Most children have very active and vivid imaginations, turning the toy pieces into a vast array of objects, as they begin to adapt in the therapy sessions, and when they begin to feel more at home with me. Their creations become more complex and elaborate, except for the few children who maintain a constricted style for some time. Sometimes the play process naturally evolves into a story-telling activity, initiated by the child or by me. This is just what occurred in the case of Anna.

Anna lived with her father, a physician, and a younger sister. Her mother had suddenly moved to Chicago a year or so earlier, to be with her new boyfriend, and left the children with their father. Anna's father was involved in suing her mother for custody and was very vocal about how annoyed he felt that the process was taking so long. He was a narcissistic man, one who expressed his feelings openly, in front of his daughter. He openly discussed his annoyance in front of Anna, saying in an angry tone, that if it took much longer he would just "give up" and let his ex-wife "have them." Each time he repeated the threat Anna became highly agitated. He seemed unaware of the panic he caused his daughter and the insecurity of leaving a home that was comparatively more protective than she felt her mother's home would be. Telling him about the chaotic effect his angry threats had on Anna did little good in stopping them. Anna never directly indicated that these angry pronouncements bothered her, but she acted out her panic by continuously literally throwing herself from one side of my office to another. Despite my admonitions, he continued to repeat his desire to leave the children with their mother. In subsequent sessions I mentioned again and again to Anna's father how destructive his words were to Anna and how frightened and abandoned she felt when she heard them, but he ignored my feedback.

Anna was quite resistant to visit her mother and became very troubled and filled with panic as the time for the next visit drew near. She hated the airplane trip, which she made at least one weekend a month, and pleaded with her mother to visit Knoxville instead. Her mother refused to come to Knoxville to see Anna and her sister. As therapy progressed, Anna visited her mother more often and she began to work through the anger she felt at her abandonment by her mother. Visits became more pleasant and the child settled down.

Anna initially approached the Toobers and Zots© in a quite chaotic manner, one that matched her interpersonal style in other therapy activities. Rapidly moving around the room, she would bounce back and forth on the couch and other furniture, mumbling softly, in a quite incoherent manner. Initially her verbalizations were bizarre and confused; she giggled, babbled, and mumbled under her breath. I began to wonder whether she might be psychotic, perhaps manic, or at least severely hyperactive (ADHD).

Anna would request that we play a game, or do one or another activity, and when we began, she quickly jumped to something else. Any efforts to calm her or focus her were ineffective. Verbal efforts to contain her movement, no matter how gentle or active, would result in even more extreme hyperactivity. Over a number of months she became calmer, less impulsive, and was able to stay with one activity or game, unless she was losing. However, she was eventually able to tolerate losing occasionally, and she became more actively focused on winning. My concerns about a serious diagnosis began to fade as Anna's behavior in the therapy room became more collaborative and less frenetic.

Anna had recently begun playing with the Toobers and Zots©, which was unusual because she typically chose more structured activities. She especially enjoyed making various objects and using them in a charades-type game, where I would have to identify the object and the activity. For example, she made an object that resembled a baton, and used it to march, as if she were a majorette in a parade. She then asked me to make an object and use it, so she could guess the object and the activity. In contrast with her behavior in the past, she stayed with this activity for almost an entire session, over a period of two months.

One day, Anna requested a change in our typical activity with the Toobers and Zots©. She asked if we could construct animals and tell stories about them. This was a substitute for drawing, she said, which she had previously declined to do. Her father had by now relaxed quite a bit, as it looked like he would be successful in his custody fight and he had stopped threatening to abandon his children to their mother.

I wanted to determine how Anna felt about her situation and whether her father's threats were still an issue for her. I made a deer with large antlers and she made a small animal, but did not specify what kind of animal it was. Ordinarily I ask the child to make up a story first, and then I make up my story, but here I wanted to see how she felt about her relationship with her father. So here I used the story as assessment, to determine the progress that hopefully had been made.

I made up a story about a cute little animal who Anna then named Lady. She named the deer with big antlers, Lonnie, her father's name. The little animal, Anna said, rested in the soft and warm spot between Lonnie's antlers.

Lonnie protected her, I said, and kept her safe all the time. They went for a walk and lions and tigers appeared. In my story Lonnie talked to them, assertively, and said, "Now look you animals, I'm not scared of you! You had better leave so I won't have to use my antlers to hurt you!" I said that he was protecting Lady and she was safe in between his antlers. I also said that the lion and the tiger knew he meant business, so they quietly left.

Then it was Anna's turn to make up a story, one which proved to be quite revealing and quite upsetting. This is her story:

Anna: They [Lonnie and Lady] always walked together and ate dinner. Let's eat dinner tonight. OK. So they were walking. On the way, Lady fell off. Lady lost *all* her lives. Lonnie was singing along and didn't know she fell off. "Lady, Lady, where are you", said Lonnie? He found her. She lost *all* her lives. All her lives came off and all of a sudden Lonnie said, "I'll never leave you again." Then all of a sudden, Lonnie smacked her with his antlers and she lost all of her nine lives. Lonnie put them back on. The story is, every time she gets hit, one of her lives is lost. She's now down to four lives. Then she got hit with a spoon, and she's down now to three lives.

Lonnie was so careful, but he hit a rock. Now there are two lives left. Then, all of a sudden, Lonnie knocked her down because he hurt his leg [her father had accidentally hurt his leg and was on crutches several weeks before], and she came over and said, "What's the matter"? And he smacked her in the face and she lost another life. Then, all of a sudden, Lady and Lonnie went to the hospital. "I'm very sorry" [Lonnie said]. "If you lose another life, you'll be dead". All of a sudden, Lonnie got out of bed. "I don't want to lose you [he said], you'll be gone forever".

Lonnie was really sad. "I'm so sorry, I'm so sorry" [he said]. He was night dreaming that he smacked her, and she lost her last life. He called 911 [emergency]. He was always sad, all his life. So they found one more life for her and put it in. But he knocked it out, accidentally and she lost her last only life and she was gone forever. The end.

Certainly, Anna did not feel protected by her father; far from it. Certainly, she had given her father chance after chance in her heart and mind, but he was damaging her, finally causing her to feel dead, mostly not by direct intent. She captured her father's insensitivity and lack of concern for her in her story.

During our next meeting I read the story to her father, who was visibly shaken by it. He then understood his daughter's unexpressed feelings about him. He promised, again and again, to be more careful when he was frustrated or angry and he became much more attuned to his daughter's feelings. After that session the relationship changed dramatically; he reassured her that he would never abandon her.

In the following session Anna spoke about her story and we decided to tell another story, together. Here is our story:

Dr. H: Once upon a time there was a deer named Lonnie and a ladybug named Lady.

Anna: Are you making up a story he *does* or *doesn't* care?

Dr. H: which one do you want?

Anna: Where he's taking care [of me]. [Note that the fantasy story has now become a story about *herself.*]

Dr. H: OK. So Lady was so sure Lonnie would take care of her. She said, "Please take care of me better. In the last story you didn't do so well." So Lonnie says, "OK, you can live up between my antlers where it's soft and safe and I will protect you from any animal that wants to hurt you."

Anna: How about if someone hunts you?

Dr. H: "Good question," says Larry. "I'm big and strong and if any animal tries to attack, I can get them to run away, if I buck up and use my sharp antlers."

Anna: So Lady says, "OK, it does look pretty soft right there, so let me get on your antlers. Can you bend down?"

Dr. H: Of course! He bends down and says, "Hop on!"

Anna: And Lady says, "Wow! This is soft up here. I'm gonna live up here the rest of my life. The end."

Dr. H: But what happens to them?

Anna: (continues) And Lonnie says, "I hope you are safe up there." And Lady says, "Don't worry, I will be." And all of a sudden Lonnie was walking and there were two tigers that walked up and said, "I'm gonna eat a ladybug! I can smell a ladybug!" "OK, I see one," one of the tigers said. And Lady screams and Lonnie says to the tigers, "Back off! I have big antlers. You can't harm me at all, me and my ladybug, Lady. I'm strong and if you come closer, you'll lose your life!" So the tigers ran away—in fear!! And Lady and Lonnie, from now on, and *ALWAYS,* stayed safe. The end.

Anna beamed with pleasure as she concluded the story. She appeared to be satisfied. Her father had finally gained some insight about his relationship with his daughter. He finally recognized the destructive effects he produced with his threats. Since that time he has softened considerably. Anna was able to process her angry feelings about her mother and was able to have a better relationship with her.

Adults

I tried using the make believe animal with adults, with interesting results.

For example, a 20-year-old female drew a huge black predatory butterfly-like animal, taking the entire page. She told me it represented her feeling about heterosexual interaction and the way she interacted with men. She was very troubled because she could not keep herself from developing a close emotional relationship with the person, and she would then quickly reject him, for no apparent reason. She would then quickly find another substitute male. She recognized that this relationship was primarily with healthy and adequate men. This became the central focus of the therapy sessions, and a closer examination of her family relationships.

Administration

Following the drawing for each administration, I asked the patient to find a name for the animal. The choice of a name often gives the clinician more information about whom the drawing choice represents. Other clinicians, whom I taught to use the administration of and interpretation of the approach, have tailored the administration to suit their own style. In a recent case study of the use of the Fantasy Animal Game with a psychotic teenage girl, Heikki Toivakka, a Finnish psychologist, listed the ways in which he has crafted the method to suit his patient population and personal style (see Toivakka, 2012, pp. 335–354).

Most of the children were able to name the make believe animal and to tell a story about it. Both Heikki and I found that a small percentage of the children could not craft a story (about 10–15%) and needed help to do so. I might help to tell a story by saying, "Once upon a time … " and then point to the child, asking him/her to continue. With some children I ask them to tell "another story" if I cannot find the message in the story the child initially shared with me. Usually, the second story is more meaningful, allowing me to find an important message.

I almost always ask the child how he/she felt about my story, in order to allow me to evaluate how well the message was heard and had affected the child. Sometimes the child will ask me to tell him/her the story again, which is a good sign that my story told to the child was effective. Sometimes I ask the child to tell me another story, to see whether I am able, through my story, to give the story some meaning for me. This is essentially what I call "symbolic feedback" that allows me to take stock of how my story, and sometimes their own, has affected the child on a deeper level.

Under no circumstances do I make any of this material conscious, unless the child or adult wanted it to be so. We allow it to be indirect and/or unconscious, unless the child chooses to make it conscious, which does not happen very often. In this manner we are doing assessment and we are doing psychotherapy too—providing insight and helping, wherever possible, to provide therapy, all at once.

Unfortunately, many assessors use the Fantasy Animal approach with their clients but do not take the next step, telling a story of their own to offer indirect feedback. They use the Fantasy Animal for diagnosis, rather than as a therapy approach as well. The process should be a collaborative one in the drawing and in the mutual story-telling process as well. The details of the drawn animal and a story about it, leads the therapist in a correct path concerning the patient's emotional needs.

References

Altman, N., Briggs, R., Frankel, J., Gensler, D., & Patone, P. (2002). *Relational child psychotherapy.* New York: Other Press.

Finn, S. E., Fischer, C. T, & Handler, L. (2012). *Collaborative/therapeutic assessment: A casebook and guide.* Hoboken, NJ: John Wiley & Sons.

Handler, L. (2007). The use of therapeutic assessment with children and adolescents. In S. Smith & L. Handler, (Eds.), *The clinical assessment of children and adolescents: A practitioner's handbook* (pp. 53–71). Mahwah, NJ: Lawrence Erlbaum Associates.

Handler, L. (2012). Collaborative storytelling with children: An unruly six-year-old boy. In S. Finn, C. Fischer, & L. Handler (Eds.), *Collaborative / therapeutic assessment: A casebook and guide* (pp. 243–268). Hoboken, NJ: John Wiley & Sons.

Mahler, M. (1975). *The psychological birth of the human infant.* New York: Basic Books.

Toivakka, H. (2012). Collaborative assessment on an adolescent psychiatric ward: A psychotic teenage girl. In S. Finn, C. Fischer, & L. Handler (Eds.), *Collaborative/therapeutic assessment: A casebook and guide* (pp. 335–354). Hoboken, NJ: John Wiley & Sons.

9

THE ART THERAPY-PROJECTIVE IMAGERY ASSESSMENT

Sarah Deaver and Matthew Bernier

The Art Therapy-Projective Imagery Assessment (AT-PIA) is a clinical interview consisting of six drawings, to be administered by art therapists in mental health venues to children, adolescents, and adults to identify developmental level, problem areas, strengths, defenses, diagnoses, and potential for engaging productively in a therapeutic relationship. The AT-PIA was developed by art therapists at Eastern Virginia Medical School in Norfolk, Virginia, beginning when the school was established in 1973. Through the ensuing years, the series of drawings was adjusted and the administration, art materials, and report format were standardized into its current form (Raymond et al., 2010). The AT-PIA was developed to provide a systematic method of art therapy assessment that is compatible with psychological tests and psychiatric evaluations. It is to be administered and interpreted by art therapists or art therapy students (under supervision) who are trained to assess mental status, personality dynamics, and diagnostic indicators expressed through artwork, verbal associations, and behavior. Interpretations are made both impressionistically (Lally, 2001; Scribner & Handler, 1987) and through matching and research-based methods (Gantt, 2001, 2004; Groth-Marnat, 1999). The AT-PIA, a direct-observation projective assessment, is based on standard clinical use of administrators' observations, interview procedures, and projective drawing tasks embellished through a wide variety of drawing materials.

Drawings in the AT-PIA

Drawing tasks were selected for inclusion in the AT-PIA based on art therapy and projective drawing literature and upon clinical utility in the experience of the assessment developers. The standardized order of administration has a clinical rationale as well: The open ended no-fail Projective Scribble Drawing (PSD) is first in the series, and the assessee-dictated Free Choice Drawing (FCD) is last in order to provide the assessee an opportunity for content and media control while finishing the assessment experience. Between these two are placed the more sensitive and perhaps affect-laden Favorite Weather Drawing (FWD), Human Figure Drawing (HFD), Kinetic Family Drawing (KFD), and Reason for Being Here Drawing (RBHD).

The PSD, which entails creating a free-form scribble and then developing that into a picture, was chosen because it is essentially nondirective yet allows the assessor to infer a number of salient aspects of the assessee's functioning. These include response to an ambiguous directive, ability to create a whole from diverse parts, evidence of planning versus impulsivity, projection of unconscious material, and capacity for abstraction (Cane, 1951/1983; Hanes, 1995; Kiendl, Hooyenga, & Trenn, 1997; Ulman, 1975). The FWD is modified from several studies that explored the meaning and diagnostic value of weather elements in drawings. For example, Gregorian, Azarian, DeMaria, and McDonald (1996) observed "black suns" in the drawings of traumatized children who were earthquake survivors. Manning (1987) studied a variation of the FWD, the Favorite Kind of Day drawing, with children with varying histories of physical abuse. She discovered differences in the line quality, size, and movement of inclement weather depending upon the degree of abuse suffered by the subjects. More recently, however, Veltman and Browne (2000) replicated Manning's study and found no significant correlations between degree of abuse and drawing characteristics. Kron (1983) studied the FWD and found that presurgery hospitalized children drew inclement weather more frequently than did nonhospitalized children. Studies of the Draw-a-Person-in-the-Rain technique suggest that this drawing yields information about assessees' coping mechanisms and stress levels (Rose, Elkis-Abuhoff, Goldblatt, & Miller, 2012; Willis, Joy, & Kaiser, 2010). We have concluded based on these studies and our clinical history with the AT-PIA that the FWD elicits information about a person's perception of and relationship to his or her environment, including coping with stress, affiliation versus loneliness, and sense of safety and security versus sense of danger in the environment.

The Human Figure Drawing and Kinetic Family Drawing are two projective techniques with which the readers of this text are undoubtedly familiar. We have included an HFD in the AT-PIA because it yields important information about developmental level (Cox, 1993; Deaver, 2009; Lange-Kuttner & Vinter, 2008; Lowenfeld & Brittain, 1987; Malchiodi, 1998), overall adjustment (Cox, 1993; Milbrath & Trautner, 2008; Yama, 1990), and sense of self (Hawkins, 2002; Milbrath, 1998; Riethmiller & Handler, 1997). The KFD provides important clues to family relationships, the assessee's sense of belonging to the family, and separation and attachment concerns (Burns, 1982; Burns & Kaufman, 1972; Kaplan & Main, 1986). We developed the Reason for Being Here Drawing (RBHD) from the experiences of our internship students. The assessee's approach to this drawing and the content depicted seem to suggest aspects of locus of control, ability to see the self in a causal chain, shame and guilt, personal responsibility versus denial or avoidance, and reality testing. The AT-PIA series ends with the Free Choice Drawing, which provides an opportunity for closure by offering a less threatening, client-directed drawing topic. Often the content of this drawing offers clues regarding the assessee's creativity and imagination, anxiety levels, and ability to self-structure.

Administration guidelines

Art therapists are as interested in the assessee's drawing process as they are in the drawings themselves (Hinz, 2009). In other words, through assessment art therapists attempt to understand not just the drawings but also the persons who drew them by directly observing them while drawing. The AT-PIA is designed around these basic principles in that not only are the six drawings clues to understanding the assessee, but the assessee's behavior toward and interaction with the art therapist, media selection process, responses to the materials, and verbal associations are also of keen interest to the art therapist.

The AT-PIA takes about one hour to complete. It should be conducted in a private office or art therapy studio, free from distractions and interruptions. To avoid a confrontational stance and allow the assessee greater comfort, the assessor and assessee should sit side by side or adjacent to each other, not directly across from each other, at a table. Art materials should be in good shape, not broken or incomplete, and displayed facing the assessee. The client should be told the purpose of the assessment, and the art therapist should explain that the drawings will be kept by the art therapist and that the assessment will be documented in the chart and may be discussed with treatment team members.

Drawing materials

Art therapists are often more interested in the expressive capacity of art materials than they are in the psychometric properties of their assessment methods. Therefore multiple drawing media are supplied when administering the AT-PIA. Standardized materials used in the AT-PIA include 9 × 12 inch bogus paper (80 lb) (grayish color); a set of 20 colors of Crayola© Washable Super Tips felt pens; a set of 24 colors of Crayola© Colored Pencils; a box of 24 colors of Crayola© Crayons; a set of 24 colors Crayola© "Portfolio" Oil Pastels; two HB drawing pencils, and one gum or vinyl eraser. These art supplies allow for mixing colors or using drawing materials singly, making changes using an eraser, detail, and elaboration; the gray paper allows white pastel, colored pencil, and crayon to be visible.

Drawing directives

The directives given to assessees are standardized and based on existing literature. In order, the directives are: (a) "Use one of these materials to scribble freely on a piece of paper," (b) "Draw your favorite weather," (c) "Draw a person from head to toe. Try to draw a whole person, not a cartoon or stick figure," (d) Draw a picture of everyone in your family doing something. Try to draw the people from head to toe, not cartoons or stick people," (e) "Draw a picture about why you are here [e.g. at the residential facility, in detention, in the hospital, etc.]," and (f) "Using any of these materials make one more drawing. This time you get to choose what to draw." If assessees have questions or seek clarification about directives, they are told to "do the best you can," and not much further clarification is offered. After each drawing is completed, the assessee is asked to turn the paper over and write a title for the drawing on the back. At that point, the administrator begins to subtly invite verbal associations to the drawing, such as "Tell me something about your drawing," or making an observation and then waiting for the assessee to expand on the observation. An example would be, "I see you have drawn lightening and rain clouds."

Documentation of the AT-PIA

The AT-PIA is documented in a standardized written report form (Raymond et al., 2010). Since AT-PIA reports are most likely read by professionals other than art therapists, the format for the report was purposely designed to be similar to psychological testing reports and psychiatric evaluations. It includes sections on Referral and Brief Bio-psychosocial History, Behavioral Observations (aligned with the Mental Status Exam), and Projective Drawing Tasks (tasks and the titles given them by the assessee). Next, the Discussion section includes identification of developmental level; clinical concerns, or problems as understood by the clinician through the artwork, behavior, verbal associations, and history; interpretations and inferences; strengths; and coping mechanisms. Finally, there are sections including Summary and Conclusions, Diagnostic Impression (using the current DSM multi-axial assessment), and Recommendations.

In the report, the problems section of the discussion is organized problem by problem rather than drawing by drawing. This reflects the art therapist's thoughtful and integrated clinical assessment of the client and avoids the tendency to simply describe individual drawings without making useful inferences. Instead, it is preferable to identify overall themes such as violence, shame, or fear and problems such as low self-esteem, depression, poor anger management, negative self-concept, poor impulse control, conflicts with authority figures, and so forth. Each problem is then supported with evidence noted in the behavior, significant history, verbal associations including titles for the drawings, and approach to drawing tasks. In looking at problems seen in the artwork, the art therapist considers manifest formal elements and drawing content and latent metaphoric and symbolic content. Interpretations and inferences about the client's psychological dynamics are supported with observations about behavior, verbal associations, and the artwork. The behavior and artwork should be congruent in terms of supporting inferences. For example, the report might state,

"Poor body image was noted both in behavior as seen in posture when drawing, attire, and verbal associations about self, and in the artwork as manifested in small, distorted human figures."

Interpretation

The AT-PIA was initially intended to be an atheoretical assessment. However, the administration procedures are an integration of psychodynamic and humanistic approaches. The use of projective drawings for assessments and the eliciting of titles and verbal associations are derived from psychodynamic approaches. The objective reporting of behaviors and the inclusion of titles and verbal associations as evidence of cognitive processes and thought content is integrative of the phenomenological, psychodynamic, and CBT approaches. Therefore, the AT-PIA could be considered an integrative approach to art therapy assessment. However, clinicians may write the discussion section of the report according to their own theoretical orientation to personality and psychological development formulation or conceptualization of mental status dynamics. For instance, references can be made to psychosexual, psychosocial, or cognitive development. Personality and mental status can also be conceptualized through psychoanalytic or archetypal interpretations, or explored existentially, trans-personally, or humanistically.

In identifying developmental level, most art therapists use Lowenfeld's (Lowenfeld & Brittain, 1987) stage theory of drawing development to classify the client's developmental level as seen in the artwork. It is important to identify if the observed drawing level is age appropriate, above age level (gifted, talented), or below age level (regressed or delayed). In addition to drawing development, especially with children, it is important to assess all developmental domains including cognitive, emotional, language, motor, and social or interpersonal as manifested during the assessment.

The initial approach to "reading" the artwork is to look at the six drawings as a whole, arranged from left to right in the order in which they were drawn. If an assessee has refused to execute any drawings, these are displayed as blank pieces of paper in the series. The art therapist can then begin to see patterns or themes that appear across several or all of the drawings. For example, color may have increased or (more likely) decreased as the series progressed. Color may exist only in the PSD, FWD, and FCD, but be absent in the HFD, KFD, and RBHD. Drawing style may have become more expansive or restrictive as the series progressed. There may be consistent content that cumulatively suggests a diagnosis such as depression or schizophrenia. Inferences are drawn and described in detail.

Interpretations are made impressionistically and through matching and research-based methods (i.e., formal elements or symbolism is consistent with many other patients with similar symptoms or life experiences). Art therapists are adept at impressionistic approaches to understanding drawings through their knowledge of human psychological development, psychopathology, and stage theories of drawing development. Further, their own personal art-making experiences, familiarity with art-based assessment methods, and knowledge of projective drawing research contribute to their interpretive skills (Deaver, 2009). Particularly with adolescents and adults, often the assessee is invited to a follow-up session to review the findings and develop treatment goals. In this regard, the AT-PIA is congruent with some of the humanistic and collaborative aspects of therapeutic assessment discussed by Finn and Tonsager (1997).

Abbreviated case example

We have derived a case example from our IRB-approved database of AT-PIAs collected for educational purposes by our student interns. For use in this chapter, we have changed certain details and created facsimiles of the original artwork.

"Susie Smith" was a seven-year-old female residing with her mother at a shelter for victims of domestic violence. She and her mother had traveled from state to state in an effort to escape the mother's abuser, finally aided by police to relocate to the current setting. The mother reported that Susie, too, was a victim; she had experienced verbal, physical, and sexual abuse at the hands of relatives and of the mother's abuser. Susie had experienced yeast infections and abdominal pain, and allegedly had been locked in closets, thrown on beds, poked with pins, and grabbed so hard that it left bruises on her skin. The mother had cut all ties with her family of origin because family members often revealed the mother's whereabouts to the abuser. The abuser allegedly attempted to teach Susie "how to kiss like an adult on the lips."

The AT-PIA was administered by the art therapist (the only clinician on site) as a routine service provided at the shelter. In light of Susie's history including isolation and lack of support from extended family, alleged abuse, and multiple moves, one objective of the AT-PIA was to determine whether or not a psychotic process was present.

Behavioral observations

At the assessment session, Susie was observed to be tall for her age and neatly dressed. She was oriented to person, time, and place. She made appropriate eye contact throughout the session and seemed to execute the drawing tasks with ease. Her speech was disorganized and at times she appeared to have difficulty verbalizing what she was thinking. Her verbal associations to the drawings did not always make sense as she demonstrated a flight of ideas and made up illogical fantasy stories. She needed help spelling words in her titles.

Her drawing approach was initially somewhat controlled in the PSD, but quickly became impulsive and disorganized, using only oil pastel and pencil throughout the series, and executing each task quickly. In the FWD, for example, Susie drew a female figure, a ground line, and some stars, and then rapidly covered the entire page with black oil pastel. Another example is that after drawing the RBHD, Susie became noticeably uncomfortable, fidgeted in her chair, removed the drawing from the space in front of her, and began rubbing broken oil pastel pieces over the tabletop. At times during the assessment, she worked so fast that she had difficulty keeping the oil pastel on the paper. Several times when Susie became distracted or perseveratively immersed in drawing, she needed to be redirected to task. She smudged the oil pastels on the drawings, her hand, and her face while she was talking, and as noted above she eventually went beyond the edges of the drawing paper and smeared on the tabletop.

Pencil, a more controlled medium that also enables greater detail than is possible with oil pastel, was first used with the KFD, suggesting that Susie's affective response to the topic of family was met by her employing greater control over the drawing process and content. This greater control was again exercised in the clearly depicted rape scene in the RBHD. Some color returned only in the details of the hand drawn in the FCD. The FCD, drawn immediately after the affect-laden and graphic RBHD, was executed by Susie by tracing around her own left hand which she placed flat onto the surface of the drawing paper. On the back of most of the drawings she encircled her name with a line; this encapsulation of figures or representations of the self is associated with artwork by children who have been abused (Cohen-Liebman, 1995; Malchiodi, 1990).

Please see Figures 9.1a–c and 9.2a–c for the facsimile drawings and Table 9.1 for their titles assigned by the assessee.

Figure 9.1a Projective scribble drawing

Figure 9.1b Favorite weather drawing

Figure 9.1c Human figure drawing

Figure 9.2a Kinetic family drawing

Figure 9.2b Reason for being here drawing

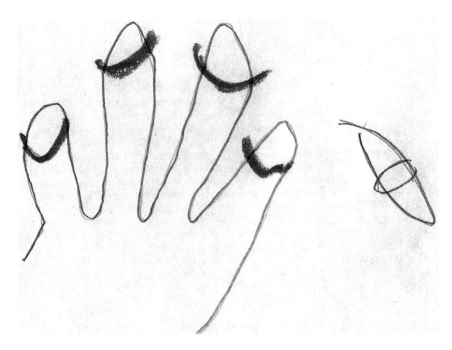

Figure 9.2c Free choice drawing

Table 9.1 Drawings and titles

Tasks	Titles
1. Projective Scribble Drawing (PSD)	1. I Like Butterflies
2. Favorite Weather Drawing (FWD)	2. Aqraba (Queen of Arabia)
3. Human Figure Drawing (HFD)	3. Rainboll (corrected to Rainbow)
4. Kinetic Family Drawing (KFD	4. Big Fish
5. Reason for Being Here Drawing (RBHD)	5. Rape
6. Free Choice Drawing (FCD)	6. Silly Eyeball

Developmental level

Susie's drawing developmental level fell on the border between the preschematic (ages 4–7) and schematic (ages 7–9) stages (Lowenfeld & Brittain, 1987). The simply drawn HFD dominated the paper and did not include a baseline or environment. Attention was given to the hair details. This was handled emotionally: The hair was drawn as large swirls of orange lines expansively filling the picture plane. Movement towards the schematic stage was evidenced in the FWD which included a baseline and stars properly placed in the night sky. Bordering between these two drawing stages is considered age appropriate for a seven year old. However, some of the drawings showed regression (low end of preschematic stage), lack of details, and poor organization which might be more indicative of an emotional response than a manifestation of cognitive delay. Furthermore, although some drawing content was age appropriate (e.g., depiction of fantasy stories) most was not.

Problems and concerns noted
in the drawings

Symbols and themes in the drawings and Susie's stories about them seemed more related to fantasy than reality. These included imagined butterflies, a windy night, a king ruining a castle, and the "Queen of Arabia" coming from the sky to build a new one. The references to the ruined castle and building a new one may refer to anxiety regarding the loss of the home and current living arrangements in the shelter. Imagery and verbal associations indicative of primitive, oral-level preoccupations include fish that are eating and fish that are being eaten, dental cavities, lip emphasis, stomach emphasis, and depiction of a bizarre family who share one body and stomach. Fear of the environment and lack of a feeling of safety were seen in the RBHD in which a "bad person" was depicted trying to scare a sleeping girl—and then raping her. Although seven year olds often include metaphors, symbols, and fantasy stories in their art and play, Susie's imagery and thoughts appeared overly erratic and loose. Furthermore, it is rare for an assessee to draw an explicit depiction of rape. Moreover, Susie's drawings contained bizarre qualities such as idiosyncratic use of color, excessive lines and overworking of the drawings, rambling stories seemingly unrelated to drawing content, and titles that were incongruent with drawing content. These qualities are typical of emotional disturbance including possible thought disorder.

There appeared to be a preoccupation with the female body. In the FWD, Susie depicted a queen that "has large breasts and lips and is very sexy." The HFD depicted a girl with massive swirling orange hair; large, smudged lips; and a heavily overworked area on the chest. This attention to female figures' breasts and lips, and the overworked area on the chest, seemed overly sexualized for a seven-year-old girl. Furthermore, Susie stated that the girl depicted in the HFD had died due to dental cavities, suggesting a fantasy that ingesting bad things would lead to death. Preoccupation with the female body and with sexuality appears linked with the graphic depiction of rape seen in the RBHD. When asked to draw the RBHD, Susie initially stated that she could not tell the art therapist the reason she was at the shelter. However, opting for a pencil, she then drew a figure on a box-like shape that she referred to as a bed. She stated there was "a bad person trying to scare a person who was sleeping." At this point, she put her fingers in her mouth. She then quietly turned the paper over and wrote the title, *Rape*. As stated earlier, such a graphic depiction from a seven year old is unusual and suggests the child may have been sexually abused or exposed to adult sexual activity or discussion.

As stated above, verbal associations to the FWD regarding external forces ruining a castle and building a new one may refer to anxiety regarding the loss of the home and current living arrangements in the shelter. When given the directive for the KFD, Susie stated, "I don't have one (a family)." In response, she drew one large "stomach," which had "lots of people hooked together" sharing the stomach. The "people" Susie drew were simply circles that represented people unknown to her who would have difficulty eating because they had "no arms" with which to pick up food. She included three fish in the communal stomach and stated the fish had just finished eating. At best, this remarkable and fantastical depiction of fish that are eating and, because they are within a stomach, are in turn also being eaten suggests a chaotic conceptualization of family, likely due to the history of abuse in the family and to the multiple moves in an effort to avoid the mother's abuser. At worst, the KFD suggests extremely primitive fantasies regarding eating or being ingested by parental objects.

Strengths and coping mechanisms

Susie presented herself as imaginative and expressive. She seemed capable of sublimating her anxiety into her artwork and fantasy stories, but was not often successful at this during the assessment. She employed the defense mechanisms of fantasy, avoidance, encapsulation, incorporation, and regression. She attempted to self-soothe through imaginative activity as well as physical actions such as putting her hand in her mouth or smearing the colors or rubbing the table with oil pastels. However, she did not demonstrate adequate age appropriate coping mechanisms to deal with her past trauma and seemed to be experiencing much primary process disorganized thought activity as well as a high level of anxiety.

Summary and conclusions

The assessment revealed impulsive, regressed, and anxious behavior and disorganized thoughts as seen in the approach to the assessment and the drawings themselves, illogical titles, and verbal associations. Susie seemed easily distracted and preoccupied by fantasy characters and stories. Given the history of severe and repeated abuse, a diagnosis of an Anxiety Disorder is usually considered. However, due to the lack of reporting (from the child or mother) or observation of specific Anxiety Disorder symptoms, a diagnosis of Acute Stress Disorder

Table 9.2 Diagnostic impression

Axis I:	Adjustment Disorder with Anxiety (Acute)
	Physical Abuse of Child
	Sexual Abuse of Child
	R/O Attention-Deficit/Hyperactivity Disorder
	R/O Psychotic Disorders
Axis II:	None
Axis III:	Hx of Yeast Infection
	Hx of Abdominal Pain
Axis IV:	Environmental Stress, Economic Stress
	Repeated victim of sexual and physical abuse
Axis V:	GAF 60

or Posttraumatic Stress Disorder could not be made. It was also difficult to account for impulsivity and distractibility by Attention-Deficit/Hyperactivity Disorder without further observation in settings such as school. Although Susie appeared oriented to person, time, and place, psychosis should be ruled out as suggested by the bizarre qualities of the artwork, titles, and stories. The client may currently have sufficient ego strength, coping mechanisms, and resilience to function despite her history of abuse. However, this assessment suggested that the client was on the verge of more serious psychopathology. Table 9.2 contains the diagnostic impression based on the AT-PIA.

Recommendations

A number of recommendations were made based on the AT-PIA including a psychiatric evaluation of the need for more intensive interventions such as medication or hospitalization. Individual art therapy was recommended to improve ego strength, decrease impulsivity and anxiety, address symptoms related to the client's history of domestic violence and abuse, and address feelings related to shelter living. In addition, dyad art therapy with the mother was recommended to support bonding and feelings of safety and security. Group art therapy to increase positive peer interactions and to foster positive community living in the shelter was suggested for the future, after Susie's anxiety had lessened and the bond with the mother had improved.

Discussion

Becoming an art therapist is an intensely personal journey for our students because in addition to rigorous art therapy, counseling, and psychology coursework, a thesis requirement, and hundreds of hours in supervised internships, introspection and reflection as well as personal exploration through artmaking are nonacademic requirements. Our students take a year-long course in which they learn the psychological and artistic properties of a variety of art processes and their application with a wide range of special populations of patients. We attempt to inculcate reflection through artistic means into the curriculum throughout the two years of study, through art-based assignments, and through students' use of visual journaling (Deaver & McAuliffe, 2009). Indeed, art therapists' continued immersion in their own art process is crucial to their optimum functioning as *art* therapists (Allen, 1992). For our students, this combination of an assessment course that is steeped in current literature about art-based assessment, the year-long art therapy processes and materials course, and personal reflection through visual journaling facilitates our students' unique capacity for empathic understanding of clients through their art productions. As Rancour and Barrett stated:

> By "sitting with" a piece of art, really "watching" it, and observing what it evokes in one's self, the observer learns something, not only about the larger world but also about one's own responses about that world, thereby forging a connection between internal and external experiences.
>
> (2011, p. 68)

Since the AT-PIA is an art-based clinical interview rather than simply a diagnostic test based on a single drawing, the art therapist's skill in observation, knowledge of research-based projective drawing literature, and ability to resonate with the assessees and their drawings are crucial elements to sensitive and accurate interpretation. Scribner and Handler (1987) concluded that an empathic and intuitive approach, supplemented by "matching" based upon the literature, may be the most successful approach to drawing interpretation. This is the approach we teach our art therapy students.

The literature is clear about the impact that culture has upon children's drawing style and content: Artistic and cultural traditions are reflected in children's drawings (Anderson, 1995; Cox, 1998, 2005; Golomb, 2002; Milbrath & Trautner, 2008; Teichman, 2001). Therefore, as the U.S. population changes, and as art therapy expands into Asia and South America, there is reason to question the contemporary applicability of our Western-based assessment methods. Art therapists are ethically mandated to develop cultural competence that includes knowledge of the artistic traditions of their multicultural clients (American Art Therapy Association, nd). In this context, our continued reliance upon Lowenfeld's stage theory of children's artistic development and upon traditional interpretations of various projective drawing techniques demand debate and further research (Alter-Muri, 2002; Wegmann & Lusebrink, 2000).

144

Keeping these admonitions in mind, however, our history with the AT-PIA suggests it is a rich assessment approach that provides in-depth data essential to initial understanding of clients, their problems, their strengths and coping mechanisms, and that is valuable in treatment planning and as a piece of a comprehensive multidisciplinary assessment.

References

Allen, P. (1992). Artist in residence: An alternative to "clinification" for art therapists. *Art Therapy: Journal of the American Art Therapy Association, 9*, 22–29.

Alter-Muri, S. (2002). Viktor Lowenfeld revisited: A review of Lowenfeld's preschematic, schematic, and gang age stages. *American Journal of Art Therapy, 40*, 170–192.

American Art Therapy Association. *Multicultural and diversity competencies.* Retrieved from http://www.americanarttherapyassociation.org/upload/multiculturalcompetencies2011.pdf

Anderson, S. (1995). Social scaling in children's family drawings. A comparative study in three cultures. *Child Study Journal, 25*, 97–121.

Burns, R. C. (1982). *Self-growth in families: Kinetic Family Drawings (KFD): Research and applications.* New York: Brunner/Mazel.

Burns, R. C., & Kaufman, S. H. (1972). *Styles and symbols in Kinetic Family Drawings.* New York: Brunner/Mazel.

Cane, F. (1951/1983). *The artist in each of us* (Rev. Ed.). Craftsbury Common: Art Therapy Productions.

Cohen-Liebman, M. (1995). Drawings as judiciary aids in child sexual abuse litigation: A composite list of indicators. *The Arts in Psychotherapy, 22*(5), 475–483.

Cox, M. (1993). *Children's drawings of the human figure.* New York: Psychology Press.

Cox, M. (1998). Drawings of people by Australian aboriginal children: The intermixing of cultural styles. *Drawing Research and Development, 17*(1), 71–79.

Cox, M. (2005). *The pictorial world of the child.* New York: Cambridge University Press.

Deaver, S. (2009). A normative study of children's drawings: Preliminary research findings. *Art Therapy: Journal of the American Art Therapy Association, 26*(1), 4–11.

Deaver, S., & McAuliffe, G. (2009). Reflective visual journaling during art therapy and counseling internships: A qualitative study. *Reflective Practice, 10*(5), 615–632.

Finn, S., & Tonsager, M. (1997). Information-gathering and therapeutic models of assessment: Complementary paradigms. *Psychological Assessment, 9*(4), 374–385.

Gantt, L. (2001). The Formal Elements Art Therapy Scale: A measurement system for global variables in art. *Art Therapy: Journal of the American Art Therapy Association, 18*(1), 50–55.

Gantt, L. (2004). The case for formal art therapy assessments. *Art Therapy: Journal of the American Art Therapy Association, 21*(1), 18–29.

Golomb, C. (2002). *Art in context: A cultural and comparative perspective.* Washington: American Psychological Association.

Gregorian, V., Azarian, A., DeMaria, M., & McDonald, L. (1996). Colors of disaster: The psychology of the "black sun." *The Arts in Psychotherapy, 23*, 1–14.

Groth-Marnat, G. (1999). *Handbook of psychological assessment* (3rd ed.). New York: Wiley.

Hanes, M. (1995). Clinical application of the "scribble technique" with adults in an acute inpatient psychiatric hospital. *Art Therapy: Journal of the American Art Therapy Association, 12*(2), 111–117.

Hawkins, B. (2002). Children's drawing, self expression, identity and the imagination. *International Journal of Art and Design Education, 21*(3), 209–219.

Hinz, L. (2009). *The expressive therapies continuum: A framework for using art in therapy.* New York: Routledge.

Kaplan, J., & Main, M. (1986). *Instructions for the classification of children's family drawings in terms of representation of attachment.* Unpublished manuscript, University of California at Berkeley.

Kiendl, C., Hooyenga, K.,& Trenn, E. (1997). Empowered to scribble. *Art Therapy: Journal of the American Art Therapy Association, 14*(1), 37043.

Kron, C. (1983). *A pilot study of the emotional environment of surgically hospitalized children as reflected in their Favorite Weather Drawings.* Unpublished master's thesis, Eastern Virginia Medical School, Norfolk, VA.

Lally, S. (2001). Should Human Figure Drawings be admitted to court? *Journal of Personality Assessment, 76*(1), 135–149.

Lange-Kuttner, C., & Vinter, A. (2008). *Drawing and the non-verbal mind.* New York: Cambridge University Press.

Lowenfeld, V., & Brittain, W.L. (1987). *Creative and mental growth* (8th ed.). New York: Macmillan.

Malchiodi, C. (1990). *Breaking the silence: Art therapy with children from violent homes.* New York: Brunner/Mazel.

Malchiodi, C. (1998). *Understanding children's drawings.* New York: Guilford.

Manning, T. (1987). Aggression depicted in abused children's drawings. *The Arts in Psychotherapy, 14,* 15–24.

Milbrath, C. (1998). *Patterns of artistic development in children.* New York: Cambridge University Press.

Milbrath, C., & Trautner, H. (Eds.). (2008). *Children's understanding and production of pictures, drawings, and art.* Cambridge: Hogrefe & Huber Publishers.

Rancour, P., & Barrett, T. (2011). Art interpretation as a clinical intervention toward healing. *Journal of Holistic Nursing, 29*(1), 68–80.

Raymond, L., Bernier, M., Rauch, T., Stovall, K., Deaver, S., & Sanderson, T. (2010). *The Art Therapy-Projective Imagery Assessment* (Rev. Ed.). Unpublished manual available from Graduate Art Therapy and Counseling Program, Eastern Virginia Medical School, 651 Colley Avenue, Suite 300, Norfolk, VA 23507.

Riethmiller, R., & Handler, L. (1997). Problematic methods and unwarranted conclusions in DAP research: Suggestions for improved research procedures. *Journal of Personality Assessment, 69*(3), 459–475.

Rose, S., Elkis-Abuhoff, D., Goldblatt, R., & Miller, E. (2012). Hope against the rain: Investigating the psychometric overlap between an objective and projective measure of hope in a medical student sample. *The Arts in Psychotherapy 39*(4), 272–278.

Scribner, C., & Handler, L. (1987). The interpreter's personality in Draw-a-Person interpretation: A study of interpersonal style. *Journal of Personality Assessment, 51,* 112–122.

Teichman, Y. (2001). The development of Israeli children's images of Jews and Arabs and their expression in Human Figure Drawings. *Developmental Psychology, 37,* 749–761.

Ulman, E. (1975). A new use of art in psychiatric diagnosis. In E. Ulman & P. Dachinger (Eds.), *Art therapy in theory and practice* (pp. 361–386). New York: Schocken.

Wegmann, P., & Lusebrink, V. (2000). Kinetic Family Drawing scoring method for cross-cultural studies. *The Arts in Psychotherapy, 27*(3), 179–190.

Willis, L., Joy, S., & Kaiser, D. (2010). Draw-a-Person-in-the-Rain as an assessment of stress and coping resources. *The Arts in Psychotherapy, 37,* 233–239.

Veltman, M., & Browne, K. (2000). An evaluation of Favorite Kind of Day Drawings from physically maltreated and non-maltreated children. *Child Abuse & Neglect, 24*(1), 1249–1255.

Yama, M. (1990). The usefulness of Human Figure Drawings as an index of overall adjustment. *Journal of Personality Assessment, 54*(1&2), 78–86.

10

THE WARTEGG DRAWING COMPLETION TEST

A New Methodology

Alessandro Crisi

Brief history of the test

This test was created in 1926 and it took its name from that of its author, the German psychologist Ehrig Wartegg (1897–1983). His first article was published in 1939 and his book in 1953. In English-speaking countries the test is known as Wartegg Drawing Completion Test (WDCT). In the present work the term Wartegg Test will be used.

Test description

The test consists of a form that contains eight boxes or squares (1 to 8), arranged in two parallel rows. Each box has a different graphic sign (Figure 10.1).

The Wartegg Test has had mixed fortunes; it is widely used in Northern and Southern Europe and in South America. The tool is unknown in North America where we have only one book (Kinget, 1952). It was described by Buros (1959) as "an interesting tool for its potential."

The Wartegg Test is a projective drawing technique, with semistructured graphic stimuli. Subjects are prone to project contents, dynamics, and organization of their personality (Rapaport, 1977). According to Bornstein (2007), the Wartegg Test can be classified as a stimulus–attribution test in which examinees attribute meaning through their interpretations' characteristics.

The Wartegg Test instructions are easily understood by examinees; it is short and quick to administer; most subjects complete it in an average time of 5–10 minutes, 10–15 minutes for scoring and computations, and 30 minutes for writing the report. It is simple in structure on a perceptive level.

The simplicity of the stimulus-signs bypasses the defensive mechanisms of the subject (Mc Cully, 1988). An easy instruction makes it suitable for subjects from four years old. The test is suitable for group administration using

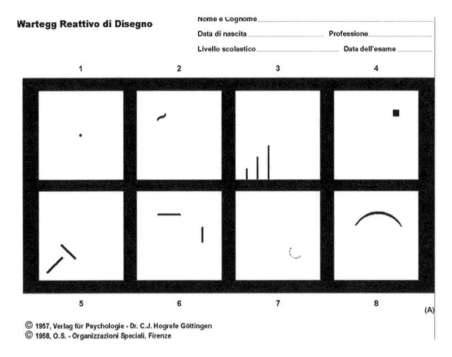

Figure 10.1 The Wartegg drawing completion test form

custom-designed software. Due to these features, it has been adopted as a selection tool by the Italian Armed Forces since 2002.

A new methodology

A new methodology for scoring and interpreting the Wartegg Test, which differs from Wartegg's, has been validated during 30 years of research and demonstrated utility in clinical assessment and research. In clinical context, it has been developed in the theoretical context of Dynamic Psychology (Crisi, 1998, 2007).

The new methodology, called CWS (Crisi Wartegg System), is based on two key elements: 1) two devised/original scoring categories: Evocative Character (EC) and Affective Quality (AQ); 2) focus on drawings' Order of Sequence.

Validity and reliability

One of the most important studies compared the Wartegg Test results and psychological tests used by the Italian Navy for admission (1999):

1) High concordance between the general evaluations of the Selection Department and Wartegg Test data.

2) Concordance (86.4 %) between Wartegg Test and MMPI-2 and (89.2 %) between Wartegg Test and Guilford-Zimmermann.

3) Other researchers found a very high (k = 0.91) inter-scorer agreement between expert psychologists (Crisi, 2007).

Evaluations and norms presented below are derived from a recent Italian standardization on samples of about 2,300 subjects (Crisi, 2007).

Administration

Clients sit facing the examiner, who hands them the Wartegg Test form (Figure 10.1) and a pencil (#2 HB) without an eraser, then gives the following instructions: "As you can see, this form is divided into 8 boxes; in each box there is a little mark. Using the mark as a starting point, make a drawing in each box that means something, preferably the first thing that comes to mind. If possible, don't make abstract drawings. You don't have to go in numerical order; work at your own pace; there is no time limit."

The examiner makes a note on the administration form of the Order of Sequence chosen by the subject and Performance Time, then asks the subject, according to the numerical order of the eight boxes, to describe each drawing and writes his/her descriptions.

Scoring

On the Scoring Form, drawings and descriptions of each box are evaluated using eight scoring categories, of which the following are the most important:
1) Evocative Character (EC); 2) Affective Quality (AQ); and 3) Form Quality (FQ).

Scoring categories description

1) Evocative character

It points to the capacity of a specific stimulus (a graphic sign) to recall and facilitate the projection of particular psychic contents.

Scoring the evocative character

Score = 1: The client picks up the implicit suggestion of the box stimulus sign and makes a drawing corresponding with its evocative character.
Score = 0.5: Drawings in which the evocative character is partially picked up.
Score = 0: Drawings completely inadequate; the subject does not pick up the stimulus–sign suggestion.

2) The affective quality

It is an evaluation exclusively based on the subject's affective connotation of each drawing. It concerns drawings of all contents not only human representations.

Scoring the affective quality

Score = 1: For positive contents such as human, animal, or natural elements.

Score = 0.5: For neutral contents such as objects, letters, numbers, symbols, mineral, architectural, or abstract.

Score = 0: For negative contents such as anatomy, weapons, explosion, smoke, cloud, or rain.

Note. To ensure uniformity of scoring between psychologists and consequently increase the reliability of the test, a huge list of contents accompanied by their scoring, are found on the website of the Italian Institute of Wartegg (www.wartegg.com).

3) Form quality

It is based on the criterion of evidence (or obviousness).

Scoring form quality:

Score = 1: The meaning of the drawing is evident and immediately perceived by the examiner and does not need to be explained by the client.

Score = 0.5: The meaning of the drawing is not immediately perceived or may have different interpretations. To become understandable, the client needs to give further explanations.

Score = 0: The meaning is quite incomprehensible, inaccurate, or arbitrary and even the client's verbalization does not permit the identification of the drawing.

Diagnostic meaning of main indexes

There are many indexes; the most important are presented below. Percentages of normal subjects are in brackets.

Percentage of affective quality (AQ + %)

This index allows us to assess the potential emotional disposition of clients; the type of affect that characterizes their emotional life; the presence of repression;

the degree of harmony that they are able to achieve in relationships with the environment; and the presence of depression.

> < 50% = depressive personalities that are scarcely interested in interpersonal relationships, unable to establish a connection with the environment, or very neurotic (repression of affect) (14%);
>
> 50–62% = Good tuning with feelings, emotions, and affects (59%);
>
> 63–75% = Excessive adaptation to surroundings and its requests; dependence and imitation of the others' behavior (25%);
>
> > 75% = Highly adjusted subjects, who are accommodating in their interpersonal relationships and conceal defenses, such as denial. These values are also compatible with high impulsivity and tendency to act on emotions. (4%)

Affective/Form quality ratio (A/F)

This ratio indicates the presence or absence of an emotional stability or an emotional balance. It is a ratio between the raw score of the Affective Quality and that of the Form Quality. The range is: 0–4 in each ratio.

> A < F: A normal value of 1–2 points on F indicate stability and mature control over feelings and emotions; affective equilibrium (65%).
>
> A << F: More than 2 points on F favors rigidity, inhibition and coercion, conformism, low spontaneity (9%).
>
> A > F: When A is still less than F but with only 0.5 point in favor of F (15.5%) and the cases in which A = F (6.5%) immaturity, dependence; impulsivity.
>
> A >> F: When A is higher than F egocentrism; acting out inclination; "explosive personalities"; affective conflicts (4%).

Analysis of sequence—1

During performance, the subject is free to choose the order of sequence of boxes and drawings. Wartegg affirmed, "The sequence of the drawings must not be considered casual because the drawings have a connection with the archetypical signs", (Wartegg, 1972, p. 32).

In 92% of performances, sequence differs from one subject to another and is called Individualized Performances, while the "numerical" Order of Succession, in which the subject makes the drawings in order (1 to 8), occurs only in 7% of normal subjects.

Based on the author's clinical experience, an original method was developed to analyze the Order of Sequence.

A) If the Box was drawn in the first half (1–4): It is appraised as:

Choice (C): if the raw score, obtained by adding the raw scores of the Evocative Character (1, 0.5, or 0) and of the Affective Quality (1, 0.5, or 0), is greater than 1.
Ambivalent Choice (AC): if the raw score is equal to 1.
Negative Compensation (NC): if the raw score is less than 1.

B) If the Box is drawn in the second half we appraise it as:

Delay (D): if the raw score is less than 1.
Ambivalent Delay (AD): if the raw score is equal to 1.
Positive Compensation (PC): if the raw score is greater than 1.

To complete Analysis of Sequence 1, we also write the obtained raw scores, in each Box, in some categories of scoring (Form Quality, Ratio A/ F, Impulse Responses).

In the case illustration below (Figure 10.2), the subject drew Box 3 first, Box 5 second, and so on. Taking into consideration the raw scores of EC and AQ each box is evaluated. So, Box 3 = C, Box 5 = AC, Box 8 = AC, and so on.

Each evaluation of the Analysis of Sequence 1 has a special diagnostic meaning.

* Choice (C): is the most positive code that a Box can obtain. Choices indicate the most developed and integrated areas. On the Basis of these key

	ANALYSIS OF SEQUENCE 1							
	I	**II**	**III**	**IV**	**V**	**VI**	**VII**	**VIII**
OoS	3	5	8	7	2	6	1	4
EC	1	.5	.5	0	1	.5	1	0
AQ	.5	.5	.5	0	1	.5	.5	0
Code	C	AC	AC	NC	PC	AD	PC	D
FQ	1	.5	.5	1	1	1	1	1
A/F	.5/1	.5/.5	.5/.5	0/1	1/1	.5/1	.5/1	0/1
I.R.			*					

Figure 10.2 The analysis of sequence 1

elements, the subject's personality structure evolved and matured. On one end, a Choice indicates an area of preference, major attunement, and integration. On the other end, very high scores (scores of 2 to be exact) can also indicate an excessive dominance of those areas in the subject's personality. These areas' hypertrophy inevitably subtracts emotional energy to other functions. In terms of prognosis, Choices represent the aspects of personality on which the therapeutic alliance can be founded

- Ambivalent Choice (AC): indicates that the subject experiences a certain degree of ambivalence of which he/she is usually aware; it shows that the subject experiences opposite feelings of equal intensity. For example, in Box 1, an AC response indicates some indecision, insecurity, and a conscious tendency to self-deprecation, which is related to a desire for autonomy and agency. In other words, AC responses are indicative of some conflict on the dimension of dependence autonomy.

- Negative Compensation (NC): indicates a higher degree of ambivalence and sharp conflict within the area of the Psyche that is evoked by the Box. These feelings are generally not within the subject's awareness, but are instead unconscious. These responses are true compensations, and, as such, tend to carry negative meaning. However, they should be understood from two points of view. While AC responses can easily confronted, because they fall within the subject's awareness, NC responses require a greater degree of psychotherapeutic exploration. Thus, when there is a prevalence of AC responses, Cognitive or Supportive psychotherapy may be appropriate recommendations. When NC responses prevail, psychodynamic psychotherapy should be recommended. Ambivalent Choices could be relatively obvious and understandable by the subject (consciously perceived). Negative Compensations require deeper psychotherapeutic work. When the ambivalent choice is prevalent, cognitive psychotherapy would be recommended. When the Negative Compensations predominate a psychodynamic orientation would be profitable.

- Positive Compensation (PC): is the most positive among the codes of the II half, as it is defined by high scores of both E.C. and A.Q. In the great majority of cases, a PC response indicates that the area of the psyche associated with it is fully comparable to a Choice (C) in terms of diagnostic value. When negative elements are present, PC responses indicate light to moderate complexity. PC indicates that the subject masters great potential (positive prognosis).

- Ambivalent Delay (AD): is also comparable to AC. However, differently than AC, AD is unconscious. Being closer to actual Delay, AD indicates that unconscious ambivalence and conflict exist in a specific area of the Psyche. These contents are subjected to deep repression, which cause generalized tensions, reactive behaviors, and distress that rules the majority of the subject's behavior. In terms of prognosis, AD carries quite a negative value and indicates that psychodynamic psychotherapy is recommended.

- Delay (D): represents the most negative code that a Box may receive. It reflects elements that the subject tends to repress and erase. These are, therefore, completely unconscious areas of the Psyche, which indirectly determine and affect all of the subject's behaviors. Delays are conflictual areas, actual challenges, that affect—mostly unconsciously—the entire personality functioning. The closer the score is to 0, the more it indicates total repression of the related area of the Psyche.

The categories represent a continuum from C (Choice) to D (Delay). From an elevated level of integration to a lesser level; from a lesser degree of conflict to a greater; from a state of awareness to one in which it is absent.

Analysis of sequence—2

Clinical experience, confirmed by statistical analysis, helped create a theoretical model about how the normal subject could carry out the order of boxes' sequence.

In the first four drawings we expect to find Boxes 1 and 8 and 3 and 6. Box 1 evokes feelings and self-evaluation, Box 8 provides information on interpersonal relationship. They are formed by the subjects' conscious level and include many Ego functions, from strictly perceptive-associational to those regulating mental operation (i.e. concept formation, memory, anticipation, and planning).

Box 3 indicates the amount of psychic energy invested in adaptation processes. Box 6 the ability to make an adequate reality testing. So, these functions include self-evaluation, social relationships, and the ability to adapt to one's surrounding (i.e., judgment, reality testing).

In the last four drawings we expect to find Boxes 2 and 4 and 5 and 7. Box 2 is connected to object relation dynamics with the maternal figure, Box 4 the paternal figure. They share characteristic of affective appearances.

Box 5 is connected to the ability to overcome obstacles, react to frustrating situations, and demonstrates aggressive energy. It is connected to the survival of mankind. Box 7 evokes dynamics related to females, sensitivity, and sexual energy.

Recap: On one hand, we have four boxes (1, 3, 6, and 8) concerning the Ego and its process of adaptation with its surroundings; on the other hand, we have four boxes (2, 4, 5 and 7) that are more concerned with the Affectivity.

Hypothesis

Normal subjects would predominantly draw Boxes 1, 8, 3, and 6 first (because they concern the Ego and its adaptation process). Then the remaining boxes (because they concern the Affectivity). That is, the Order of Performance would be: Boxes 1 and 8 first (choices); 3 and 6 second (choices or ambivalent choices); 2 and 4 next (positive compensations; 5 and 7 (positive compensations) last.

This hypothesis was statistically significant at the .001 level, (Crisi, 2007). In more than 75% of the sample (N = 2300), three or four boxes concerning the Ego were drawn in the first half of the Order of Sequence.

Theoretically, a normal subject should not "initially" present ambivalent delays, negative compensations, or delays.

The order of succession in this theoretical model is very important. It is of great psychodiagnostic relevance when the subject strays away from this succession. The sequence of the 4 pairs (1 & 8), (3 & 6), (2 & 4), and (5 & 7) represent the theoretical model of succession. In the illustration below, the subject drew first Box 3 and second Box 5 (instead of 1 and 8), as in the theoretical model. These boxes obtained Choice and Ambivalent Choice, respectively. As third and fourth drawings (instead of the Boxes 3—6), the subject drew Boxes 8—7 with Ambivalent Choice and Negative Compensation evaluations.

The meaning of the analysis of sequence 2

Do the four pairs represent specific areas or functions? And which are the reciprocal interactions amongst them?

The boxes that are drawn first and especially the first two indicate the psychic areas that are mostly used by the subject in his adaptation; the last two drawn boxes indicate the less used and less developed areas of personality.

So, for example, those who are very devoted to work and are usually very rational often draw as first the two Boxes 3 and 6. Or, adults still tied to parental figures draw in the first half Boxes 2 and 4. Or, very insecure adolescents with difficulties in their relationships draw Box 1 and 8 last.

The psychodiagnostic report

The Wartegg indices contribute to assess personality organization within a test battery to connect results and make a significant evaluation about the structure and thought processes organization (Rapaport, 1977).

The following illustration shows how to obtain a clinical profile from the Wartegg Test.

Illustration: A clinical case

Case history

David, a 37-year-old male was married without offspring. He had a high school diploma. David sought psychotherapy for two reasons; first, going through a very hard marital period, and second, lamenting a state of "existential" malaise in social relationships. In addition, he experienced bulimia and attributed induced vomiting to avoiding fatness.

His parents were at odds with each other and lived apart at home. Since his mother's death, a few years before, the relation with his father was almost completely interrupted. The client also reported a very bad relationship with all members of his family of origin, in particular his twin sisters (one of them was schizophrenic). In his relationships with women, his behavior was "Don Juan" like.

The Wartegg report

Wartegg report is based on two integrated results: (a) formal indexes; and (b) Analysis of Sequence 1 and 2. In clinical practice these two parts are interconnected.

Formal indexes

The client cooperated with the psychologist and did not try to modify his self-image.

He presented a moderate cognitive level, with a tendency toward an upper level (FQ + % = 94, Content P 6 with EC = 1 and Evaluation = C). Judgment and of reality-testing abilities were intact and integral (P 6 = C, FQ + % = 94); signs of formal thought troubles were not highlighted (a slight Personalized answer in P 4).

His thought content appeared adequate in thinking about his community and was characterized by good creative ability and criticism.

Activity levels present themselves accentuated (P 3 was first in the Order of Sequence). But they do not appear functional or well aimed toward achieving a goal (P 3 with EC = 0.5, AQ = 0.5, evaluation = AC). As for the level of

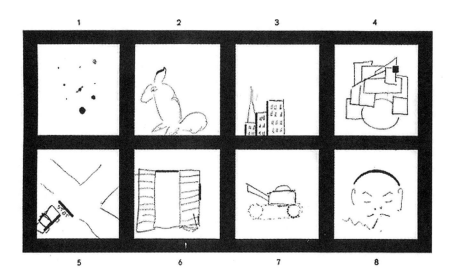

Figure 10.3 The Wartegg test of David

manifest behavior, there was a dispersion of interests and a pressure for high anxiety. At the same time, he started by multiple activities without properly evaluating his capacity to accomplish them.

This accentuation of activity levels is attributed to the deep conflicts that characterized his personality (only one C and D in Boxes 5 and 4, AC in Boxes 3 and 8).

Social relationships presented several difficulties; (P 8 with EC = 0.5, AQ. = 0.5); they were managed in a conflicted manner (P 8 = AC); the presence of dependence traits:

(That is, Impulse response of oral type in P 8); narcissistic traits (Personalized answer in P 4); and a strong tendency for autonomy and freedom (Contents of P 1, P 1 with EC = 1, A.Q = 0.5, PC Code). In view of these considerations, we could assert that a real interest in social relationship does not exist, but rather a propensity to use others (aggressive dependence on others). Affective life presents a strong repression (AQ + % = 44, reported A/F = 1.5: 3.5) and was characterized by strong strains and by marked immaturity, ambivalence, and egocentrism (IIT-1 = 1.4; CB; MI blocked in Box 5, MI rotated in P 1). In fact, the areas of aggressive dynamics (P 5 with EC = 0, AQ = 0.5, Code = D) and of sexual dynamics (P 7 with EC = 0, AQ = 0, Code = NC) were notably disturbed and not managed in a functional way.

The psycho-affective dynamics connected to the aggressive instinct were strongly repressed by consciousness (P 5 with Code = D). They determined, in manifest behavior, inadequate and unsuitable reactions to circumstances and to frustrations (P 5 with Code = D, and early in the Order of Sequence).

In addition, the psycho-affective dynamics connected with the sphere of the sexuality presented strong conflicts (P 7 with EC = 0, AQ = 0) and aroused an accentuation of sexual behaviors that had the characteristics of an obsessive-compulsive disorder; thus this must be interpreted as his real compensation (P 7 early in the Order of Sequence but evaluated as NC). It is possible to hypothesize that the subject lives his sexual relations under the pressure of a deep conflict with the female figure (P 2 evaluated as PC and deferred in the Order of Sequence).

Finally, the relationship with the paternal figure (P 4 = D) was characterized by strong feelings of anger. This condition negatively influenced all his relations with authority figures.

Analysis of sequence 1 and 2 report

ANALYSIS OF SEQUENCE 1

There is only one box evaluated as Choice (Box 6, Figure 10.2). Since the choices are the best evaluation that a subject can get, we would have expected to find more of them especially in an adult case. Quantitatively, this consideration leads us to understand this poorly adapted client.

Based on the meaning of the "evocative character" of this box (rationality), this element showed that the defensive rational structure of the subject constituted a fundamental role in his personality organization.

Two Boxes (4 and 5) are evaluated as D (delay). This indicates that the areas connected to the relationship with the father and authority (P 4) and to aggressive energy (P 5) were completely conflicting areas. So, in a latent and negative way, they determine and affect the subject's behavior. Such evaluation testifies to the presence of very deep and conflicting complexes.

ANALYSIS OF SEQUENCE 2

First Pair (Figure 10.2) was Boxes 3 and 8, instead of the expected 1 and 8. Both were evaluated as AC (Ambivalent Choice). Box 3 comes early and replaces Box 1. This configuration initially meant that activity levels were accentuated. But, seeing that P 3 is evaluated as AC, such accentuation should not be interpreted in a productive sense. We were facing the subject's attempt to fill the sense of inner uneasiness by recurring to action. Action is not always well geared to achieving a purpose. Such pretense was confirmed by the fact that the performance in Box 3 did not amount to a continuation toward the top of the stimulus-sign (EC = 0.5). The subject seemed to perceive himself more in what he does rather than in what he is.

In addition, social relationships (Box 8 = AC) were characterized by the presence of contrasting feelings. The equilibrium of "dependence-autonomy" was very unstable, determining a conflicted condition. The verbalization in Box 8 ("A bald Chinese who smokes") contained various interesting elements. The subject drew a person of a country geographically remote from his, with a completely different culture to those in Europe. All this seemed to accentuate the sense of separation and extraneousness that the client felt about his social environment. The fact that the drawn person presents an "aesthetic defect" ("he is bald") seemed to accentuate the importance that the subject attributed to his own physical appearance. Finally, the "Chinese is smoking" inserted an oral element that is clearly connected with dependence and social anxiety.

Second Pair was Boxes 7 (NC) and 6 (C) replacing expected Boxes 3 and 6. Box 7 came quite early in the Order of Sequence and obtained an evaluation of NC. The negative compensational points presented a high degree of ambivalence and conflict regarding sexual dynamics. The client presented notable disguised uneasiness not amounting to a conscience level and manifest behavior using compensating mechanisms. The overall configuration of this box, together with the verbalization ("A tank"), allowed us to hypothesize the activation of a deep conflict area. On an apparent behavioral level, the sphere of sexuality and relationship with females appeared very inadequate and unsatisfactory.

Box 6, evaluated as C and situated in the expected position within the Order of Sequence, confirmed the very high intellectual level of the subject and his tendency to use this asset in his relation with the environment.

Third Pair was Boxes 5 (D) and 1 (PC) replacing the expected Boxes 2 and 4. Box 5 came early but had a negative value (D). The aggressive dynamics were submitted to total repression and, on an unconscious level, they determined and affected the subject's behavior. It should be emphasized how the performance and the verbalization obtained in this Box ("A crossing with a stationary car") and the presence of a blocked inanimate movement testified to the inner situation of blockage lived by the subject. It was possible that such situation would give rise to attitudes and behaviors characterized by disguised aggression and maybe by the use of irony and sarcasm. Also in this box, the evaluation of D suggested the presence of a conflicting area.

Box 1 brought deferred and evaluated PC. The subject had latent potential and capabilities that could be improved in psychotherapy.

Fourth Pair was Boxes 2 (PC) and 4 (D) replacing expected Boxes 5 and 7. Both boxes were deferred. The relationship with both parents was disturbed and determined the subject's behavior on an unconscious level.

The statement in Box 4 "a usual drawing of mine" revealed, in a symbolic form, an obsessive thought connected with the paternal image which came to consciousness. But it was totally unhooked by the content underlying it.

In addition, the performance in Box 2 was fairly significant. The client drew a rabbit, an animal element that is a representative of repressed instincts. The rabbit may have recalled themes of tenderness and need of affection on one hand, but it brought up insecurity, fear, and accented sexuality, on the other hand (data particularly in tune with the exposed psychosexual sphere).

Final diagnosis

In light of these elements, the subject presented high levels of widespread ambivalence, both in the sense of ambivalent affectivity and of ambivalent way to relate to others. Although there were many Positive Compensations and the client had good cognitive and cultural levels, the prognosis was very moderately positive, on account of the presence of deep and unconscious conflicting areas (D = 2).

Points of contact with the draw a person test

The subject drew the face of a woman with closed eyes and head lightly bent downward (Figure 10.4). The graphic stroke was very uncertain and presented accentuation particularly in the drawing of the eyebrows and the mouth. As a whole, the female figure conveyed a feeling of passive delay and resignation.

The second figure was a man's bust, without hands and part of the arms (Figure 10.5). The graphic stroke was uncertain and presented defensive strokes in the eyes, mouth, and shoulders. The eyes appeared marked but somewhat feminine (the accentuation of the eyebrow on the left eye); the shoulders were very wide and mighty. An earring adorned the left ear of the figure. As a whole, the male figure conveys a feeling of ambiguity due to the contrast between the upper part (certainty and determination) and the lower part (slovenliness and imperfection).

Figure 10.4 The first drawing

To draw at first a person of the opposite sex could be a sign of difficulty in the sphere of sexual identification; in addition, to only draw the head (contrary to the second drawing) pointed out partiality of rationality rather than affectivity. Considering all elements of the test, the rational and multiple instinctual connotations attributed to the female figure (in contrast with raising the levels of activity in the sexual sphere) could be explained by obvious compensation via the desire to contain and control this situation.

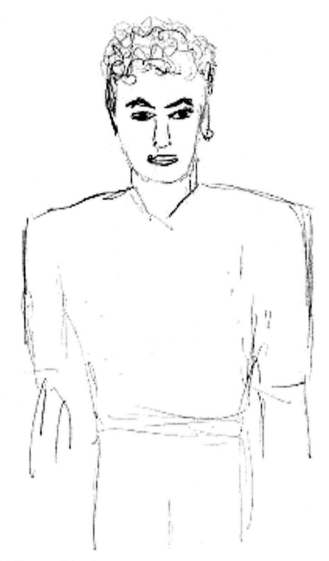

Figure 10.5 The second drawing

The first drawing was acceptable as being "a bust." But the second drawing had part arms and part below waist. The lack of legs and feet in the latter was an index of insecurity, insufficient contact with the practical and concrete aspects of life. The lack of hands pointed out the presence of problems in the aggression sphere. The subject then, was very anxious, had impulsive traits, and above all a clear conflict concerning his sexual identification.

Congruences between the draw a person test and the Wartegg test

- Presence of anxiety;
- Strong repression that characterized aggressive and sexual dynamics;
- Deep conflict in the relation with the female figure;
- Traits of accentuated narcissism; and
- Difficulties in sexual identification.

Summary

This chapter briefly displays the history of the Wartegg Test. The CWS is a new methodology, within the theoretical context of Psycho-dynamic Psychology, for scoring and interpreting the test was developed, based on the analysis of thousands of clinical cases some of which were combined with the Rorschach (Crisi, 1999, 2007).

Extensive evaluation of the eight Boxes in the Wartegg's test is presented, based on several categories, such as Evocative Character, Affective Quality; Form Quality; Contents, and the Order of Sequence. Of prime interpretive importance is the Analysis of Sequence, which describes the organization of personality. An Illustration case draws links between the new Wartegg interpretation and the Draw a Person Test.

References

Bornstein R. F. (2007). *Toward a process-based framework for classifying personality tests: Comment on Meyer and Kurtz.* Journal of Personality Assessment, 89, 202–207.

Buros, O. K. (1959). *The fifth mental measurements yearbook.* Highland Park: Gryphon Press.

Crisi, A. (1999, July). *Some similitudes between the Evocative Character of the Wartegg Boxes and that of the Rorschach Plates.* Paper presented at the XVI meeting of the International Society of Rorschach, Amsterdam, The Netherlands.

Crisi, A. (2007). *Manuale del test di Wartegg.* [Handbook of the Wartegg Test] (2nd ed.). Roma: E. S. Magi.

Kinget, G. M. (1952). *The drawing completion test: A projective technique for investigation of personality.* New York: Grune & Stratton.

Mc Cully, R. (1988). *Jung e Rorschach.* [Jung and Rorschach]. Milano: Mimesis.

Rapaport, D. (1977). *Il modello concettuale della psicoanalisi.* [The conceptual model of psychoanalysis]. Milano: Feltrinelli.

Wartegg, E. (1936). Gefuhl und Phantasiebild. [Emotion and imagination]. *In Industrielle Psychotecnik, 13, 251–255.*

Wartegg, E. (1939). Gestaltung und Charakter. [Formation of gestalts and personality]. *Zeitschrift für Angewandte Psychologie und Charakterkunde, 84,* Beiheft 2.

Wartegg, E. (1953). *Schichtdiagnostik: Der Zeichentest (WARTEGG TEST).* [Differential diagnostics: The Drawing test (WARTEGG TEST)]. Gottingen: Verlag fur Psychologie Hogrefe.

Wartegg, E. (1972). *Il reattivo di disegno.* [The drawing test]. Firenze: OS.

11

DRAW-A-PERSON-IN-THE
RAIN TEST

Eva Fishell Lichtenberg

Introduction

Human figure drawings have been used as an assessment tool since the early part of the twentieth century. The Goodenough Draw-A-Man Test attempted to measure intelligence and to quantify the data to yield an IQ score (Goodenough, 1926, 1928). However; studying individual drawings often uncovered clinical findings unrelated to the subject's intellectual level. These observations led to the development of Machover's Draw-A-Person Test that is used primarily as a projective technique rather than simply a means of evaluating intellectual capacity (Machover, 1949).

Although the Draw-A-Person Test (DAP) is frequently included in batteries of personality tests, questions have been raised about its merit as an assessment device (Roback, 1968; Swenson, 1968). Several authors have attempted to shift from Machover's specific indicators to more global, comprehensive ratings in using figure drawings as a projective test (Kahn & Jones, 1965; Lewinsohn, 1965).

Moreover, a number of variations have been devised to enhance the value of drawings as a clinical tool and increase their predictability of personality dynamics. Patients have been asked to draw objects other than a person; these techniques include drawing a car (Loney, 1971) and more popularly drawing a house, tree, and person with the H-T-P Test (Buck, 1948). The Kinetic Family Drawing, that is drawing a family doing something, has been a relatively well-accepted procedure as well (Burns & Kaufman, 1971).

Another figure-drawing extension, originated by H.M. Fay in 1924, was designed to measure intellectual maturity; the test was administered to children between the ages of 7 and 12 who were instructed to draw "a lady walking in the rain" (Fay, 1924). It was later revised and standardized by Wintsch (Wintsch, 1935) and subsequently standardized again with a scoring system adapted from Goodenough by Andre Rey (Rey, 1946, 1947; Goodenough, 1926; Taylor, 1959). Clinicians found this tool useful and added their own qualitative observations.

Arnold Abrams modified the instructions of drawing a *lady walking* in the rain to facilitate using the method as a diagnostic personality assessment tool (Hammer, 1958). He directed subjects to "draw a person in the rain" (DAP-R) without stipulating gender or activity. Moreover, in clinical settings the figure in the rain usually followed the administration of the classical "Draw-A-Person Test" so that comparisons could be made between the two initial drawings (a person followed by the opposite sex) and the third one. In other situations, Abrams sometimes used the rain drawing alone as a screening mechanism. For example during a three-year period in the 1960s, Abrams and the author screened applicants for the Chicago police force to indicate individuals with severe psychopathology who then were interviewed before possible elimination. To that end the single rain figure drawing was administered in addition to the computer-scored Minnesota Multiphasic Personality Inventory (MMPI) and a brief written test of cognitive functioning.

Some studies have indicated that it is possible to predict adolescent patients' diagnostic category—neurosis, character disorder, psychosis, or borderline psychosis—from drawings of figures in the rain; a high positive correlation between psychiatric diagnoses and psychologists' assessments were found (Verinis, Lichtenberg, & Henrich, 1974). Moreover, when drawings collected from hospitalized adolescents were rated for the experienced amount of stress and the strength of present defenses, the ratings correlated significantly with those independently given by the patients' psychologist (Verinis, Lichtenberg, & Henrich, 1974).

Another study (Carney, 1992) found the DAP-R to be a useful measure of depression and stress in adolescence. A quantitative scoring system for the DAP-R was developed as part of this investigation to differentiate between healthy and pathological groups. Used initially in the pilot phase of the study, the scoring method provided validity between the initial findings and the second administration a year later.

The DAP-R was included as an instrument for assessing adolescent boys' personality and behavior in a long-term residential drug and alcohol treatment program (Page, 1989). The technique was one of several methods used to evaluate the total emotional and behavioral functioning of the students. After completing a six to nine months' treatment program, the students were reexamined one year after admission. For all examinees, the later rain drawings exhibited an umbrella although initially half the group had drawn no protection whatsoever and a third of the drawings had displayed inadequate protection. The study concluded that despite indications of remaining serious concerns, the students had become more self-controlled and purposeful.

Since working with Abrams, the author has routinely included the DAP-R when administering the Draw-A-Person Test in clinical practice and has used it for other purposes, such as screening groups. The author has found using these three drawings together invaluable for formulating clinical impressions and considers the combination much superior to using the classical figure drawing test alone.

Rationale

Drawing a person in the rain is a more complex task than drawing a person. This is corroborated by the fact that few children under the age of seven are capable of producing such a drawing; developmentally these younger children lack sufficient perceptual-motor ability to cope with the situation. However, as they mature, nearly all will have experienced rain. In most western societies it is customary to protect oneself from the rain in some way, i.e., umbrella, raincoat, boots, tree, awning, etc. This added task, both in the increased complexity of drawing and conceptualization, involves finding protection against an uncontrollable act of nature. Thus the rain is hypothesized to symbolize stress. How an individual perceives and represents the stress as well as how it is defended against reflects important personality dynamics.

Comparing the figure in the rain with the drawing of simply the person provides additional valuable data. Equally as important as the absence, presence, or intensity of the rain and the adequacy of the protection method, are the observable qualitative changes in the figure representation itself. These alterations, occurring in symbolically stressful conditions, reveal much about the nature of the subject's coping mechanisms. Therefore, whenever possible, the DAP-R should be administered not in isolation, but rather following the more conventional administration of the Draw-A-Person Test.

Two examples dramatically illustrate the power of this technique:

Mr. A., a 39-year old "successful" business man, drew Figures 11.1, 11.2, and 11.3. He was hospitalized because of inability to sleep, excessive reliance on tranquilizers, and general inability to cope, partially precipitated by his wife's pregnancy. His father had died when he was 19 years old, and as the oldest of three children, he had quit school to support the family. The Rorschach was replete with texture responses and other regressive signs.

Ms. B, a female art student in her thirties, drew Figures 11.4, 11.5, and 11.6. She was hospitalized following a serious suicidal attempt. Rorschach results indicated a diagnosis of borderline schizophrenia.

In both instances, the quality of the rain drawing differs markedly from the initially drawn persons and is laden with meaning. Note the regression to childhood in Mr. A's rain drawing, and note the disintegration of Ms. B's artistic abilities under stress.

Administration

Unless a brief screening technique is desired, the "rain drawing" is solicited after the classic administration of the Draw-A-Person Test. That is, after drawing a person on a blank sheet of paper followed by a person of the opposite sex of the first figure on another sheet of paper, the subject is asked to "draw a person in the rain" on a third page. After the completion of all three drawings, a story about each of them can be solicited. Each drawing is returned

Figure 11.1

Figure 11.2

Figure 11.3

to the subject for viewing as he or she tells a story, or failing that, describes the picture.

It is very important that no further directions or cues are provided to the subject in order for the task to be performed. If the subject requests additional guidance either before beginning to draw or during the process, the original directions are to be repeated and the subject should be encouraged to proceed; the subject should not be given any other information so that he or she must

Figure 11.4

rely entirely upon inner resources. A projective drawing should reflect the "artist's" own feelings, impulses, and attitudes, not anyone else's.

The above restrictions are emphasized because it has recently come to the author's attention that all too often the Draw-A-Person-in-the-Rain Test is being incorrectly administered with the examiner providing additional cues or suggestions. The Internet text regarding this test states that the subject is directed to "draw a person in the rain, with an umbrella . . . and to be sure to draw all three parts: the person, the rain, and the umbrella" (Niolon, 2003). These directions not only defeat the purpose of the test, they invalidate it. It is the presence or absence of these elements as well as their characteristics that reveal personality dynamics.

The test is suitable for administration to individuals seven years or older, although it can be attempted with highly intelligent children as young as six

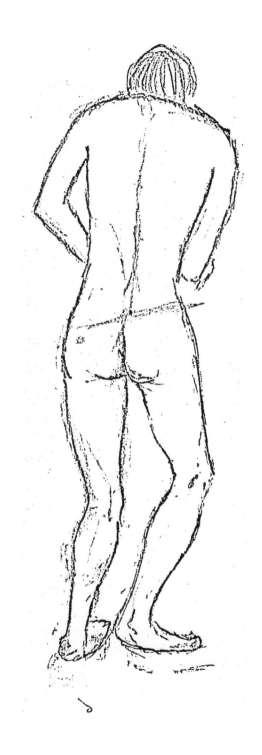

Figure 11.5

Figure 11.6

or six-and-a-half years of age. Children younger than seven frequently lack sufficient fine visual-motor coordination skills to draw an umbrella; one bright six-and-a-half-year-old boy told the author, "I know he should have an umbrella, but I don't know how to draw one." One source reports that children under the age of eight years are unable to draw an umbrella (Piaget & Inhelder, 1969), but in the author's experience many slightly younger children with only average intelligence are able to do so.

Interpretation

Initial inspection of the rain drawing focuses on the absence or presence of rain as well as the latter's intensity and pervasiveness. In addition, one looks for the presence or absence of raingear and its adequacy in protecting the figure. Based upon this examination, one can often categorize the subject as being more or less healthy, neurotic, psychotic, or as having a character disorder.

Relatively normal people tend to draw figures of their own gender in a frontal presentation with a moderate degree of rain and some appropriately placed protective gear such as an umbrella or raincoat. Neither the rain nor the protection is excessive, and the figure is intact. Deviations from this pattern can be analyzed for their possible meanings. The subject's verbalizations about the figure sometimes contribute helpful diagnostic information as well; in talking about their drawing, healthy subjects do not exaggerate the figure's discomfort in the situation nor do they dwell upon the measures taken to protect themselves. However, neither in their drawings nor in their remarks do they deny the rain's presence; it is acknowledged as being part of the scene.

Neurotics can be characterized as feeling very anxious and distressed but whose defensive structure is sufficiently adequate not to regress or decompensate into psychosis. The modal neurotic drawing contains excessive rain, sometimes with extras features such as clouds, lightning, or puddles, but always with at least partially adequate protection against the rain; in fact, the defenses might also be extreme or disproportionate to the symbolic stress. Verbalizations might include expressed fears of getting wet or even sustaining some degree of wetness; if psychologically prone to somatising, the subject might also mention the possibility of illness caused by the rain. The drawn figure, however, is intact and not unduly distorted.

In character disorders, symptomatic behavior is ego-syntonic rather than ego-alien as in neurotic reactions; denial is a favored defense mechanism, and subjectively experienced stress is minimal; instead of the latter, stress is often created for others. Character disorder drawings feature little or no rain although the figures are frequently well protected with rain gear, often excessively so. That is, defenses are present despite feelings of stress being minimal or totally denied. Verbalizations sometimes mention rain despite its absence in the drawing itself. Furthermore, the figure's body boundaries are intact.

Psychotics or borderline personalities experience much stress with sufficient intensity to impair the ability to function; defensive structure is weak, and regression and decompensation may occur (Bellak & Loeb, 1969). Drawings have unusually heavy rain and stormy weather is present, sometimes just concentrated upon the figure; and unlike neurotic drawings, protection against the torrential rain is absent, minimal, or grossly inadequate. The figure is depicted as largely defenseless. Moreover—not uncommonly—the figure itself is not intact or the drawing is relatively primitive or otherwise distorted. Suicidal risk can sometimes be discerned in missing body parts and defective body boundaries.

Although the DAP-R has been used for tripartite diagnostic categorization (Verinis, Lichtenberg, & Henrich, 1974), it is more valuable for assessing the subject's stress level and the nature and strength of defenses. If a diagnosis is desired, the qualitative impressions gained from the drawings can be combined with other clinical data to assist in formulating a diagnostic conclusion. Applying clinical insight with global interpretation of the drawings and the descriptions or stories if available is preferable to rigidly using a quantified scoring method. The information holistically gained is often considerably richer than that obtained by adding single characteristics to yield a numerical score.

Furthermore, it is preferable to compare the rain drawing with previous drawings of a male and a female to note what figure alterations have occurred. In many instances significant qualitative differences would be observable. Variables including changes in size, gender, presentation (frontal, profile, rear view), age, detail, symmetry, proportions, integrity of line, degree of completion, body transparencies, placement on page, stance of figure, background, introduction of additional figures, and overall artistic quality among other features are considered in interpreting all three drawings together.

A noticeable increase or decrease in figure size in the rain drawing compared to the original figures drawn is a good indicator of how the subject reacts to stress in regard to expansiveness versus constriction. A larger person suggests expansiveness, looseness, or relaxation of self-control under stress whereas a smaller figure indicates emotional constriction, repression, or depression when subjected to stress.

When the figure in the rain is the opposite sex of the drawer, regardless of the initial drawing's gender, questions about sexual identity issues are raised. Some other concerns or difficulties in normal identification are suggested by figures that differ from the age or race of the subject. (See Figures 11.1, 11.2, and 11.3) Profile or rear-view figures in the rain compared to frontal presentations in the original drawings lead to speculations about evasiveness or the need to hide something. Loss of detail, deterioration in representation, introduction of ancillary figures, or including elaborate backgrounds in rain pictures unlike in nonrain ones have interpretive implications. (See Figures 11.4, 11.5, and 11.6) In these instances, the drawings obtained under conditions of symbolic stress reveal personality dynamics not so readily apparent in those executed under less stressful circumstances.

Stories or descriptions concerning the drawings provide additional meaningful information. For example, when the person in the rain is described as being soaking wet and perhaps also sustaining illness following the incurred wetness, one has evidence of anxiety and feelings of defenselessness or helplessness and perhaps tendencies to somatize. If possible, interpretive inferences should be drawn and integrated from a totality of the data: all three drawings, verbalizations about the pictures, and observable behavior during test performance, and other projective test findings should be considered as well. Sometimes, however, only the drawings are available for interpretation.

Illustrations are considered below—in the absence of drawings—showing that artistic talent is not correlated with drawn or described comments.

A 38-year-old woman drew and described her drawing. The artistic quality is better than average, yet it demonstrates psychopathology. The female figure is older and rather unglamorous in appearance, perhaps reflecting the subject's own self-image. The rain's intensity is mild but the protective measures taken are disproportionately great: head covering, hands hidden in sleeves as though the latter are a muff and boots. Moreover, to ensure the woman is not getting wet, she adds a man to hold an umbrella over her. The presence of a second figure is relatively uncommon; when this occurs, it is usually interpreted as reflecting dependence upon others for support. In this instance, the extra person is a chivalrous man, indicating probable reliance upon males for meeting her needs; rather than just sharing the umbrella, the man somewhat neglects his own welfare to protect her. The line beneath the two persons, probably representing a sidewalk, suggests the subject's need for external props for stability. Self-reliance seems to be lacking.

Another example illustrates how the rain drawing adds to the clinical impressions gained from the Draw-A-Person Test alone. The figures were drawn by a highly educated 44-year-old woman, a business consultant, unable to work because of various unclear somatic symptoms and therefore on disability insurance. All three drawings depict children. The first two drawings clearly demonstrate the subject's regression; the stories about them concern a young happy girl having a lovely day—reflecting wishful thinking and attempted denial—and a boy looking for his "mommy" in a grocery store where he is scared. Dependency issues are obviously present. The rain drawing and its story, however, indicate greater psychopathology; the defenseless figure is approached by lightning through a cloud in addition to mild or moderate rain; this picture evokes a story of getting caught unaware in the rain without an umbrella, getting hit by lightning, and becoming wet and maybe electrocuted. The subject not only experiences regressive longings but more significantly, feels overwhelmed and endangered. Based on these as well as findings from other tests, the subject was diagnosed as having a major depressive disorder with psychotic features and an underlying borderline personality disorder

Two drawings were made by an 11-year-old boy in psychotherapy and include stories evoked by the drawings. Noteworthy in the drawings is the slightly feminine quality of the boy—reflecting the patient himself—and the rain figure's being a female. Moreover, in the female drawing, the subject erased frequently. Sexual identity problems are suggested. The first drawing is better executed than the rain drawing; the neck in the original drawing is thick but a neckline is indicated; the neck of the figure in the rain is unduly elongated and a neckline is missing. Impulse control problems might be present. Obvious deterioration is visible under stress. Unsuccessful attempts at denial are indicated by the fact that the rain in the picture is not heavy whereas the patient's story describes it as intense—in fact hail; in both the drawing and the story, the umbrella is not very functional; and in both stories maternal figures are much involved. Unresolved dependency issues in relation to his mother are suggested.

The first story, described in the first person, concerned a boy food shopping for his mother when a dog jumped on him; he mentioned his previous fear of dogs and expressed pride in overcoming it. The second drawing: A female is described as becoming soaking wet because her umbrella broke in a hailstorm. Moreover, because her mother would not return home until later, she had to go to a friend's house in the meantime. When her mother returned, she bought her a sturdier umbrella. (After being depicted as neglectful, the mother becomes protective by making amends. The patient appears to be both dependent upon her as well as angry at her).

The psychotherapist's report corroborates the above impressions. The patient dislikes any kind of pressure and cannot cope when stressed. The therapist also reports that the patient has difficulty dealing with his conflicted feelings about his mother whom he regards as demanding but feeling very dependent upon her, he fears antagonizing her by being self-assertive. His mother is seen as the stronger parent in the family. The therapist further describes the patient as displaying strong feminine proclivities such as great interest in feminine apparel, wearing velvet clothing, and exhibiting feminine body mannerisms. Years later, he "came out" as a homosexual.

Figures 11.7, 11.8, and 11.9 were drawn by an 11-year-old girl with superior intelligence; she was referred for evaluation to determine her need for psychotherapy. Her mother was concerned about the consequences of divorcing her daughter's father to marry an alcoholic; this marriage was on the verge of dissolution. The drawings are mature for a girl her age, and despite the defensiveness apparent in the rain drawing, no gross psychopathology is evident. Erasures are manifested on all three drawings indicative of the patient's excessive concern about the adequacy of her performance and some lack of self-confidence.

The figure in the rain is not inferior in quality to the others, but its uptightness is obvious at first glance as are the absence of rain and the presence of an umbrella. Moreover, the figure wears a raincoat emphatically buttoned from top to bottom. All her defenses are raised against nonexistent stress indicating denial of any distress she might be experiencing. However, rain is mentioned in the patient's story. The drawn figure takes piano lessons to which she takes a bus, sometimes in the rain; thus, she has some awareness of discomfort. The examiner concluded that the patient was neither motivated nor receptive for psychotherapy at that time, but that possibly in the future her feelings toward therapy might change. Seen by chance socially forty years later, she disclosed that she had eventually been psychoanalyzed and had become a successful psychotherapist herself.

Applying the DAP-R as described below exemplifies interpretive techniques.

Some applications

The DAP-R can be used to assess progress in psychotherapy. Nancy, an adopted child displaying a number of behavioral problems, was referred for diagnostic evaluation when she was seven years old. The test battery included the DAP and the DAP-R. Rain is totally absent in the latter drawing despite the presence

Figure 11.7

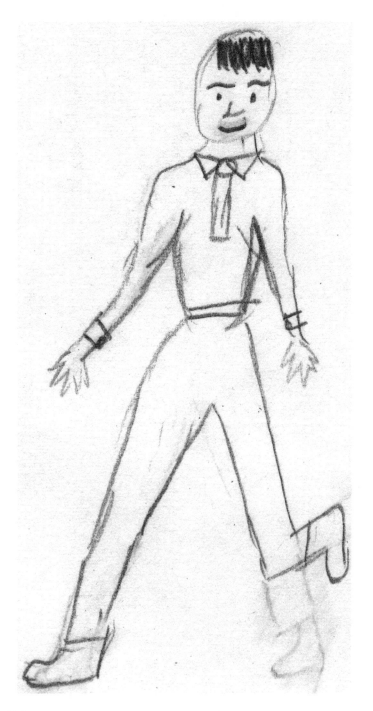

Figure 11.8

Figure 11.9

of a relatively large umbrella which only partially covers the figure; an inter-preter's first impression is one of "massive denial, defensiveness, and inadequate coping mechanisms." The figure being male rather than female is corroborated by Nancy's story which explicitly mentions the rain; in fact, she describes the rain as being sufficiently stressful as to make the ground "too slippery." This necessitates going home to his mother to obtain salt for the sidewalk, which in turn suggests unmet dependency needs. Based on the complete evaluation, she was referred for intensive psychotherapy.

Five years later, when Nancy was 12 and still in therapy, the figure drawing test was repeated. All three drawings were artistically more mature, that is, age appropriate. The figure in the rain is definitely female and in fact, secondary sex characteristics are emphasized, perhaps reflecting sexual preoccupation consistent with incipient adolescence. The rain is very much present, the person seems to be crying, and boots on her feet are her only defense. Comparing this to her initial rain drawing, one sees that Nancy has become able to express her feelings of distress although she continued to feel helpless and coped inadequately. Nancy's story explains that the figure is crying because while on her way to a dinner party after getting her hair done the rain began. She had no coat and her hairdo was ruined which meant not looking good upon arrival; moreover, she would be "all wet"; she cried as she did not know what to do and finally decided to return home instead of going to the party. The story also reflects that concern for her appearance is obviously important, something not unusual for an incipient adolescent. Nancy's therapist maintained that although progress had been made in therapy, particularly in regard to reducing guardedness and denial, she nevertheless needed to continue in therapy.

The DAP-R is also useful as a means of group screening, especially in conjunction with other easily administered psychological tests. Screening candidates for the police force has already been mentioned. A research project conducted at a teaching hospital serves as another example. It tried to predict how students admitted to nursing school would perform. An attempt was made to determine which of the students would have a relatively successful training experience and which ones would encounter difficulties, perhaps sufficiently severe as to require expulsion. The students in the entering first-year class were administered the following tests: DAP-R, Rotter Sentence Completion Test, and MMPI computer scored and interpreted. The identity of all respondents was unknown to those interpreting the tests. (Admission or retention was not conditional on the test results nor were the tests compulsory; however, most of the students agreed to cooperate). More often than not the various test findings for a specific student were consistent. Occasionally, however, seemingly contradictory findings were apparent. Attempts were made to integrate and explain the data. Regardless, a personality profile was derived for every student, and predictions were rendered regarding possible problems that might arise during training. In some instances, supervisors were asked to relate behavioral observations. Sometimes, they were alerted to test results demonstrating potential problems so that appropriate support could be provided in a timely manner.

The next examples summarize a few individual test results and illustrates how the drawings contributed to the obtained personality impression.

A student who was regarded by her teachers as well-functioning drew a sidewalk scene or pathway with a few plants and flowers on an adjacent lawn. Despite the figure's being of the opposite sex—a possible reflection of some identity difficulties—both rain and umbrella were present. The smiling face and added flowers suggest a need to put a positive spin on whatever happens, a Pollyanna tendency; "to make lemonade if given a lemon." (To some extent, such an attitude was welcomed and encouraged in nurses.) The other tests show her to be energetic, ebullient, and sociable as well as someone who wants acceptance and approval.

A student regarded as somewhat uptight and overly controlled, but who was seen as improving with time, drew a girl with clothing details including collar, sleeve cuffs, and buttons down the front of her dress to her waist. The figure in the drawing appears stiff, prim, and perhaps somewhat childlike. (At that time, however, it was customary for nurses to wear starched, white uniforms including caps on their heads). Both legs and feet turn sideways in one direction in an otherwise frontal presentation to suggest some degree of inner conflict. That the rain is slight with an umbrella looking more like a large hat on her head suggests some denial of stress. The MMPI profile shows her to be conventional, moralistic, and conforming while her handwriting on the sentence completions is very small indicative of tight control.

A drawing with two figures of a male and a female dancing was done by a student whose supervisor reported that she was unrealistic, glorified nursing, and "did not have her feet on the ground." In fact, the dancing female does have one leg off the ground raised into the air; she was further described as easily disillusioned and lacking maturity. The romantic heterosexual couple that she drew is in the rain without any protective covering; there are also some clouds in the sky. The presence of two figures in the rain instead of just one suggests excessive dependency in addition to some difficulty following directions. Her sentence completions indicate someone seeking excitement, disliking routine, and resisting authority; moreover, she explicitly stated that she was in love with love. The MMPI characterized her as extremely feminine in a then stereotypical way—that is helpless, dependent, and feeling inferior to men.

A rather different drawing was made by a male student who resigned from the program shortly thereafter. In the drawing, the tiny figure sitting beneath a large tree, which pose and defense are passive, seems lost in overwhelming surroundings: Two other small trees are discernible in the distance and clouds and rain fill the top three fifths of the page. The MMPI profile is pathologically elevated and indicates great distress. His responses to incomplete sentences demonstrate insecurity as well as questioning of his own stability. Background information from an outside source indicated that this student had a renowned and authoritarian father who overshadowed him.

Another student did not indicate his gender on the MMPI answer sheet. Because a sentence completion test response referred to a wife, interpreters assumed the subject was male. The drawing, including rain and puddles on the ground, was replete with guardedness and defensiveness: Profile stance, raincoat, boots, hand in pocket, and an umbrella that hides his head, as though chopping it off, are pathological features.

The MMPI profile is pathologically low, that is guarded, except for the elevated social introversion scale and some manifestations of anti-establishment attitudes. His responses to the sentence completion test are similarly guarded; they espouse excessively high standards and express intolerance of others' weaknesses. They also indicate his refusal to recognize external authority. After a few months during which he displayed difficulties with supervisors among other problems, he was asked to withdraw from the program.

Summary

The Draw-A-Person-in-the-Rain Test is a way of enhancing the utility of the Draw-A-Person Test for children and adults. Although the DAP-R can be used by itself, its primary purpose is to augment the findings obtainable from the DAP. Using the two projective techniques together for clinical evaluations as well as for research studies frequently yields significant insights into the subjects' personalities. Under the conditions of symbolic stress stimulated by this test, subjects unwittingly tend to reveal their feelings of distress as well as their defenses and coping mechanisms.

This chapter provides directions for administration and illustrates methods of interpretation. Numerous test applications are presented to facilitate readers using the DAP-R themselves.

References

Bellak, L., & Loeb, L. (1969). *The schizophrenic syndrome.* New York: Grune & Stratton.

Buck, J. N. (1948). The H-T-P Test. *Journal of Clinical Psychology, Clinical Psychology Monographs, 5,* 1–120.

Burns, R. C., & Kaufman, S. (1971). *Kinetic-Family—Drawing.* New York: Bruner/Mazel.

Carney, S. M. (1992). Draw-a-Person-in-the-Rain: A comparison of levels of stress and depression among adolescents. *ETD Collection for Pace University.*

Fay, H. M. (1924). Le depistage des arrieres à l'école. [The tracking of school underachievers]. *La Medecine Scolaire, Décembre,* 282–290.

Goodenough, F. L. (1926). *Measurement of intelligence by drawings.* Yonkers: World Book.

Goodenough, F. L. (1928). Studies in the psychology of children's drawings. *Psychological Bulletin, 25,* 504–512.

Hammer, E. F. (1958, 1971). *The Clinical application of projective drawings.* Springfield: Charles C. Thomas.

Kahn, M., & Jones, M. (1965). Human figure drawings as predictors of admission to a psychiatric hospital. *Journal of Projective Techniques, 2,* 319–322.

Lewinsohn, P. M. (1965). Psychological correlates of overall quality of figure drawings. *Journal of Consulting Psychology, 29,* 504–512.

Loney, J. (1971). Clinical aspects of the Loney Draw-A-Car Test: Enuresis and encopresis. *Journal of Personality Assessment, 35,* 265–274.

Machover, K. (1949). *Personality projection in the drawing of the human figure.* Springfield: Charles C. Thomas.

Niolon, R. (2003, Spring). *Notes on projective drawings.* Chicago School of Professional Psychology. Retrieved from http://www.psychpage.com/projective/proj_draw_notes.html.

Page, V. B. (1989, March). *Draw-a-Person in the Rain (DAPIR).* Antioch High School, Allendale/PREP Program.

Piaget, J., & Inhelder, B. (1969). *The psychology of the child.* New York: Basic Books.

Rey, A. (1946). Epreuves de dessin temoins du developpment mental [Drawings as evidence of mental development]. *Archives de Psychologie, Décembre,* 369–380.

Rey, A. (1947). Epreuves de dessin temoins du developpment mental (Drawings as evidence of mental development). *Monographies de Psychologie Appliquée, Février,* 145–149.

Roback, H. (1968). Human figure drawings: Their utility in the clinical psychologist's armamentarium for personality assessment. *Psychological Bulletin, 70,* 1–19.

Swenson, C. (1968). Empirical evaluations of human figure drawings. *Psychology Bulletin, 70,* 20–44.

Taylor, E. M. (1959). *Psychological appraisal of children.* Cambridge: Harvard University Press, 1959.

Verinis, J. S., Lichtenberg, E. F, & Henrich, L. (1974). The Draw-a-Person in the Rain technique: Its relationship to diagnostic category and other personality indicators. *Journal of Clinical Psychology,* July 1974, 407–414.

Wintsch, J. (1935). Le dessin comme temoin du developpment mental. [Drawing as a witness of mental development]. *Zeitschrift fur Kinderpsychiatrie, August.*

12

THE TREE TEST

A parsimonious projective drawing technique

Yann Le Corff, John Tivendell, and Charlotte LeBlanc

Projective techniques have been around since the end of the nineteenth century but perhaps one of the earliest examples of a drawing test was Machover's (1949) adaptation of Goodenough's (1926b) Draw-A-Person (D-A-P) test. Soon after Goodenough's work, Jucker would start using a tree drawing task in his own work in 1928 (Webster, 2008). It was a short time after the D-A-P that Wartegg presented a somewhat corollary measure, his Drawing Completion Test (WZT; Wartegg, 1939; Roivainen & Ruuska, 2005), a structured projective and drawing task that consists of a series of unfinished lines or dots that the examinee is instructed to complete. Although Jucker was his mentor, it was Koch who developed the Tree Drawing Test (Baum test; Koch, 1949, 1952, 1957), which involves the drawing of a "fruit tree." Later Buck would integrate the tree test into Goodenough's D-A-P to produce the now well-known House-Tree-Person test (HTP; Buck, 1948). Today the Tree Test is still quite popular in continental Europe (ESPD, 2007) and in Japan (Stevens & Wedding, 2004). There was also Raven's Controlled Projection Test (Cohen de Lara-Kroon, 1999), a British method which combined a drawing task with the story-telling method (in children's version, the examinee is invited to make a drawing and, while doing so, tell a story about it), and Van Lennep's (1958; in Cohen de Lara-Kroon, 1999) drawing task, which requires the drawing of three trees: a fruit tree, a fantasy tree, and a dream tree.

Although Goodenough (1926a) had initially proposed that the D-A-P be used to measure intelligence, her contemporary Jucker—a vocational counsellor—was the first to use the Tree drawing as a psychological test. At that time, he used an entirely intuitive interpretation approach, looking for what the drawing could reveal as problematic aspects in the subject (Koch, 1952). However, the methodological use and study of the Tree Test began with Hurlock and Thomson (Stora, 1978). In the same year Schiebe (Stora, 1978) proposed to use the test to assess personality. Two decades later Koch (1952), in his book *The Tree Test*, proposed the Tree drawing be used as a psychological diagnosis method.

Previous studies

In literature, there is much less on the reliability and validity of Tree drawings than on other projective tests. To date, there are only a few empirical studies on the Tree Test or even on the House-Tree-Person Test. Although the Tree Test is sometimes seen as a part of the House-Tree-Person test, many authors including those cited, consider the Tree Test as a test in its own right. In the authors' experience the material elicited by the Tree drawing is—at least slightly—affected when in interaction with the House and the Person drawings, justifying our quest to understand it independently of these.

The few studies dealing with the validity of the House-Tree-Person could lead one to conclude that it is at best a "rough and non-specific measure of psychopathology" (Handler, Campbell, & Martin, 2004). As for the Tree Test alone, more supportive results were observed. The test appears to succeed not only in differentiating psychiatric patients from controls (Inadomi, Tanaka, & Ohta, 2003; Mizuta et al., 2002), but also in distinguishing different psychopathological states. Indeed Tree characteristics such as its branches, leaves, and trunk significantly distinguished between schizoaffective disorders, delusional disorders, and nondelusional psychiatric inpatients (Keisuke et al., 2001) and between paranoid and nonparanoid schizophrenia (Inadomi et al., 2003).

Meanwhile it should be noted that Buck (1948) reported an important finding for his Tree drawings, which has since been used in interpretation of the Tree test. That is, the presence of knots or mutilations on Tree would be an indication of past trauma or victimization. In addition, Buck hypothesized that the proportional positions of knots or mutilations on the Tree would correspond with subjects' age at the time when those traumatic events occurred. In a recent study Torem, Gilbertson, and Light (2006), reported that the number of indicators on the Tree (such as scars, knots, and dry and broken branches) was significantly correlated with the duration of physical abuse in psychiatric patients as well as in non-psychiatric subjects. In another study (Devore & Fryrear, 1976), it was found that only 12.36% of a large sample of juvenile delinquents had scars or holes in their Tree drawings (albeit as part of the House-Tree-Person). The authors concluded that Buck's hypothesis could not be supported, as they assumed that all delinquents would have had traumatic experiences in the past. However, the presence of past trauma itself was not assessed and thus this study cannot be considered as a valid test of Buck's hypothesis.

In experts' comments, the Tree is said to better reflect a person's emotional history and tap a deeper level of one's personality than the drawing of a Person, according to both Koch and Hammer (Hersen, Hilsenroth, & Segal, 2004). So far we were able to find only one study testing the ability of the Tree Test to inform on personality (Bon & Bon, 1984), but less than convincing results were reported. Bon and Bon's study however provided empirical support to the Tree Test's convergent validity, given that interconnections with the Draw-A-Person test were observed in children in terms of developmental indicators.

Advantages of projective drawings

One of the main advantages of projective drawings is rooted in their underlying psychometric theory. That is, by presenting an unstructured stimulus that leads to a symbolic creation, it is assumed that this can circumvent unconscious defenses as well as conscious resistances. They are therefore considered harder to falsify (Lemaire & Demers, 2008), in particular when compared to the obviousness of the material used in most self-report questionnaires and interviews today (Furnham, 1997; Rothstein & Goffin, 2006). The examinees, or at least most examinees, are not likely to know neither what can be revealed through their drawings nor how this will be interpreted (Koch, 1957). Projective drawing tests are also by their nature less threatening or intrusive, which is advantageous with apprehensive clients. Moreover, as it does not require reading questions or providing verbal responses and needs only very simple instructions, it should be useful even with clients who have poor verbal skills or who are highly introverted.

Tree test description and administration

The Tree Test, it is argued, is one of the simplest projective drawing tests to administer. The required material is limited to a white letter-sized sheet of paper and a pencil (even though some authors have also suggested using color pencils; i.e., Fernandez, 2005). Instructions are simply "draw a fruit tree, but not a Christmas tree" (see Koch, 1957 for variations). The administrator is however allowed to add an encouraging word or two when a client is particularly inhibited, such as when he or she professes an inability to draw or a lack of artistic competency (Fernandez, 2005). Thus this test can be administered to just about any person, whether a child, an adolescent, an adult, an elder person, a psychiatric patient, or a person from the general population (Thomas & Jolley, 1998).

Scoring and interpretation

Scoring of the Tree Test is not so much quantitative as qualitative and thus should only be done through the careful study of interpreted drawings and coaching/mentoring. As for interpretation guidelines, several books have already discussed this matter in great detail (e.g. Bolander, 1977; De Castilla, 1994; Fernandez, 2005; Koch, 1957; Leibowitz, 1999; Stora, 1978). It is beyond the scope of this chapter to attempt to summarize these references.

Some key interpretation guidelines

Some of the most obvious interpretations involve looking at roots, trunk, branches, or crown and any added features such as presence of fruit or flowers (Koch, 1952).

The *trunk* for example is said to represent the structure of the subjects' personality, in particular his or her emotional life. Knots on the trunk indicate past trauma and holes indicate culpability. An open trunk at its top indicates impulsivity. A trunk larger at the base indicates that elements of the past have an important place in the person's life.

Crown and *branches* indicate subject's relation with the outside world, both in social and intellectual aspects. Extroverts and sociable people tend to draw loops in their crowns. Rational people tend not to draw leaves. Falling branches indicate depressive affect, as does darkening trunk or crown.

The presence, size, and depth of any *roots* is said to indicate a personality that is not in full contact with reality, a personality that needs a phase of firm footing in reality (Fernandez, 2005). *Flowers* could indicate narcissism, as do drawing of *fruit* when instructions do not specify to draw a fruit tree specifically. Some authors also discuss the importance of Tree's position and inclination on the sheet and drawing boldness, but not all authors agree on these points.

Recently, there have been some interesting innovations proposed. For instance in Hungary we find the Expert System for Projective Drawings (ESPD), an expert system for psychological interpretation and analyses of personality via drawings. It is a rather sophisticated artificial intelligence type of software, designed to interpret projective drawings, such as House-Tree-Person test, Human Figure Drawings, Tree Drawings, Animal Drawings, and Free Drawings, and provide results in a psycho-diagnostic report (ESPD, 2007; Kirady, 2007). Another interesting recent innovation is a program written to help reduce reliability problems and ultimately validity, in interpreting projective drawings, such as that of our Tree test, which is proposed by three Japanese psychologists (Takemura, Takasaki, & Iwamitsu, 2005). However, most computerized interpretations are unable to take into account past experience with the test and other subjects' antecedents that might affect test interpretation (Thomas & Jolley, 1998).

Some further empirical data

Hypotheses

One of the authors (LeBlanc, 1988) conducted a study testing two of Buck's (1948) hypotheses. That is, (a) participants reporting "high traumatic" events will also draw "mutilated" Trees, while subjects who report "low traumatic events" will draw little or nonmutilated Trees, and (b) the proportional position of a "knot" or another "mutilation" on the Tree will correspond with subjects' age at trauma occurrence, compared to their present age.

Participants

Participants were 187 volunteers, 15 incomplete cases were eliminated, with 172 retained protocols. The sample consisted of 138 university students and 34 young adults diagnosed with socio-affective problems, who had same age range as students. Socio-affective participants were added to counterbalance the assumption that university students were more likely to be trauma-free than even the general population. Participants were 94 females and 78 males between the ages of 17 and 25 years ($M = 19.2$, $SD = 2.2$).

Comparisons were made on the basis of drawn Trees. That is, participants who drew mutilated Trees (having a scar, a knot, or a broken or dry branch) versus those whose Trees were free of any such mutilation. Both these groups included university students and socio-affective participants.

Material

Along with a minor variation to Koch's (1957) instructions, participants were issued a pencil and a blank paper and asked to draw a tree. In accordance with Koch's instructions (1957) were asked to draw "a fruit tree but not a Christmas tree." They were also asked to complete a questionnaire, inspired by Lyons's (1955). In addition to demographic questions, it included 15 items to describe objective and subjective qualities of their most traumatic event (including age at which it happened). Seven-point Likert scales were used to evaluate its level of unpleasantness and current impact on them, (available in LeBlanc, 1988).

Two judges, both well-trained graduate students in psychology and in projective measures, independently scored drawings. To calculate height of mutilation on Tree, as related to subject's age, Tree height was measured and divided by subjects' age to produce an age-related scale. For example, if an 18-year-old female drew a Tree 6 inches high, each one third inch represents one year of her life. Thus, if she drew a mutilation (e.g., a broken branch) 3 inches from Tree bottom, one would expect traumatic event to have occurred when she was 9 years old.

Results

According to LeBlanc (1988) it was expected that subjects reporting a severe traumatic experience would draw a mutilated version of their Tree, when compared to less traumatized subjects. Briefly, 78 subjects drew nonmutilated Trees, while the remaining 94 subjects drew mutilated Trees (including 13 broken branches, 47 with knots, and 34 multiple mutilations).

To test hypothesis (a), that mutilated Trees indicate presence of a severe trauma, the two groups (mutilated vs. nonmutilated tree) were compared resulting in a significant difference in the reported level of unpleasantness of their most traumatic life event ($t(170) = 3.05$, $p < .05$).

Hypothesis (b), that one's age at the time of a reported trauma would be related to the position of mutilation drawn on the Tree, was tested on the 94 subjects who drew a Tree with one mutilation or more. Results showed that their reported age at the time when trauma occurred was significantly correlated with the height at which the knot and/or broken branch was placed on Tree trunk ($r = .28, p < .05$.).

These results support the argument that a subject's drawing can be related to a previous traumatic event, in terms of both presence and chronology (Bolander, 1977). However, although all subjects who included a knot or another mutilation in their drawing reported having endured a "disagreeable" event, not all subjects reported having had a *traumatic* event. Also, although statistically significant, the correlation between age of traumatic event and height of mutilation is moderate, indicating that this measure provides only a rough estimate of age of traumatic event.

Figure 12.1

Illustrations

Taken from a recent unpublished data set collected by the authors, the following figures illustrate what we consider a little and very mutilated Tree. For instance, a 21-year-old male drew the nonmutilated Tree in Figure 12.1. It has no knots, scars, or dry or broken branches. The young man did not report any trauma in his response to the Life Events Questionnaire.

Figure 12.2 represents a mutilated Tree, having a large scar on the trunk and a small dry branch on Tree side. It was drawn by a 19-year-old female. She was expected to have a sexually charged experience at age five and a second experience at age six, respectively. She was however, fully functioning and seemingly a well-adapted person, as evident in her responses to Life Events Questionnaire. The width of the trunk suggested a strong personality and the large crown

Figure 12.2

suggested extroversion and a rich social life (Fernandez, 2005). Her level of psychological functioning could have been anticipated according to Tree Test's interpretation guidelines discussed above (although never empirically tested).

Discussion

Together these data lend some empirical support to both Buck's (1948) original hypotheses and, consequently, to the Tree Test criterion validity. Indeed, a significant difference was found between traumatized and non-traumatized subjects in terms of presence or absence of mutilations on their Tree drawings. In addition, the age at which trauma was reported to occur significantly correlated with the height at which the knot and/or broken branch was placed on Tree. On one hand, we can recommend the use of Tree Test when assessing possible presence of past trauma. On the other hand, given that not all subjects who reported having had a traumatic event included a knot or broken branch in their drawing, we cannot recommend its use as a unique measure to identify past trauma such as sexual abuse. Such drawings can certainly help a clinician formulate hypotheses about possible past trauma, albeit ones that need be corroborated with other valid instruments, as Koch himself (1957) argued. Indeed, it is well understood that no clinical decision should be taken based on a single test result. In their training, psychologists and vocational counsellors are strongly encouraged to use batteries of multiple tests that complement each other (Anastasi, 1994), batteries in which Tree Test has a place of its own.

References

Anastasi, A. (1994). *Introduction à la psychometrie* [Introduction to psychometrics]. Boucherville: Guérin Universitaire.

Bolander, K. (1977). *Assessing personality through Tree drawings.* New York: Basic Books.

Bon, N., & Bon, M. (1984). Analyse des correspondances des tests du bonhomme et de l'arbre. [Analysis of the correspondences between the Draw-a-Man test and the Tree test.]. *Psychologie Française, 29,* 303–307.

Buck, J. N. (1948). The H-T-P technique, a qualitative and quantitative scoring manual. *Journal of Clinical Psychology, 4,* 317–396.

Cohen de Lara-Kroon, N. (1999). *The history of projective testing (emphasizing the thematic apperception test).* Retrieved from http://www.cohendelara.com/publicaties/history.htm

De Castilla, D. (1994). *Le test de l'Arbre: Relations humaines et problèmes actuels* [The Tree test: Human relations and present problems]. Paris: Masson.

Devore, J. E., & Fryrear, J. L. (1976). Analysis of juvenile delinquents' hole drawing responses on the tree figure of the House-Tree-Person Technique. *Journal of Clinical Psychology, 32,* 731–736.

ESPD. (2007). *Psychological analysis of drawings: From artificial intelligence systems in psychology (AIS).* Budapest. Retrieved from http://download.cnet.com/ESPD2007-Psychological-Analysis-of-Drawings/3000-2054_4-10583991.html

Fernandez, L. (2005). Le test de l'Arbre: Un dessin pour comprendre et interpréter [The Tree test: A drawing to comprehend and interpret]. Paris: Éditions In Press.

Furnham, A. F. (1997). Knowing and faking one's five-factor personality score. *Journal of Personality Assessment, 69,* 229–243.

Goodenough, F. (1926a). A new approach to the measurement of intelligence of young children. *Journal of Genetic Psychology, 33,* 185–211.

Goodenough, F. (1926b). *Measurement of intelligence by drawings.* New York: World Book.

Handler, L., Campbell, A., & Martin, B. (2004). Use of graphic techniques in personality assessment: Reliability, validity, and clinical utility. In M. Hersen, M. J. Hilsenroth, & D. L. Segal (Eds.), *Comprehensive handbook of psychological assessment: Vol. 2. Personality assessment* (pp. 387–404). Hoboken: Wiley.

Hersen, M., Hilsenroth, M. J., & Segal, D. L. (2004). *Personality assessment: Volume 2. Comprehensive handbook of psychological assessment.* London: Wiley.

Inadomi, H., Tanaka, G., & Ohta, Y. (2003). Characteristics of trees drawn by patients with paranoid schizophrenia. *Psychiatry & Clinical Neurosciences, 57,* 347–351.

Keisuke, I., Kiichiro, M., Naoki, K., Satoshi, H., Keiichiro, M., & Hisao, M. (2001). Diagnostic evaluation of the "Baum" test in mental disorders. *Neuropsychiatry, 47,* 129–136.

Kirady, A. (2007). Application of artificial intelligence in military aptitude tests. *Academic & Applied Research in Military Science, 6,* 785–790.

Koch, C. (1949). *Der Baumtest: Der Baumzeichen-versuch als psychodiagnostisches Hilfmittel* [The tree drawing as psychodiagnostic aid]. Bern: Huber.

Koch, C. (1952). *The Tree Test: The Tree-Drawing test as an aid in psycho diagnosis.* Berne: Huber.

Koch, C. (1957). *Le test de l'arbre: Le diagnostic psychologique par le dessin de l'arbre* [The Tree Test: Psychological diagnosis using the drawing of a tree] (3rd ed.). E. Marmy & H. Niel, (Trans.). Paris: Animus et Anima.

LeBlanc, C. (1988). *Mutilisation de l'Arbre comme symbole traumatiquedans la technique du House-Tree-Person test* [Tree mutilation as a traumatic symbol in the House-Tree-Person technique]. Unpublished master's thesis, University of Moncton, Moncton, New Brunswick, Canada.

Leibowitz, M. (1999). *Interpreting projective drawings: A self psychological approach.* Ann Arbor: Taylor & Francis.

Lemaire, M., & Demers, S. (2008). Réflexion sur la pertinence des tests projectifs en expertise psycholégale [Reflections on the appropriateness of projective tests in the psycho-legal expertise]. *Revue Québécoise de Psychologie, 29,* 43–48.

Lyons, J. (1955). The scar on the H-T-P tree. *Journal of Clinical Psychology, 11,* 267–270.

Machover, K. (1949). *Personality projection in the drawing of the human figure.* Oxford: Charles C. Thomas.

Mizuta, I., Inoue, Y., Fukunaga, T., Ishi, R., Ogawa, A., & Takeda, M. (2002). Psychological characteristics of eating disorders as evidenced by the combined administration of questionnaires and two projective methods: The Tree Drawing Test (Baum Test) and the Sentence Completion Test. *Psychiatry & Clinical Neurosciences, 56,* 41–53.

Roivainen, E., Ruuska, P. (2005). The use of projective drawings to assess Alexithymia: The validity of the Wartegg Test. *European Journal of Psychological Assessment, 21,* 199–201.

Rothstein, M. G., & Goffin, R. D. (2006). The use of personality measures in personnel selection: What does current research support? *Human Resource Management Review, 16,* 155–180.

Stevens, M. J. & Wedding, D. (2004). *Handbook of international psychology.* London: Routledge.

Stora, R. (1978). *Le test de l'arbre* [The Tree Test]. Paris: Presses Universitaires de France.

Takemura, K., Takasaki, I., & Iwamitsu, Y. (2005). Statistical image analysis of psychological projective drawings. *Journal of Advanced Computational Intelligence and Intelligent Informatics, 9,* 453–454.

Thomas, G.V., & Jolley, R. P. (1998). Drawing conclusions: Are examination of empirical and conceptual bases for psychological examination of children from their drawings. *British Journal of Clinical Psychology, 37,* 129–139.

Torem, M. S., Gilbertson, A., & Light, V. (2006). Psycho-diagnostic processes: Projective techniques: Indications of physical, sexual, and verbal victimization in projective tree drawing. *Journal of Clinical Psychology, 46,* 900–906.

Wartegg, E. (1939). Gestaltung und Charakter [Form and character]. *Zeitschrift für angewandte Psychologie und Charakterkunde, 84.* Leipzig: Barth.

Webster, R. (2008). *Flower and tree Magic: Discover the natural enchantment around you* (p. 143). Woodbury, MN: Llewellyn Woldwide Ltd. Retrieved from http://www.llewellyn.com/product.php?ean=9780738713496

13

USING THE SQUIGGLE GAME IN THE CLINICAL INTERVIEW OF ADOLESCENTS

A case study of psychodynamic therapeutic assessment

Shira Tibon Czopp

Introduction

This chapter explores the Squiggle Game, a drawing technique that Winnicott (1971) developed for use with children, as representing a relational psychoanalytic model in which the clinician plays with the child freely and spontaneously within a context of mutual, though asymmetric, interaction. When using the Squiggle Game, usually during the clinical interview, Winnicott would make a squiggle, a twisted or wriggly line, spontaneously drawn on a piece of paper. The child was then invited to add elements to the drawing and both would comment on the collaborative product. Winnicott would then transform a drawing made by the child and both would further comment on it. Whose drawing is it? Is it the child's or the clinician's? This question is discussed in the present chapter by describing the use of the method in the clinical interview of Dan, a 12-year-old exceptionally gifted boy who, on referral, clearly defined what he was looking for: a psychologist who would provide him with a glimpse of his internal world, enabling him to discover his true self, and would serve as a mediator between him and the external world.

Assessing adolescents

As suggested in case studies of adolescents' assessment (Bram, 2010; Exner & Weiner, 1995; Exner & Erdberg, 2005; Tibon & Rothschild, 2007) clinicians who interview adolescents should be aware that normal developmental demands induce regressive experience and primitive defensive reactions.

However, except for severe psychopathological states (within the schizophrenic or the affectively disordered spectrum), most of the adolescents seen in the clinical practice might be more reasonably viewed as demonstrating problems evolving from a developmental crisis rather than psychopathological states. Given that well-synthesized personality style in adolescents is not yet fully developed and patterns of defenses are not fully crystallized, the personality structure and effective defensive strategies can be more vulnerable to disruption by contextual factors (e.g., exposure to trauma) that exacerbate subjective distress. Accordingly, when assessing adolescents, one must consider in addition to issues related to the stormy developmental stage, contextual factors, and the vulnerability of existing structures along with the potential for rapid recovery. Indeed, because major mental disorders are often present in atypical forms during adolescence, assessing mental functioning in youngsters might be more complicated than in adults. However, rather than providing a diagnosis in terms of the *Diagnostic and Statistical Manual of Mental Disorders* (*DSM-IV-TR*; American Psychiatric Association, 2000) the assessment is usually aimed at describing the psychodynamic picture, evaluating cases of faltering personality development, detecting risk factors, and understanding subjective experience of symptom patterns.

It is quite infrequent that adolescents themselves search for professional help. Usually it is either the parents or the school teachers who initiate the referral. As a result, many adolescents seen in the clinical practice are reluctant of being interviewed, tested, or treated which makes the assessment process even more complicated. Although this was not the case with Dan, the use of the Squiggle Game in the initial interview with him is offered as an illustration of the ways that various aspects of traditional psychological testing, particularly those of the developing intersubjective experience, can enhance and even be essential to the assessment process and its results.

The Squiggle Game as integrating assessment and therapy

Winnicott's (1958, 1971) description of the Squiggle Game is quite detailed, and one can feel his playfulness and enjoyment of the method. The elaborated description has inspired many psychoanalytically oriented clinicians, who have found the game to provide them with a creative tool and a useful metaphor for conducting both assessment and therapy, particularly with children and adolescents. Winnicott describes how he introduces the game, how he encounters possible anxiety, how he allows the child to decline the invitation to play, and how he observes and analyses his own and the child's drawings and comments.

Playing the Squiggle Game within a supportive context can enable youngsters revealing current emotional difficulties, and even more important opening the door for authentic mutual communication. From theoretical perspective, the Squiggle Game is based on the view that creative communication and play both occur in what Winnicott (1971) defined as potential or transitional space between reality and fantasy, between infant and mother, between self and object, and between patient and therapist and/or examiner. This is an experiencing space that is not challenged, a space in which overlapping of subjectivity occurs. Handler (1999) applied the construct to introduce his approach to the utility of the Rorschach in therapeutic assessment. In line with this approach, the Squiggle Game is used in the present case study as both an assessment and a therapeutic tool.

Historically, Winnicott (1958, 1971) used the Squiggle Game as a technique of communicating with children in the initial interview. The use of the technique followed the integration of the Spatula Game (Winnicott, 1958) as part of the interview. In the Spatula Game Winnicott left a shining spoon on his desk while observing a mother–infant pair within the initial interview. Winnicott describes how the infant hesitated before reaching for the spatula and how he checked back and forth the mother's and Winnicott's face before picking it up. Gradually, the infant took the spatula, played with it, bit on it, sucked it, and threw it on the floor to play with it. Likewise, the squiggles drawing was perceived as part of the interview aimed at assessing simultaneously the child's major difficulties and therapeutic response. However, from its inception the game, which was initiated as a diagnostic tool, became a therapeutic technique in itself. Aron (1992) applies both the use of the spatula and the squiggle drawing as a metaphor for an interpretation. The clinician provides the patient with an interpretation and observes the way in which this previously unknown, apparently surprising and exciting piece of information is handled by the patient. In line with this approach, the present illustration focuses on the interpretative utility of the Squiggle Game within the context of *Psychodynamic Therapeutic Assessment* (Tibon Czopp, 2010).

Case history

Dan is a nice looking boy who was born in Israel as the first son of an upper-middle class couple. His two younger brothers are 10 and 3 years old. Both parents own an academic degree. His father has made a career as a computer expert and his mother, who originally graduated as an engineer, works as a high school teacher, and seems to be quite satisfied in her job. The couple has a wide range of intellectual and cultural interests. The extended family from both sides is in close relationships, and the grandparents, who live in the same neighborhood, take an active part in raising the children. Socially, they have a close group of friends, with whom they frequently go to family trips and have collaborative activities.

Since infancy, Dan was recognized as a gifted boy, with wide-range exceptional abilities in both verbal and performance domains. As a result, upon reaching the third grade he was referred to a special class for gifted children with whom he currently continues to study. Dan appears to be well integrated in the class, both academically and socially. Although admitting that he has no specific difficulties with his familial or social immediate environment, Dan reports that something causes him quite elevated tension from within.

The Squiggle Game: The Eye-Fish and the crown

As noted, this is a self-referral that followed Dan's initiative to see a psychologist.

When entering the interview Dan looked mostly tense and reserved. Emotionally, he gave the impression of being in some kind of depressive mood, lacking the capacity to play (Winnicott, 1971). Following a few introductory phrases I suggested Dan to do a collaborative drawing (i.e., the Squiggle Game) and he accepted it enthusiastically.

Unlike the usual procedure, in which the clinician starts with the first squiggle drawing, I thought it might be more important to observe Dan's initial step in coping with the blank sheet, rather than investigating his response to my drawing.

We started with Dan's drawing of an oval shape with a small triangle on the left side (Figure 13.1) which seemed to me to be a fish. Accordingly, I added the sea,

Figure 13.1

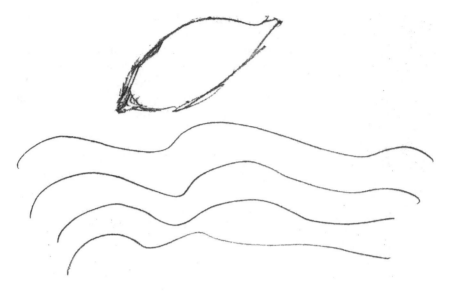

Figure 13.2

being represented by waves (Figure 13.2). At this point Dan added some slashes on the upper part of the oval shape and a circle in the middle (Figure 13.3).

By locating the circle in the middle Dan successfully transformed my initial interpretation and I said: "I can now see that you meant to draw an eye, not a fish, as it seemed to me when you drew the oval shape and also the slashes on its upper part. However, when you added this circle in the middle, my inter- pretation changed. I can see it looks like an eye, observing the external world. Isn't it?" Dan looked playful and satisfied. He succeeded to communicate his original idea of drawing the oval as representing his experience in the world as a participant observer.

Dan then drew another shape (Figure 13.4) which was much less ambiguous. I interpreted this shape correctly as a crown adding some jewelry (Figure 13.5). Dan looked at the decorated crown and seemed to be disappointed. He took the pencil and added two triangles (Figure 13.6) that made the crown three dimen- sional. His search for depth instead of shallow decoration of his narcissistic needs of recognition (represented by the crown) was quite obvious.

Discussion

The advantages of using performance-based assessment tools, previously defined as projective methods for evaluating mental functioning of adolescents are not limited to the diagnostic task. Rather, it might also be applied for therapeutic

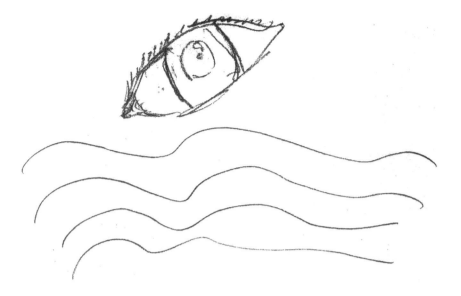

Figure 13.3

interventions. The contemporary clinical practice, in general, and that with children and adolescents, in particular, is different from the traditional, in which the practitioner's two major tasks, assessment and therapy, were viewed as being sharply differentiated. Assessment, according to this approach, was mainly used as a method of collecting data, usually followed by psychotherapy. Assessment and therapy were thus typically conducted by two different clinicians and perceived as two separate tasks. In contrast, the current model of *Psychodynamic Therapeutic Assessment* (Tibon, 2010), fits into Handler's (2007) suggestion to use an assessment process which is designed to be transformative, in the sense that it is considered to be a therapeutic intervention in itself. In line with this approach the use of the Squiggle Game as an assessment tool constitutes a real challenge to the sharp distinction between free association and interpretation, between data gathering and analyzing our observations, which are central for classical psychoanalytic-oriented techniques.

The present case study illustrates the use of the Squiggle Game for assessing an adolescent whose subjective distress brought him to look for someone who would help him to explore his internal experience and would serve as a mediator between him and the external world. The analysis of the squiggle drawings proposes a shift from the traditional view of assessment and testing as an observation made on the patient's personality dispositions and dynamics, to a view of assessment as a meaning-making and mutual communication process.

Applying a psychoanalytic relational perspective, Aron (1992) uses the Squiggle Game to explore the mutual and subjective aspects of interpretation.

Figure 13.4

He argues that like interpretation, collaborative drawings such as the Squiggle Game, belongs neither to the clinician nor to the patient:

> Like an interpretation, in Winnicott's view, it does not come from the analyst or from the patient, but rather it emerges from the transitional space between them. When Winnicott squiggles his line, he does it spontaneously. He has the patient in mind; however, he does not deliberately or intentionally plan his squiggles. On the contrary, they express his spontaneity; they are reflections of true self, spontaneous gestures. He does not necessarily know what will come out when he begins to draw. If he did, it would feel contrived and false . . . Winnicott fundamentally altered our understanding of the meaning and function of interpretation.

Figure 13.5

"Where analysts had previously focused on gaining understanding, Winnicott insisted that the analyst must be able to tolerate not knowing".

(Aron, 1992, p. 486)

Relational psychoanalytic thinking acknowledges that every clinical activity inevitably consists of an interaction between two subjects who meet together in what is called "meeting of minds" (Aron, 1996). When we refer to a psychoanalytic interaction, we mean an interaction between two complete psyches, and the realization that this is so has been exerting an increasing influence on the way we think about what actually takes place in the clinical practice. However, the relational approach to psychoanalysis is considered to be a powerful guide

Figure 13.6

to issues of techniques used in clinical work. Nonetheless, while the fundamental conception we hold is of psychoanalysis as an interaction between two complete psyches, clinicians are usually expected to eliminate personally motivated action. Renik (1993) explores the construct of Irreducible Subjectivity in the psychoanalytically oriented practice and describes the current state of affairs as a bit confusing. While tolerance for interest in the intensely personal nature of an analyst's participation in clinical work has gained an increasing place in theoretical thinking about psychoanalytic process and technique, many clinicians still conceptualize the patient's psyche as a specimen to be held apart for examination in a field as free as possible from contamination by elements of the analyst's personal psychology.

While Irreducible Subjectivity in the clinical practice is considered to be quite obvious when we talk about psychotherapy, it is more challenging when we look at assessment procedures, which are usually considered as being aimed at providing an objective, scientific-based, and evidence-supported picture of the personality.

However, psychoanalytic theories of assessment agree that regardless of how standardized the assessment procedure might be, the observed data reflect also the intersubjective relationships between the assessor and the patient (Lerner, 1998; Schafer, 1954). Accordingly, transference and counter-transference issues should also be considered while interpreting test results. This is particularly important when using the Squiggle Game which involves mutual, collaborative activity.

Indeed, the Squiggle Game provides the clinician reference data to the patient's current emotional difficulties and most often also to their roots in developmental and structural reality. Nonetheless, it also reveals some aspects of the clinician's internal world. Bollas (1987) suggests that within this context of being a participant-observer, the clinician can establish himself or herself as a subject in the analytic field, and disclose mental content, psychic process, emotional reality, and authentic self-state. Obviously, the collaborative nature of the Squiggle Game drawing task points out the clinician's position as a subject in the intersubjective analytic field. Furthermore, clinicians' awareness of their emotional responses as they arise in the clinical encounter necessarily follows translation of those responses into action. These responses enable them to profit from subsequent exploration of incorrect interpretations. In the present case study, the incorrect interpretations (interpreting an oval shape as a fish instead of an eye and adding decoration instead of a third dimension to the crown) appeared within mutual though asymmetric relationships and enabled the clinician to use the Squiggle Game not only for assessing the patient's difficulties but also for pointing them out within the clinical practice.

This case study shows however that traditional assessment tools such as the Squiggle Game can be employed by clinicians within the context of modern psychoanalytic thinking, not only for evaluating mental functioning and investigating sources of current difficulties but also for enhancing therapeutic interventions.

References

American Psychiatric Association. (2000). *Diagnostic and statistical manual of mental disorders (DSM-IV-TR)*. Washington: American Psychiatric Association.

Aron, L. (1992). Interpretation as expression of the analyst's subjectivity. *Psychoanalytic Dialogues, 2*, 475–507.

Aron, L. (1996). *A meeting of minds: Mutuality in psychoanalysis. Relational perspectives book series, Vol. 4*. Hillsdale: Analytic Press.

Bollas, C. (1987). *The shadow of the object*. London: Free Association Books.

Bram, A. D. (2010). The relevance of the Rorschach and patient-examiner relationship in treatment planning and outcome assessment. *Journal of Personality Assessment, 92,* 91–115.

Exner, J. E., & Weiner, I. B. (1995). *The Rorschach: A comprehensive system* (Vol. 3 Assessment of children and adolescents) (2nd ed.). New York: Wiley.

Exner, J. E., & Erdberg, P. (2005). *The Rorschach: A comprehensive System* (Vol. 2. Interpretation) (3rd ed.). New York: Wiley.

Handler, L. (1999). Assessment of playfulness: Hermann Rorschach meets D.W. Winnicott. *Journal of Personality Assessment, 72,* 208–217.

Handler, L. (2007). The use of therapeutic assessment with children and adolescents. In Smith, S.R., & Handler, L. (Eds.). *The clinical assessment of children and adolescents: A practitioner's handbook.* Mahwah: Lawrence Erlbaum.

Lerner, P. M. (1998). *Psychoanalytic perspectives on the Rorschach.* Hillsdale: The Analytic Press.

Schafer, R. (1954). *Psychoanalytic interpretation in Rorschach testing: Theory and application.* New York: Grune & Stratton.

Smith, B. (1990). Potential space and the Rorschach: Application of object relations theory. *Journal of Personality Assessment, 55,* 756–767.

Tibon Czopp, S. (2010). *Using the Rorschach Inkblot Method in therapeutic assessment.* Paper presented at The III Brazilian Congress of Psychology: Science & Practice, Sao Paulo, Brazil.

Renik, O. (1993). Analytic interaction: Conceptualizing technique in light of the analyst's irreducible subjectivity. *Psychoanalytic Quarterly, 62,* 553–571.

Winnicott, D. W. (1958). The observation of infants in a set situation. In *Collected Papers: Through Pediatrics to Psychoanalysis.* New York: Basic Books, pp. 52–69.

Winnicott, D. W. (1971). *Playing and Reality.* New York: Basic Books.

14

SECTION 1: THE HUMAN REPLACEMENT TECHNIQUE©

Antoinette D. Thomas and John W. Getz

Location in the main stream

Children spontaneously draw people, trees, houses, birds, clouds, and sun. At least up until adolescence, the human figure remains central in children's drawings. Absence of human figures in children's free drawings reflects difficulties in interpersonal relationships (Di Leo, 1973). Though children with emotional difficulties can be easily led from drawings to verbal expressions (Hammer, 1986), sometimes such verbal expressions are sporadic.

This technique was devised and implemented to help these children associate with their drawn objects. Such additional medium would help them express their feelings toward family members and significant others in their lives. The Human Replacement Technique (Thomas, 1995) facilitates dealing with their difficulties in drawing human figures.

Upon completion of a Free Drawing, the interviewer would praise the child's production, then say, "let us play an imaginary game. This car (flower, bird etc.) looks like or reminds you of someone you know, who is it?" And so on pointing to each drawn object. Children and adolescents usually get interested. If a child says he does not know what to do, the examiner would add, "there are no right or wrong answers, look at your drawing and you will find out whom this car (flower, bird) looks like or reminds you of someone you know."

Laying pencil colors before children provides a chance for more emotional expressions. Since colors symbolize emotions, they are expected to add an affective element (Hammer, 1986) to projective drawings that elicit submerged levels of human feelings (Hammer, 1981). Hammer has recommended the use of crayons to draw with, as subjects do with a pencil. Wooden collared pencils are better, as they provide almost similar line accuracy to lead pencils and therefore provide more comparable comparisons than thick crayons. Usually children chose to draw first with a pencil then color their units. In all variations, colors still add emotional value to drawings.

It is fascinating to open a new door to children's stored perceptions of significant persons in their lives. They make their own interpretations of their graphic productions. A child may draw two small birds on a tree and a big flower on the ground. Intrigued by the new imaginative task, birds may be her twin brothers and flower herself. Her responses might reflect her need for more space in the family and a distinct position apart from her siblings. This additional material adds valuable meaning to our usual, literature-based interpretations of drawings. Both approaches contribute to our understanding and therapeutic work.

Illustrations

A. Jean

Jean was 11 years old when interviewed at the time her parents were in couple counselling with the therapist. She drew and colored Figure 14.1.

Jean readily responded to the Human Replacement Technique: "The sun is my grandmother (paternal) who is the sunshine in my life, clouds are my mother they are standing in the way of sunshine, rainbow is my father, he makes everybody feel better, tree is my cousins they make a beautiful day, falling apples

Figure 14.1

are our relationships falling because of her (mother), tree roots are my sister, I love her." She looked timid when asked about the flower. She accepted with a smile the therapist's suggestion "you." Mother had prevented visits with the paternal family.

Jean's replacements confirmed some classical drawings characteristics and their inferences. Apple trees with falling apples employed by dependent children express their feelings of rejection by the maternal figure (Hammer, 1964). They also provide several new symbolic concepts and emotions attributed to significant others. Jean's human replacements and affective comments complemented other verbal accounts concerning her relationship with each parent. She resented her mother and supported her father. Her associations also opened the door to investigate possible underlying paternal family dynamics, which could have contributed to such a negative perception of the mother. The paternal family was involved in conflicts between her parents.

B. Steve

Steve's mother was unable to care for him due to her serious mental illness. His father disappeared from the picture since his birth. He was sexually abused—at age five—by an adult male and suffered from other forms of ill treatments at one of the foster homes he was placed in.

A psychiatrist assessed Steve at the age of seven, when he was in another inadequate foster home. His foster father had sexually molested him. Steve was described as "apathetic, dysphonic, aloof, extremely hyperactive, cannot sit still for more than ten minutes." His social worker's reports included that he made a lot of noise at school, distracted other children, and functioned very poorly. He was manipulative, isolated, felt deprived, and often threw temper tantrums. When he was eight years old, he landed in an excellent foster home. The childless foster parents accepted a foster baby girl after six months. For about three years, the family of four had a good life. During this period, Steve attended school at a Day Treatment Centre, where he showed marked improvement. Steve and his adoptive parents had to deal with the painful loss of the foster girl, when her biological mother claimed her. The Clinic provided emotional support and assistance.

At 12 years of age, Steve was in his first year of a high school, without failing any grade. However, he started to face several interactive problems. He was adjusting to high school environment, to adolescence changes, and to the loss of foster sister. In addition, he overheard plans about adopting a baby girl. He was excluded from the decision-making process. In spite of social service intervention, the relationship between Steve and his foster father gradually deteriorated. Steve would lie and perform petty thefts from foster parents, yet he would return money when they confronted him. School performance declined.

He started seeing his biological mother in supervised monthly visits. He informed his social worker about his wish to live with her. Though realistically unattainable due to her mental illness and consequent inability to care for him, this wish seemed to add fuel to existing problems with foster parents. Steve would not talk freely with his social worker. The Day Treatment team decided to offer Steve a short-term psychotherapy with the author, to help understand his internal psychodynamics, which would precede a long-term psychotherapy elsewhere. Steve, a tall skinny youngster, was well-behaved and very quiet. He seemed rather depressed and preoccupied. Occasionally, a friendly smile would brighten his face. Steve would rarely and briefly respond with superficial clichés to any direct questions about his family.

Steve's silence was dealt with by employing two low-verbal techniques, through which support and humor therapies were employed. The first was the Human Replacement Technique used with free drawings, which he was known to be good at, to delve in his inner life. Steve would draw with a lead pencil; he was systematically offered pencil colors, which he occasionally used. The second technique was the mathematical version of the "Domino" game. To gain points, the numerical addition of the four edges should add to units of five, thus gaining one point for each unite. Steve was discretely made to win. This helped enhance concentration, self-confidence, and the joy of achievement. As Steve gained mastery, the therapist would occasionally win, to help him tolerate similar loses elsewhere, in basketball which he loved and life in general.

Steve's drawings are divided into self and family presentations.

Self-presentations

In his early drawings, Steve identified with a tall well-built 30-year-old basketball player, shown in Figure 14.2, in response to," draw what you want."

The drawn Person was said to be cheerful and successful. Steve colored his figure in red, drew details on his outfit, scoreboard, ball, and basket. The name of the winning team, Bulls, accounted for an added masculine prowess. Steve invested interest, considerable time, and care to produce his drawing. Basketball playing was about the only area of success in his life. Another self-presentation figure was a same-age—13-year-old boy—with "peace sign" on his T-shirt, engaged in the pleasant activity of flying a kite. Other objects in the drawing were: a sun with a smiley face and a tree. The sun is often considered as a paternal symbol (Di Leo, 1983). Steve's Replacement of the sun was nonhuman objects, "a dog or a cat." These pets are often children's attachment objects. Yet, Steve's association was not a human male figure, which would have represented the paternal figure, "a women who is not related to the boy" replaced kite and tree. That is, a maternal figure was brought to the front, but distance was set between her image and the drawn boy.

Steve considered the boy's figure as someone else in Replacement exercise. It would represent what he would like to be in classical drawing interpretation: A same-age boy having fun. Objects filled the page; the figure had adequate size suggesting reasonably desired presence of self in the environment.

Figure 14.2

The next drawing was a neatly colored mouse, without any other objects. Choosing a helpless animal—a mouse—drawn much smaller (2 square inches) than Persons drawn in the two previous human figures, reflected comparable inner feeling of helplessness. Missing eyes stood for Steve's tendency to shut off visual input as he was gradually becoming withdrawn, both at home and at school. The mouse had earrings, which may point to his tendency to conform to some teenagers' style. Steve's foster parents would have never allowed him to wear earrings. Therefore, they probably symbolized difference of opinion between him and his foster parents. Used colors were: gray for body, black for earrings, mouth, and nose, pink for large ears, yellow for face, and red for tail. Soft colors and light pressure may suggest willingness to reveal some soft emotions. Ears' large size may refer to Steve's interest in overhearing family plans concerning him as well as the prospective adoptive sister, since he was excluded from their plans. Mouse Replacement was, "a 20-year old person, could be anybody, just standing and happy." Positive verbalized affect was consistent with the use of colors and softness, in suggesting some mild positive inner feelings.

Subsequent self-presentations were predominantly drawn only with pencil, rejecting invitations to use colors, suggested resistance in revealing affect. Change from chromatic to achromatic colors also reflected sadness. In the next drawing, Steve drew two clouds, a sun without face, and a good-sized sailboat in water, with a reversed sail and a top flag. Sail reversal may reflect opposition or a need to be distinct, similar to the mouse's earrings. There were no Human Replacements, just animals: a fish, a dog, and a cat replaced boat, sun, and clouds. Replacement Technique failed to illicit human associations. Thus only symbolic value of docile animals was added to drawings' classical characteristics.

The next drawing symbolized Steve's aggressive tendencies combined with depression. The drawn rocket, a male symbol, labeled NASA depicted violence and desired power. Dark black lines as well as shading reflected his sadness. In response to the Replacement question, he said, "Four strangers were travelling out of space. They were going to crash and die." He was not sorry for them. Such associations revealed the intensity of his aggressive feelings, whether addressed toward others, turned against self or just stored inside.

Steve's utmost sadness was expressed in the next color drawing (Figure 14.3), as well as in Replacements. "A dead fish on a wooden board beside a sharp butcher's knife will be cut up by the butcher and sold. The fish could be replaced by anybody and sold to anybody." The act of cutting up the dead fish

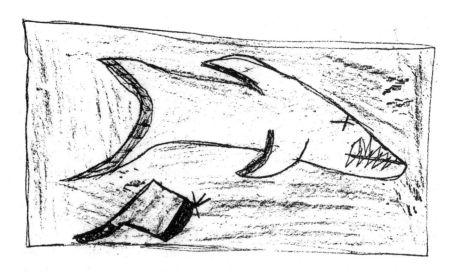

Figure 14.3

(notice the sign of sharpness) as well as embedded helplessness of the dead fish in this response suggested aggression directed against self. Therefore, would support direction of "turned against self or stored inside," in NASA figure.

Five months later—when he was moved to a group home—he drew Batman's speed car, in pencil, on the bottom of a page. The car's location and its small size reflected his withdrawal and his limited interaction with his environment. However, sense of power implied in the speed car and its supernatural fictitious owner, suggested compensatory defenses compared to sense of death, vulnerability, and self-destruction, seen in the NASA and dead fish drawings.

Family relationships

Free Drawings representing family relationships were interwoven, in sequence, with Self-Presentations. Steve carefully drew a house, three family members, a tree, and a sun, in mostly bright colors.

Figure 14.4 shows self and maternal figure—almost touching hand to forearm—on one side of the house, while the paternal figure is on the other side. This may reflect the presence, the memory or the need for closeness to the maternal figure. Not only self-presentation was distant from the paternal figure, but also relatively bigger, therefore reflecting a need to be more important or powerful compared to paternal figure within the family. Maternal and paternal figures lacked hands, a communication symbol.

Figure 14.4

Maternal figure's clothes were fully colored, were half colored for the paternal figure, while self-presentation uncolored. Thus, different corresponding degrees of affect were invested in each figure, with concealed emotions in self-presentation. The apple tree suggested yearning to a childhood phase and to mother's loving care. It would be his early three years in this foster home. The 2 by 3 inches drawing was placed high on the page, probably reflecting configurations in fantasy. This notion was supported by Steve's response to the Replacement question about the house, "for fun, not a real house."

Emotional distance between self-presentation and paternal figure—noticed in the previous drawing—reappeared in two subsequent drawings. The *first* colored drawing had two trees, each at far end of a horizontal, a sailboat in a lake with boundaries with a flag and a stick person, three clouds, two birds, and a sun with a full human face. Steve would not respond to the Replacement question concerning trees. Steve readily identified the stick person as self. Stick persons usually refer to low human value, in this case low self-esteem. A face in a sun is a childish characteristic, probably suggested perception of the paternal figure as he was in previous years. One of the two birds was flying upside down, probably symbolizing the presence of two opposing trends: conformity with what is common and ordinary versus opposition and distinction. Clouds usually symbolize anxiety; the number may refer to his household size. His verbal Replacements indicated that self-presentation, "was going anywhere and the whole scene was anywhere too," a projection of Steve's perception of himself: no direction in life, lack of a sense of belonging, and location within the environment. Steve spontaneously added, "a friend is walking on the beach, but not present in the drawing." Could this "friend" symbolize a hope for a person to be an emotional support, probably his social worker or therapist? Replacing the boat was "A visiting child, a foster cousin." A particular foster cousin had a positive relationship with Steve in real life. Colors, which corresponded with natural ones, indicated realistic awareness of the environment.

The *second* relevant drawing was done in pencil: Two trees, at each end of a horizontal page, separated by a ground line and water, a sun with a face and four clouds. "A father and a son" Replaced trees. When asked, "would you like them to come close to each other?" he nodded in the affirmative. Trees' extreme positions, on each side of water, symbolized the emotional distance between self- and paternal presentations. The Replacement Technique confirmed such meaning and added an unspoken wish for closeness. Sadness and feelings of restriction were reflected in this drawing as compared to the sailboat in a lake, that is absence of colors, smaller trees, smaller lake, light line pressure in trees and clouds.

After summer holidays, Steve drew a small house resting on the lower edge of a page. House placement suggested need support associated with feelings of insecurity and low self-assurance (Buck, 1948; Burns &

Kaufman, 1972; Hammer, 1967; Burns, 1982). Windows were barred; the door was closed and based on three layers of bricks above ground level, all of which made it inaccessible. Houses usually stand for family settings. Inaccessibility of this house could be added to series of associations and drawing characteristics describing tension at home. Colors were refused, reflecting resistance to getting in touch with deeper emotions, since he used them before.

Two months later, Steve drew a black and white castle. Similar to the previous house, this castle was completely inaccessible. Door and windows were barred, in addition to the nature of castles as being hard to access. He was asked similar questions to those posed about the House in House-Tree-Person (H-T-P) technique (Buck, 1966), to help him associate to his drawing. Responses were: "Nobody lived in, empty, it belonged to a king who lived in another one, never came here, it was haunted by ghosts, can't tell if males or females. An ugly castle, nothing could be done to make it pretty.;" No replacements were made or needed. Drawn houses are believed to portray family environments. Steve verbally and graphically projected his feelings about his family: empty, ugly, irreparable, and even scary.

Figure 14.5

Call for action

At this point, the therapist was strongly convinced that it was in Steve's best interest to be placed elsewhere, before interpersonal relationships with his foster parents reach a point of no return. Positive memories derived from years back were assumed to furnish a basis for new relationships. Occasional visits with the present foster parents would hopefully lead to more positive interactions. Steve would also maintain his supervised visits with his biological mother, provided his fantasy of being reunited with her is dealt with. The two involved social workers agreed. They explained benefits to Steve and foster parents.

The very last drawing produced by Steve was done three months later when he was placed in a group home. Figure 14.5 occupied the whole page, though colors were refused. There were several units of four: clouds, high mountains, and sets of branches on a Christmas tree. Number four may symbolize the time when the foster sister was part of the family, the happiest time in Steve's life. It is interesting to notice ice covering mountaintops, a clear symbol of cold affect. The sun lost its usual face, which is age appropriate. Steve's Replacement for all units was "all strangers," which spoke of his perception of the present state of what used to be his happy family.

SECTION 2: DOODLING AND FREE DRAWINGS: BLIND INFERENCES

Antoinette D. Thomas and John W. Getz

This study is based on blind drawings interpretations compared to clinical material in patients' files, at a psychiatric hospital in the United States. The second author, a clinical psychologist, provided drawings along with little or no information such as diagnosis, age, or background. He wrote, "I have interesting doodling done by a female patient who was exposed to abuse." The type of abuse was not specified. Blind inferences were carried out by the first author, a clinical psychologist in Canada, then mailed back. Upon reception, he wrote, "many of your interpretations were accurate, on target." These statements were *underlined*.

Case 1: Doodling

Blind inferences checked

Large filled-in-black water drops—in Figure 14.6—may be seen as <u>tears</u>. Wax dripping from candles are very similar in shape to tears, which reinforces this impression. As candles potentially give light, they are often used as a metaphor for, <u>"someone lights the way for others by diminishing oneself".</u>

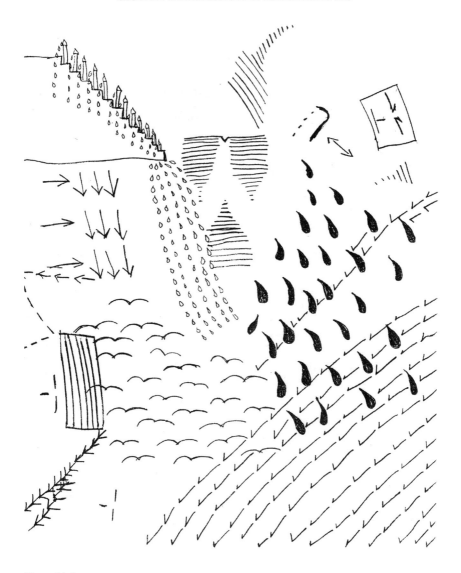

Figure 14.6

Candles on the stairway seem to go downward as noticed in their size, they get smaller, as seen on the right side. This may symbolize depression, "going down." (They would be interpreted as hope had they gone upward). There is a strong obsessive defense throughout the repetitive units (birds, arrows, check marks).

A human face could be seen in a box (upper right corner). As such, it is an abstract form that gives you the feeling of a grim expression. There are two other attempted similar faces near lower left edge (without boxes). Sad subjects tend not to draw proper eyes, they draw dashes or dots, which symbolizes visual avoidance of outside stimuli associated with unhappiness. Horizontal rectangular face, instead of the usual adult vertical oval one, is also an indication of perceived stiffness in humans. Check signs (lower right corner) may reflect a wish for setting things right or correcting them. Birds, which are often done this way in children's drawings, may reflect anxiety.

Arrows (far left edge) may symbolize an attempt to find a way, however, following them through dashes lead to what looks like thorns. Arrows and thorns suggest pain. Nearby vertical rectangular box with vertical lines suggests no way out, the lines are locked in. The double direction arrow (upper–right corner close to face) also indicates no direction. I have some difficulty or hesitation in trying to understand groups of lines in upper-middle place. They may be a far-fetched interpretation if you see them as penetration of the lower group in the direction of the space provided by the upper two. Impasse at the top may suggest a contraceptive, or refusal of a sexual act. The whole thing may otherwise show a blocked pathway, on an abstract level.

Clinical material

The patient was a 33-year-old married woman, mother of three children. Her primary diagnosis included Anorexia Nervosa and Depressive Disorder. Her depression had an obsessive flavor along with an anxiety component. She had occasional suicidal ideation. She would not easily relate to people. She had ideation of being trapped and locked in. She has had a distorted body image since age 13. Several traumatic events had occurred in her life. She was impregnated by her biological father and aborted at age 16. Her half-brothers sexually abused her.

The patient had three hospitalizations as well as treatments in two outpatient part-time programs. Doodling was done half way into her two-year individual psychotherapy with Dr. Getz.

Upon termination, she achieved several gains. Taking anti-psychotic medication had diminished her suicidal thoughts. Her eating disorder subsided. She had the courage to divorce her husband following his conviction in a homosexual attack in a public place. She held a decent job and was accepted in a university program next fall.

Case 2: Free drawings

Getz wrote, "I'll send *two* drawings done by another patient which you will find interesting." Upon receiving *three* drawings, Thomas was not sure whether they pertained to one or two subjects. After submitting drawing impressions in writing, she was informed that they belonged to one person.

Blind inferences checked

A. Hands on Head

Erasing in Figure 14.7 resulted in improvement, therefore it is a sign of good perceptual judgment. The angle of the portrayed human figure, looked at from above, provided an unusual view, yet very accurate in terms of perception. She seems to be intelligent. Her graphic skills are very good. That is, proportion and perception are superior, which show high cognitive potential according to human figure drawing scoring systems (e.g., House-Tree-Person, Buck, 1948).

As for emotional content, the rather small figure size (2 1/4 square inches) suggests inadequacy feelings. The gesture of hands over head readily conveys grief, sadness or serious thought disorder, as if saying, "my head is about to split." The fact that there were no facial features reflects a strong attempt to hide; unwillingness to face others including the therapist. She seems to find it difficult to let you know her feelings and life events. Body is naked, but private parts are not exposed. She is not seductive yet clothes do not protect her. There is no hair either, suggesting loss of her "crown," as women's hair is often referred to. The overall picture of inadequacy feelings, troubled thoughts, splitting head, sadness, naked body, and hair loss, point to sexual abuse, with desexualised interest suggested by nonexposed private parts and face.

B. Back to the viewer

Assuming the same patient did both drawings, Figure 14.8 seems to be drawn at a relatively better psychological state than the first drawing. That is, the figure has added female hair and splitting head gesture is absent. Yet the person feels she is captive, her hands are tied, and they are in a spider's web. Drawing characteristics and inferences in Figure 14.7 are applicable here, such as hiding face, nakedness without exposing private parts, and small size. Likewise, comments pertaining to perception also apply here. In addition, the well-done figure's shadow shows excellent perception.

C. Two close women (two female standing figures hugging each other)

If the same person did this drawing it shows a lesbian choice. Once more figures are rather naked but no private parts are shown. Bodies are like "silhouettes." There is a sense of tenderness between the two figures re-enforced by bodies' soft lines, relative position of holding each other, and extra lower lines which give the impression of skirts. Very similar hair styles suggest a need for an auxiliary ego, "someone exactly like me to love and support me." Absence of facial features is consistent with previous drawings.

Figure 14.7

Clinical material

The patient was a 35-year-old married woman, mother of a young child. She was hospitalized for Substance Dependence and Major Depression with psychotic features. She also presented auditory and visual hallucinations as well as insomnia and suicidal ideation. As a registered nurse, she started with excessive doses of medications then moved to street drugs. She was sexually abused by an older neighbor between the ages of 14 and 19.

Figure 14.8

At the time of the drawings, she was an outpatient, individually treated by Dr. Getz. She was treated for insomnia and chronic fatigue. She was described as "a very bright person." In therapy she was very much "'on guard." She readily protested and detached herself from her feelings. She became involved in a lesbian relationship with her husband's female coworker, looking for love by another woman. The "two close women" drawing was done in the presence of her lesbian partner, who attended the therapeutic session. Later, the patient decided to give up this relationship to keep upon her marital commitment.

SECTION 3: WHAT COULD IT BE?©

Antoinette D. Thomas

Location in the main stream

This technique (Thomas, 1995) is a modification of Winnicott's (1985) magnificent clinical use of squiggles. Winnicott would draw vague curves, occasionally combined with angles, done with eyes opened or closed. The child would try to make sense of them by adding other lines. Vagueness of squiggles aimed at reaching deep internal material to facilitate communication during initial interviews, prior to more intensive psychotherapy.

"What could it be?" technique consists of completing unfinished common objects, drawn by the clinician as well as the child. The interviewer would draw, in one color, a small portion—relative to the child's cognitive level—of a common object, such as an apple. The child is asked, "What do you think this could be when complete? Draw the rest with another color. Then it will be your turn to draw part of something and I will try to finish it." The clinician cheerfully accepts whatever object the child draws, pointing to its relevance to the stimulus. If both agree on the final product, the interviewer would say, "you and I saw the same thing." In case they differ, an appropriate comment would be, "(name the child's object) and (name your object) are good completions." Humor and enthusiasm are employed throughout the game. The exchange is done until the page is full. Children 6 to 13 years find this technique amusing and often ask for it.

At the end, the clinician goes a step beyond mutual enjoyment. He or she would link the graphic experience of similarity and differences to life situations. "This game is very much like what we do every day. Sometimes we think the same way as our brothers, sisters, and parents. Some other times we think in different ways. It is OK either way." The technique promotes two important processes: empathy and tolerance to disagreements. The graphic, concrete level facilitates the emotional, abstract level.

The present technique differs from Winnicott's squiggles. First, the squiggles are not part of any specific form or object. Second, the clinical objective is different. However, both techniques employ humor and guessing.

This technique also differs from Drawing Completion Test (Hammer, 1967). First, in Drawing Completion Test, the stimuli are standardized. Subjects are asked to complete different tiny geometric figures within eight boxes. Second, the interviewer does not participate in drawings.

Illustration

Sam's background

Sam was 11 years old when he started individual psychotherapy. He was living with his father and stepmother for two years. When his parents were divorced he lived with his mother for a similar amount of time. Sam had an older half-sister who lived with his biological parents before the divorce. Later she lived with their mother and stepfather, during the time he lived with his mother.

Sam was doing poorly at school. Some behavioral and emotional problems had recently emerged such as: lack of self-confidence and aggression at school and sadness and crying for slight reasons at home. Sam was not suicidal according to a previous evaluation. The father had exhausted all kinds of rewards and punishments excluding physical punishment.

As for family dynamics, the two reconstructed families maintained neutral positions, they neither communicated nor bad-mouthed each other. Sam's stepmother sincerely loved and cared for him. The only default perceived by the father was her controlling of Sam regarding healthy food. Her perceptions of the father's limitations were "shouting at Sam, repetitive moral lectures and lack of demonstrative expression of love and appreciation."

The graphic game

Sam enjoyed "what could it be?" game, shown in Figure 14.9. The therapist attempted to probe aggressive tendencies by drawing two spikes (D1 and D4). Instead of perceiving a weapon in these unfinished objects, he drew pleasant ones. The completed shapes were a sun and a flower. Similarly, when she drew two elongated thin rectangles, Sam completed them as a pencil and a picture frame (A5 and D3). In the absence of projected explicit aggressive objects, sublimation seemed to be at work.

Comments concerning emotional and cognitive tolerance of disagreements in outcomes stemming from one initial beginning, the graphic experience led to a new emotional issue. He reported a recurrent fantasy following the game; that his biological parents were reunited. Sam's initial family ended up in two outcomes, requiring emotional adjustments. Dealing with this fantasy using analogies from "what could it be?" game was a key element in the therapeutic work with Sam. Though a common fantasy for children of divorce, it was not brought up before in six sessions and facilitated termination.

Other projective techniques

Forerunners to this fantasy appeared in responses to other projective techniques. However, it was not dealt with until verbalized after "what could it be?" game. Using the Human Replacement Technique, significant persons in Sam's life were projected on his free drawing during the first session.

The main objects represented his father's reconstructed family. Two attached clouds were his father and stepmother, reflecting their close relationship. A near-by cloud was self-presentation, neither too far nor enmeshed with them. Sam spontaneously replaced two other objects. He replaced a sun and a tree by himself. The sun was Sam's own warmth, and the blooming tree was his deeper self-image; two dry branches within the flourishing foliage were his stressful experiences of divorce and moving out of his mother's house to live with his father and stepmother.

His attic room was self-presentation. His room would not have appeared in the drawing, located on the other side of the house, across from his father and stepmother's room. His choice of the attic room in the drawing symbolized his space in the family. That is, being on a different level had similar inference as the three clouds (close enough but not enmeshed with his father and stepmother). The house was colored in orange, a friendly symbol. His initial family, his mother, her daughter, his father, and himself, replaced the four black birds.

Sam was asked to draw his family, which represented his present one. Self-presentation was close to the paternal figure, in shape of clothes style and hair. This reflected his wish for emotional closeness to his father. The position of the left arm in self-presentation was similar to the father's, in a gesture to "greet the neighbours." Stepmother's importance was reflected in her figure being drawn first. Similarities between self and stepmother figures were: the right arms' positions and both figures' clothes were pink. In addition, pink as feminine symbol, explained the father's complain: "He is too sensitive, anything makes him cry."

The Thematic Apperception Test (TAT) shed light on Sam's relationships. All themes reflected desired positive feelings between family members within the father's reconstructed family. For example, (Card 2) parental figures scolded self-presentation then apologized, sadness became contentment. Paternal figure confined in self-presentation, who was thrilled to keep a secret (Card 7BM). The paternal figure was healed after an operation (Card 8BM). Family members

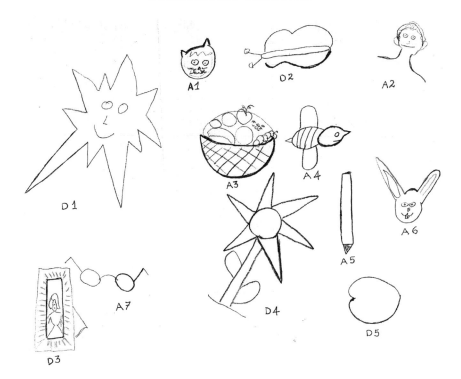

Figure 14.9

had fun engaging in a sport activity, a real life experience (Card 16). There was no sign of aggression.

References

Buck, J. N. (1948). The H-T-P technique: A quantitative and qualitative scoring manual. Monograph supplement. *Journal of Clinical Psychology, 5*, 1–120.

Buck, J. N. (1966). *The House-Tree-Person technique, revised manual.* Beverly Hills: Western Psychological Services.

Burns, R. C. (1982). *Self-growth in families: Kinetic Family Drawings (K-F-D) research and application.* New York: Brunner/Mazel.

Burns, R. C., & Kaufman, S. H. (1972). *Actions, styles and symbols in Kinetic Family Drawing (KFD): An interpretative manual.* New York: Brunner/Mazel.

Di Leo, J. H. (1973). *Children's drawings as diagnostic aids.* New York: Brunner/Mazel.

Di Leo, J. H. (1983). *Interpreting children's drawings.* New York: Brunner/Mazel.

Hammer, E. F. (1964). *The H-T-P clinical research manual* (3rd ed.). Beverly Hills: Western Psychological Services.

Hammer, E. F. (1967). *The clinical application of projective drawings.* Springfield: Charles C. Thomas.

Hammer, E. F. (1981). Projective drawings. In A. I. Rabin (Ed.), *Assessment with projective techniques: A concise introduction* (pp. 151–186). New York: Springer.

Hammer, E. F. (1986). Graphic techniques with children and adolescents. In A. I. Rabin (Ed.), *Projective techniques for adolescents and children* (pp. 239–263). New York: Springer.

Thomas, A. D. (1995). *Two graphic techniques: Children's free drawing.* Copyright Office records, Form TXu 711–610.

Winnicott, D. W. (1985). *Therapeutic consultations in child psychology.* London: Hogarth Press & Institute of Psychoanalysis.

15

SYMBOLIC FAMILY DRAWING AND ABSTRACT REPRESENTATION TECHNIQUES

Heidi P. Perryman and Juliann W. Hanback

Two drawing techniques are developed by the authors in their psychology practices from exposure to art therapy techniques. The first author developed the use of symbolic substitutions or metaphors for clients' family members. The second author has clients draw abstract representations of self and others using primarily color and shapes, although symbolic objects can be incorporated as well. Art therapists have been using various techniques involving symbolic and abstract art in treatment and evaluation for over 40 years (Kwiatkowska, 1967).

Being novel tasks, the two techniques described herein are more likely to allow for less conscious elements of the individual's psyche to be revealed. They allow difficult or conflictual material to be addressed in a less threatening context, similar to displacement in play therapy. These techniques can reveal a sense of the client's openness to self-exploration and capacity for insight. They can spur insightful and therapeutic discussions, either with individuals, couples, or families, and are therefore useful both in assessment and therapy.

I. Symbolic family drawing technique

Symbolic Family Drawing provides a pathway to access insights children may have about family issues or their role in problems but are unable to articulate. Directions are simple: "I'd like you to try another drawing for me that's kind of a puzzle. Draw me a picture of your family, only no one can be shown as people. They can be animals or objects, or whatever you choose, but no one can be a person. Everyone should be in it, including you."

Sometimes, when teenagers scoff at the task, I allude to a case of a five year old, who represented her parents as a dog and cat because they always fight, to facilitate the task.

Case illustrations

Case 1, Kristen

Kristen was a 16-year-old girl, raised by her grandmother because of her parents' addiction. She had entered therapy when guardianship was transferred and she was fairly secretive with adults in her life. Therefore, the therapist introduced journaling to their work, and was alarmed by one entry in which Kristen described suicidal thoughts. The therapist was uncertain how serious a threat this represented for self–harm, and wanted to communicate to the teen that her message of despair had been effectively delivered and received.

Figure 15.1

Figure 15.2

Kristen's Comments

"Mountains, because people think I'm a rock, I'm the strong one. But I
   have a dormant volcano and will erupt."
"Rat with witch's hat is my sister because she always rats on me and acts
   like a witch."
"Fire with halo is my grandmother because she acts so sweet but at home
   she is a demon."

With Kristen's drawings we are able to sense the stark difference between what
is on the surface, and what is beneath it. Her grandmother's dual presentation

(acts sweet, has a halo vs. fire, and a demon) marks her as a deeply unsafe adult who isolates Kristen from the world by making her feel she's the only one who can see it. Her own dormant volcano is masked by a steep mountain range whose stability everyone takes for granted. Only her sneaky sister is difficult outside and inside (which might be a welcome relief in Kirsten's life because outsiders may notice her inner anger). Based on these and other findings I was able to communicate that Kristen felt real threat in her suicidal ideation and suggest ways the therapist could address this through more frequent contact, identifying a support network (which included her sister) and reviewing the criteria for hospitalization.

Case 2, Conner

Conner was a 15-year-old male whose parents were embroiled in one of those bitter divorces that never seem to settle. They had been separated for five years but one area of ongoing contention was that of the teen's behavior and how either parent responded to it. The mother complained that the father allowed their son to ignore responsibilities and indulged in his more destructive behavior in order to stay popular. The father felt his ex-wife was overly harsh and demanding, unfairly criticizing the son in much the same way she had berated him.

Conner's Comments

"Okay, I am the sun from Coca Cola commercials, I just love that."
"This is my dad because he wants to be scary like the devil. But he can't help it. He's always nice to me. So he has a flower."
"This is my Mom. She's a snake because she always goes back on her deals. She promises me something then makes me keep working for it."
"This is my brother because he's a turd (nerd), and I do not like him."
"This is my stepmother. She is a rock because rocks are just there, they do not do anything."

The drawings emphasize the omnipotent power that this youngster felt over his parents (the large sun on top). After five years of a vicious custody battle he was well aware of the lethal importance he had to both households. He was also sensitive to the dilemma between how limits were set, and his father's own inconsistency (scary devil and giving in to him). His anger at his mother is clearly communicated (makes me work for what she had freely promised), but also his sense of longing and betrayal (a snake, backs up on her promises). Finally, his drawing of his stepmother eloquently makes the point that examiners cannot rely on their own judgment to determine the meaning of a particular symbol (a rock is not strong, rather good for nothing). In this instance "Like a rock" is not a compliment. The inference must be discussed with the child, to get a better understanding of how that particular symbol was chosen. This teen's assessment was used to force the parents to recognize the need for family therapy, so that his father could learn to provide more structure, and his mother could practice more positive, warm parenting.

Case 3, Jason

Younger children can also provide useful information about their role and perceptions of their family members, through symbolic family drawings. Figure 15.3 was done by a nine-year-old boy who was refusing visitation at his father's home. Jason's father insisted that he refused because of his mother's persuasion, who wanted to sever their relationship. Jason's mother, a recovering alcoholic, denied this, and expressed fear that his father was overly punitive with him.

Jason's Comments

"Mom's a table because she's always trying to get the right table."
"Dad's an eyeball because he sees things brighter than us."
"Brother is an egg because he's always cracking."
"And I don't know what I am, art teacher taught us to draw this in perspective" (a rod).

Jason's drawing gave support for the idea that his refusal reflected fear that contact with his father would "leak" information about his mother's behavior (father can see) and further destabilize her sobriety. Regardless of his mother's preoccupation and inaccessibility, he was protective of her. Refusing visitation expressed such concern. Jason worried that spending time with his father would cause problems for his mother, escalate the custody battle for both children, and further complicate his life. His drawing also allowed him to communicate the stress (is cracking) he thought his younger brother who was going freely between houses, felt upon parents' mistrust. Jason's inability to figure out who he symbolically represent, may reflect avoiding the examiner's penetration into his inner world. The drawn rod, however, may symbolize his need to be perceived as strong and unbending.

Case 4, Matthew

These next drawings are from a highly intelligent boy. Twelve-year-old Matthew was failing middle school despite his impressive early academic performance. His teachers noted that he lacked focus and there was a question of ADHD inattentive type. He was referred for evaluation to learn whether medication might be appropriate. Matthew's behavior in the world had become more odd and isolative, especially when he was transferred from a private school (where his parents felt he was not trying and therefore did not justify the money) to a public school. Matthew's testing and history did not support ADHD but indicated an overwhelming internal life that probably *did* interfere with his attention at times.

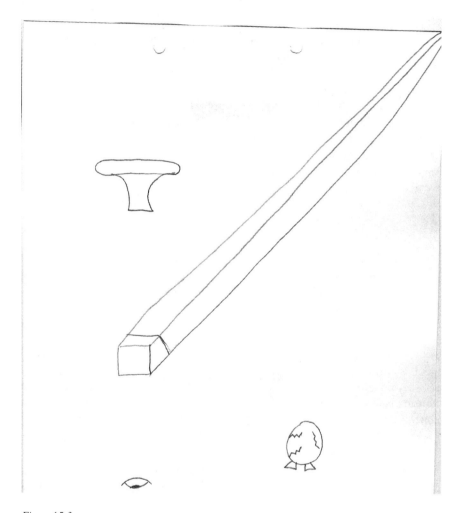

Figure 15.3

Matthew's Comments

"Dad is dragon, head of the family."
"Mom's a car because she drives around all the time."
"I'm a time bomb because I like explosions."
"(Elena) Sister is a rock because she's stubborn."

Matthew worked hard in his drawing to show the severity of his problems. He recognized it was getting harder and harder to control himself (a time bomb) and worried about the consequences. His symbolic family drawing communicated his awareness of his impending difficulties, as well as his fear that his parents would respond to his needs with either aggression or abandonment (father is a dragon with sharp teeth and mother is always out of the house driving car). Matthew was referred for intensive psychotherapy, with a possible medication evaluation delayed until treatment was underway. Once more, a rock does not symbolize strength, rather a negative characteristic (stubbornness).

Summary

These examples demonstrate how Symbolic Family Drawings can augment our understanding of child and adolescent difficulties. We can see that capacity for insight through drawings can harness a child's understanding in other ways. This harness can be used to help pull a child out of a painful situation onto solid ground with more sure footing. We can use drawings to learn more about the way youngsters see themselves, their impact on others, and their readiness for

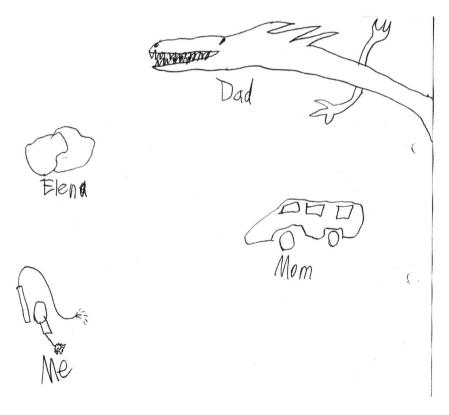

Figure 15.4

change. Specific challenges and strengths can be identified and even very secretive subjects can disclose meaningful information. Drawings offer a nonverbal, and therefore more oblique, way to communicate. Using a child's symbolic family drawings in a feedback session can be a powerful way to communicate a message that would otherwise be overlooked.

II. Abstract representation of self and others

For the second drawing technique, Abstract Representations (AR), clients need to reach sufficient mental age to be capable of abstraction and self-reflection. They are given blank paper, pencil, crayons, colored pencils, and markers. The clinician needs to explain the difference between figurative, representational art (portrays humans, animals, or objects concretely, as they appear to our eyes) and abstract or nonfigurative art (ignores external reality and focuses on intangibles or inner nature).

First, clients are asked to draw self-representations. Colors, shapes, spacing, and size are possible elements to symbolize emotions, qualities, and concepts. Clients' use of concrete objects to symbolize aspects of themselves (a heart for love, a computer to represent being a workaholic) is permissible, but should not be suggested or encouraged. They are asked to explain the elements of their drawings. The process is repeated by asking clients to draw significant "others" in their lives (sibling, parent, or spouse). An abstract representation of the family explores a client's perception of family relationships and dynamics. In couples counseling each person makes an abstract depiction of self and partner as well as the relationship.

Illustrations

Case 1—Chronic temper outbursts

Patty, a 12-year-old girl, was a sixth grader who was an excellent student and model citizen at school. At home, however, she was a time bomb who frequently erupted. She was embarrassed and remorseful about her temper outbursts. Individual and family therapy were carried out for nine months, and she was gradually able to contain her emotions and the frequency of outbursts diminished. However, six months after termination, she returned to therapy because of a re-escalation of such outbursts. A formal evaluation was conducted by another psychologist.

Her history of irritability and tantrums from an early age suggested an underlying temperament issue. Good behavior at school and her efforts to contain her outbursts at home during the first course of therapy seemed to be related to her wanting to please adults and to obtain attention by performing well. This hypothesis of her desire to please and to look good was confirmed on the Rorschach ($R = 32, W = 11$). The Rorschach also pointed to a lack of resources that could account for emotional dyscontrol in response to minor stressors ($EA = 4.5, D = -2, Adj D = -2$). Significant defenses against self-esteem issues and preoccupation with unmet needs was also indicated ($Fr = 3; FM = 9$).

Her Human Figure Drawing and Kinetic Family Drawing (KFD) were stylized and not highly revealing of a conflict or a tendency fueling her explosive behavior.

However, her female drawing, thin and graceful, yet curvaceous with long flowing hair and gown, was remarkable in a glamorousness that was quite in contrast with the client's stocky, pre-adolescent body, straight brown hair, and bespectacled face. Apparently, her ego ideal was highly focused on superficial female traits that would make any 12-year-old girl feel inferior.

The administered projective tests (Rorschach and TAT) were not indicative of a person with strong aggressive drives or underlying anger and resentment toward authority that might cause her outbursts. Since the procedures revealed considerable distress and a tendency toward emotional constraint, her tantrums did not appear to be in her conscious control as a means to manipulate her family. The source of the conflict seemed to revolve around her family, as that was where the outbursts occurred. In therapy she talked about her brother and her resentment that he never got into trouble.

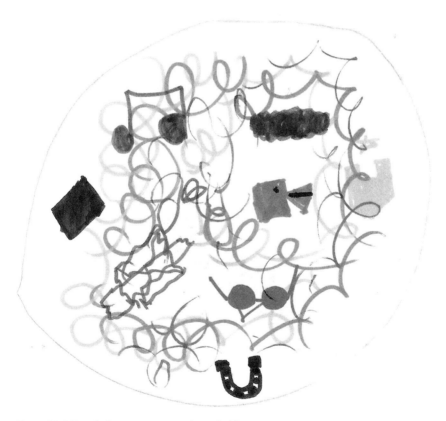

Figure 15.5 Patty's abstract representation of self

Seeking more insights than the formal evaluation provided, Patty's therapist introduced the AR. A bright, creative girl whose WISC IQ was in the Superior range, Patty was able to grasp the concept of the task. She started with a large square, quickly reconsidered, and then turned the page over and drew a large circle (Figure 15.5). She drew small objects to represent her interests in horseback riding (horseshoe), chorus (musical note), swimming (swim suit), and her pet birds (bird head).

She also had abstract elements of different colors with reasons for each:

> *Circle,* "because I am well-rounded"; it is *Green,* "because it's my favorite color."
> *Brown squiggle,* "brains, because I am brainy."
> *Glasses,* "because I wear glasses."
> *Black,* "I am bold."
> *Weird blue squiggle,* "I am weird, odd (what do you mean?) I do odd stuff and say weird stuff."
> *Red & Yellow Swirls,* "I'm lively."

Figure 15.6 Patty's abstract representation of brother

Then she was asked to draw an abstract representation of her brother (Figure 15.6). She provided the following comments:

Green squiggle (bottom right), "because he's weird."
Orange shape (middle right), "represents that he talks a lot."
Black shape (bottom left across to right), "he's big and bold."
Yellow circle (top), "because he's perfect."

This inquiry led to a discussion in which she spontaneously spoke of her many feelings of competition with her brother. She then recalled an early memory of feeling jealous of his certain male aspect. She also related her feeling that her mother likes her brother "better" than her. However, Patty was able to eventually master some defenses against her feelings of rejection and negative comparisons, concluding the session with the notion that, while she has to wear glasses now, her brother will have to get them in college like her father did. She also connected to her mother, "I have eyes like my mother's."

Later she spoke of her resentments of her brother for not siding with her to bedevil her parents and his investment in his friends over the family "animals." Both her Kinetic Family Drawing and her AR show her to be very identified with her pets. Thus, her statement reflects feeling slighted by her brother, who was more socially successful than her and choose his friends over her.

The discussion alone from this procedure produced remarkable insight into Patty's feelings and conflicts even before delving further into analyzing the drawings. However, a quick comparison between the two AR drawings suggests issues surrounding gender (including her initial square, replaced by a circle). She used her favorite color, green, to represent the one aspect of her brother she feels most similar to "being weird" in which she took some pride. Looking at the pictures side by side, one gets better sense of Patty's internal struggle. Her drawing of her brother looks clear, focused, organized, "big and bold" freely filling the page. But her representation of her "self" looks like a weakly contained ball of confusion. Thus, at some subconscious level she conveyed her precarious containment of unmanageable distress.

While history and the formal psychological evaluation provided understanding of many elements to Patty's loss of control, the AR confirmed and enhanced these findings. The AR was most informative in clarifying her areas of conflict and sensitivity that led to her temper outbursts, helping to focus therapy.

Case2: Marital discord with Asperger's

The diagnostic usefulness of the Abstract Representation technique in marital work may be seen in the case of a couple struggling with the husband's Asperger's symptoms.

Asperger is essentially a neurological condition. It involves deficits of the right hemisphere, such as complex and rapid visual analysis and processing.

Clients are often highly adept with the left brain aspects of language (i.e., vocabulary and reading) but have noticeable deficits of speech nuances (i.e., intonation and rhythm) so that their speech is usually flat, with odd intonations. As children, they tend to be clumsy and throughout their life have odd eye contact; some avoid eye contact while others make too intense eye contact. Therefore, Asperger's clients differ from rigid, overly rational people whose symptoms stem from conflicts and trauma resulting in a defensive structure.

The AR can be useful in clarifying this diagnosis. It is important to differentiate Asperger's clients from those with psychologically based difficulty with emotions and empathy because it is not responsive to insight therapy and is best treated with cognitive-behavioral methods as well as helping clients learn how to monitor their deficits and compensate for them; such as verbally reminding themselves to smile when greeting someone. They can learn to remember to ask their wife how she feels but they have difficulty empathizing. Rigidity does not really change for these people once they reach adulthood.

They sought couple counseling to address the impact of the Asperger's characteristics on their relationship. Despite being married over 20 years, the wife remained frustrated by her husband inability to understand and consider her feelings. The AR demonstrates both their differences and the signs of the husband's Asperger's Syndrome.

The wife's abstract self-representation was a swirl of bright colors gradually increasing in size around a red and purple heart. Her drawing represents her emotional complexity (four different colors), warmth (yellow swirls), and radiating love and caring (red and purple swirls emanating out of the middle heart). With just color and lines she also represented a self view that includes her personal growth (green lines), energy (movement of the lines), reaching out (lines being sent off the swirl, filling the page). Her groundedness and connection with her world is represented by several green lines touching a wavy green horizontal line at the bottom. Her drawing demonstrates that she is an emotionally focused and interpersonally oriented individual. It is not surprising that she reports frustration with a spouse who is not able to relate on these terms.

In contrast, the husband completed his abstract self-representation (Figure 15.7) in a graphite pencil using concrete objects to depict his experiences and likes (tree, sky, sun, and moon represent enjoying being outdoors). An intelligent man, he was able to analyze and self-reflect, metaphorically portraying his difficulty fitting in (square peg in round hole). The two-headed arrows on his peg represent attempts by others to affect him and his attempts to affect the world. He drew his peg with a side missing to represent his unknown aspects. His failure to progress as he wishes is seen in his spinning dreidel (spinning in place; +1 and −2, representing one step forward and two steps backward). The loss of his ability to bounce back, from various pressures he feels set on him, is represented as a trampoline with several broken springs.

Figure 15.7 Husband's abstract representation of self

While he is verbally able to self-reflect and see varied personality aspects (as opposed to a less astute individual who might have more superficial qualities, such as "being a hard worker"), his metaphors and symbols are left–brain lan-guage products and he lacks the intuitive, emotional component seen in his wife's drawing. This would be in keeping with his Asperger's diagnosis and his further difficulty to access such right brain abilities, is seen in his use of words ("Go" and "Where" to represent his getting started but not knowing what his goals are) and concrete objects.

His approach is intellectualized; his limited access to and comfort with emo-tions is also reflected in his black and white drawing. When asked about using a

Figure 15.8 Wife's abstract representation of husband

graphite pencil, he commented, "I like pencil because it keeps it simple." How-ever, more clarity about color is seen in a spontaneous comment during the Rorschach that he ignored the colors, "because they do not mean anything to me."

His Abstract Representation of his wife was symbolic but also a concrete object. His drawing focused on her general steadiness and resilience represented by an electroencephalograph print out with mostly even waves, a brief increase in amplitude (representing an upset) and then a return to the baseline of low even waves. While he is able to depict an aspect of her personality, his insensitiv-ity results in his ignoring the aspects of herself (emotional connectedness) that she considers most central and valuable.

The wife, in contrast to the warm vibrant colors and open expansive design of her self-drawing, drew her husband (Figure 15.8) as a contained system of tun-nels or tubes primarily in the coldest color (blue). Blue dashes represent his flow through this rigid system that has many ups and downs, as does her husband's moods. She did add a touch of green, which she said represented the changes and growth she has experienced since he entered therapy. The drawing conveys not only her frustration with his introversion and lack of emotional connection, but also her perception of his frustration (depicting him is spinning at the bot-tom of a vertical tube).

Summary

The case of Patty demonstrates how the AR can help clarify intrapsychic issues, such as conflicts and self-image. The second case shows how it can be useful in providing evidence for diagnosis and to delineate personality and cognitive differences that interfere with a couple's communication and mutual understanding. By asking the client to use more abstract, nonverbal representations it can help define problems clients have with the more emotional, intuitive right-brain functions, such as in Asperger's. By exploring the inherent symbolism of shapes and colors, as well as the individual's intentions and personal symbolism, the AR can provide a dialogue with (or among) the clients that can lead to greater insight and understanding.

Reference

Kwiatkowska, H.Y. (1967). Family art therapy. *Family Process, 6,* 37–55.

16

CASE STUDY

Jason, "A Little Boy with a Lot Inside"

Dennis R. Finger

Jason was a small, eight-year-old third grader at the time of intake. His parents were divorced when he was four. He had a younger brother age six. An earlier psycho-educational assessment placed Jason in the average to above average range of intelligence. His ability to process information was significantly below average.

Presenting symptoms

Jason was having trouble with school progress and home behavior. He seemed depressed and was described as keeping feelings to himself. He had a reading delay of two years and writing difficulties. His essays in school contained violence, a world where bad things happened. Pictures contained skulls, bones, and explosions. He was described as "a little boy with a lot inside of him." Jason was characterized as a daydreamer with attention problems. He also had nightmares, vivid dreams, and was a sleepwalker. At the time of intake Jason was suspended from school for threatening another student.

He was not taking any medications. Socially, he reportedly had one friend and seemed shy in social situations. He complained about not knowing how to make friends. Jason enjoyed martial arts and chess.

The projective drawing battery

The projective drawing battery consisted of two approaches: House-Tree-Person Projective Drawings (H-T-P-P), achromatic and chromatic (Hammer, 1958), and Levy Animal Drawing Story (LADS, Levy & Levy, 1958). Kinetic Family Drawing (KFD, Burns & Kaufman, 1970) was attempted and rejected. In addition, "Squiggle Game" (Winnicott, 1971), was utilized during the course of therapy. Having multiple drawing trials allows children several opportunities to express their deepest inner feelings: fears, angers, wishes, and hopes.

Children might choose, consciously or unconsciously, to reveal their hidden world through any one of the drawing tasks.

Initial meeting

Cautiously, but directly and with curiosity, Jason entered the therapy room. He related that his favorite subject was math but he disliked reading and writing because "I'm bad at it." For fun, he liked to watch television especially "Sponge Bob," who lived in a pineapple under the sea. He also enjoyed drawing cartoons with guys having big heads and just regular-sized bodies.

Pretherapy H–T–P–P achromatic

Jason drew a House with a lot of floors and remarked that "the hands are the second floor, third floor, fourth floor and fifth floor." When asked who lived in the House, Jason quickly replied "a chipmunk, a superhero chipmunk." When asked if he'd live there he said, "I don't know, some houses look okay outside but not inside." When asked if the House was built well or poorly Jason answered, "The House is built well but it has curves which could make it fall down easily." When queried as to which room he would like for himself, Jason told the examiner a story, "When I was six I looked out the window and it looked scary . . . I saw a big spider crawling on my window. I smacked it with a pole and it died. I don't like spiders." The House looked immature with an anthropomorphic quality with hands and a face-like front. A superhero chipmunk is a reflection of Jason. He's small but is also a junior black belt in karate. He compensates for feelings of psychological smallness and inadequacy by utilizing the grandiose image of a superhero. Jason expresses feelings about his family falling apart by his projected sense that the House could fall down easily. He fears the spider—a parent representative—as something that may hurt him. Jason fears being harmed and decides to kill the spider before he can be killed.

During inquiry phase of Tree drawing, Jason said that the hole, which was anxiously blackened, was made by "creatures that want to get to a hideout away from bigger animals who could hurt them." "Beavers made the hole to get to a secret area so predators won't find them." Jason related that, "diamonds and steel are in the tree so that bears can't break it." When asked what beavers do inside the Tree Jason replied, "They party, listen to music and drink soda."

Tree drawing, which reflected more unconscious emotions about self (Hammer, 1958), shows Jason's deep fears of being hurt by others, especially by larger predators which are representative of authority figures in Jason's life. His defense is to hide, avoid, and isolate himself. This activity would coincide with his friendship difficulties. Hiding though is not enough; he also utilizes magical thinking with a steel, diamond tree for protection. At the end he shows a capacity to have fun and enjoy himself.

When asked to draw a Person, Jason had a question, "Can it be an alien?" Jason decided it would be a dead guy who "died from jumping off a cliff . . . He ran away from home and fell off a cliff." When questioned further, Jason told the following story:

> He ran away. He doesn't like his life. Doesn't like his parents, they were mean to him, yelled at him. His mother was mean about everything she could think about. She let all of her anger out on him. His younger brother is mean, annoying . . . blah, blah, and does mean things. His dad once jumped on him and was so heavy he almost killed him. He told his dad to get off and his dad yelled at him. His dad yells at him because he hates his boss and his job.

When asked what will happen in the future to this drawn guy, Jason said: "Nothing, he's dead. He feels nothing." This inquiry and reply show how projective drawings can be used as an excellent technique for eliciting the child's deeper feelings and thoughts about his life and his subjective view of the world. Here is the theme of being hurt by his closest family members; his mother, father, and brother. Hammer (1958) stated that in the Person drawing the subject draws what he feels himself to be.

Jason protects himself by making himself dead. If you are dead no one can hurt you. He encases his feelings and self in a dead body as he did earlier in his steel, diamond tree. His initial question, "Can it be an alien?" shows some movement away from the world of humans and is consistent with his dead guy. This is also evidence of some depersonalization.

Jason's second Person drawing is his younger brother who's smiling and feels good because his older brother is dead. Perhaps this is Jason's own anger projected onto the younger brother.

Chromatic

According to Hammer (1994), pencil drawings bring out subject's strength and overt defenses while crayon drawings reveal deeper recesses of a person's personality. Color drawings tap the person's deeper emotions.

After drawing the black House Jason related that "an evil scientist lives in this house. He has lasers to blow up the world. The evil scientist was born evil and has lots of technology in his house, gadgets to destroy things." In the end the evil scientist will destroy the world. Rather than a house, Jason's drawing looks like immense laser guns on a platform pointed at Earth. This chromatic phase taps the deep rage inside Jason; he wants to destroy everything. The drawing of a House taps the person's feelings about home- life. For Jason, the house is not a home but a place of war. Jason identifies with the evil scientist who wants everything to explode.

Jason remarked that crayon Tree was the same as pencil Tree with a hole for the beaver to use as a secret hideout and steel inside to protect the tree. Here we have consistent theme of avoiding environmental contact with others and a deep need to protect himself. Again he utilizes magical thinking: steel tree, to further shield himself. Jason is filled with intense rage and fears being hurt by his own rage or by the rage of others.

Jason's first color Person is a guy with an immense blue head, tiny body, and a small person in the man's mouth. Jason told the following story about his drawing:

"He's always eating somebody. He's always hungry. When he was born his mom died, his head was too big. Now he's eating somebody who tastes yummy." The Person drawing relates to feelings of self as well as relationships with significant others. Very large head is associated with an emphasis on fantasy life. Jason's world is one in which small people are gobbled up by big people. He feels the closest persons in his life will devour him, at the same time perhaps he would like to take them into himself in order to make them his own.

The second Person drawing is a red young boy singing, "La la la." So far Jason has used blues and blacks in his chromatic drawings, colors which are associated with emotional constriction and repression (Hammer, 1997). Color red has been associated with conflict which has characterized his relationship with his younger brother.

Jason refused to draw a picture of his family doing something (KFD), He said: "My mom is mean and my brother is mean," and he did not want to draw his family. The examiner believes that this task was too emotionally painful for him.

Using Levy Animal Drawing Story (LADS), Jason was asked to draw his favorite animal and then to make up a story. He chose a turtle, a small animal that is encased in a shell with the ability to retreat into the shell for protection, a reflection of Jason; physically and psychologically. He told the following story:

> One day Jack the turtle was swimming to shore and then he saw a guy scuba diving but then a shark came and then Jack swam as fast as he can but it missed Jack because his shell was too hard and ate the scuba dive and then some dolphins came and killed the shark. In the end Jack swim to safety and lives happily ever after.

Jason again is threatened by a large scary predator but he is able to out-maneuver the shark that kills someone else. Also, dolphins come to his rescue; perhaps he senses that his family and his new therapist will help him. This story also shows a positive outlook for treatment.

Discussion

Jason had much strength and many difficulties. His strengths included average to high average intelligence; athletic prowess and interests; a long involvement and success in martial arts and continuous relationships with instructors; excellent math and science skills; a desire to play on a soccer team; interests in skiing and skateboarding; involvement and satisfaction in a school aftercare program; concerned though divorced parents; and involved and caring grandparents.

His difficulties included intense, constricted rage and a marked fear of being hurt by others or by his own anger; a tendency to avoid contact with others and isolate himself; ongoing effects of divorced parents at age four and minimal contact with his father; an overworked mother; problems with his younger brother; a two-year reading delay and writing problems; and the recent loss of a loved babysitter.

Diagnostically Jason showed significant adjustment reactions as well as signs of deeper pathology consisting of intense inner rage, some depersonalization, paranoia, depression, anxiety, and a marked constriction of feelings.

Jason's treatment plan recommendations were ongoing play therapy to have a safe place for Jason to express his deeper feelings of anger and fear; parent guidance sessions; parental involvement including more frequent contact with his father; immediate playdates with friends and potential friends at a twice a week schedule; involvement in group activities along with joining a soccer team and ski group; increasing the parents' empathy for Jason's feelings of anger and aloneness; tutoring in reading and writing; and de-emphasizing his watching scary movies. This plan was discussed with his parents and therapy began.

During therapy projective drawings

Therapy, lasting about one year, consisted of individual play therapy and parent guidance sessions. During Jason's therapy projective drawings were used as a vehicle for Jason to express his inner emotions, especially the Squiggle Game (Winnicott, 1971). In the Squiggle Game the therapist spontaneously makes a "squiggle," a twisted line using a crayon on a piece of paper. The child then adds his own lines to the squiggle and then there's conversation about the drawing. This process continues until the spontaneous, joint adding of lines and the subsequent therapeutic discussion ends. In the beginning Jason and the therapist's squiggle drawings were simple and constricted. Over time the drawings became more expressive and revealing culminating in an intense startling squiggle. The squiggle, mostly Jason's production, became a ferocious dinosaur-like monster with sharp spikes emanating from its back.

This creature with razor-sharp teeth is drawn devouring a boy. Jason worked hard and long on this enraged red and black monster. He was quite animated when telling about the contents of the picture, and how the monster was eating the little boy. Jason decided to give the drawing to the therapist to hold for him.

Here the therapist acts as a container for Jason's rage. His rage cannot hurt him or others. Jason is safe to continue in his life and the therapist becomes the guardian of his anger and fears, holding and keeping them out of harm's way. Together the child and therapist have created an "area of experiencing" (Winnicott, 1971). Through his emotion-laden drawing, Jason was able to have a direct cathartic experience with his therapist in a safe, accepting place. Besides the projective drawings, Jason and the therapist played games including chess.

Jason became increasingly aggressive in the chess game as therapy progressed.

Later in therapy, he told a story about being lost in the forest and he meets a guy who helps him find his way out of the forest. Perhaps Jason viewed his therapist-guide as helping him through his "life forest."

Therapeutic progress

Jason made substantial progress during his treatment. His improvement was due to many variables. Besides his treatment Jason joined a soccer team, made friends, and was successful; his social life improved significantly culminating in becoming part of a group of peers; he received a cell phone and maintained closer connections with his parents and friends, and a new babysitter entered his life who also tutored him.

In therapy, Jason was able to express experience and own more of his anger. He more constructively channeled his aggression through athletics, martial arts, and chess. He was able to begin enjoying his changed family life including the beginning of his own second family in his group of peers. Overall, he became less constricted and "the boy with a lot inside was expressing it outside." He began talking about his dreams, eventually his angst lifted, he became alive.

References

Burns, R. & Kaufman, S. (1970). *Kinetic family drawings: An introduction to understanding children through kinetic drawings.* New York: Brunner/Mazel.

Hammer, E. (Ed.). (1958). *The clinical application of projective drawings.* Springfield.: Charles C. Thomas.

Hammer, E. (1994, July). Annual projective drawing workshop. New York City.

Hammer, E. (Ed.) (1997). *Advances in projective drawing interpretation.* Springfield: Charles C. Thomas.

Levy, S., & Levy, R. (1958). Symbolism in animal drawings. In E. F. Hammer (Ed.) *The clinical application of projective drawings.* Springfield: Charles C. Thomas.

Winnicott, D. (1971). *Therapeutic consultations in child psychiatry.* London: Hogarth Press.

17

FOUR CASE ILLUSTRATIONS

Antoinette D. Thomas

1. Mark: A multiple-problems adolescent

Background

Mark's parents had difficulties; his father was often absent from home, he was alcoholic, short tempered, and self-centered. His mother loved and cared for him but was submissive to his father. The strong, big man was not impressed with his tiny, skinny son. Mark commented on his relationship with his father by saying, "he spent short, low-quality time with me." An adult neighbor sexually assaulted him at age eight. At age 11, his father died; his mother got a job and a live-in male companion, whom Mark hated.

At school, Mark's performance went from bad to worse, in spite of his high average intelligence. In a couple of years he was moved to an alternative program. Peers in both programs rejected him. At the age of 15 he joined an adolescents' group psychotherapy for a few months. His group therapist described him as "an anxious, depressed and obsessive adolescent. He presented occasional Borderline features when fantasies become over-expansive." He was in individual psychotherapy with the author for two years.

First session

Mark talked about his interest in classical music, which he listens to all night, making it impossible to attend school on time. He drew a circle representing the world (the globe), with a horizontal line in the middle and triangles up and down based on it, representing pyramids. Listening to music put him at the top of a pyramid; when depressed, he would descend several steps below it in horizontal lines. Mark's fluctuation between elation and depression associated his drawing. Illogical link between a circle and the world depicted a Borderline feature. Poor graphic quality reflected anxiety and inadequacy.

246

Two weeks

Mark expressed strong hatred for his father associated with sadness. He was asked in the first session to write positive and negative paternal characteristics. The negative list was four times the length of the positive one.

Mark made a free drawing (Figure 17.1). He spontaneously explained: The small brown patch near the left edge was "me" but in a few minutes became "dad." The larger patch became "me." Mark added, "Me and dad fishing together." A tender sparkle was conveyed in his voice. He wrote on the drawing what his objects were. When he came to "a rose flouting on water," he drew a larger flower to illustrate his concept. Self as well as paternal representations were far from being identifiable as persons. At his age and intelligence, this would be considered as a distortion of reality. Yet, the closeness as well as the interchangeable roles clearly reflected the enmeshment and the symbiotic attachment to the paternal figure.

The sun—a common paternal symbol—showed aggression presented in teeth. It was also very present, as suggests its large size. Thus, a predominantly negative paternal image was likely incorporated. Depression may have resulted from perceived paternal detachment, intensified by death.

Figure 17.1

Yet, Mark seemed to have loved his father and craved for his attention, which surfaced in the drawing, his comments about self and paternal representations lumped together, as well as his tender voice tone. A therapeutic goal was to help Mark get in touch with such feelings. He needed to internalize a paternal figure that basically loved him, though rarely explicitly demonstrated. The feeling of "not being loved" by a parent is hurtful throughout one's life. In addition, children' self-concept is partly derived from internalized parental figures in childhood. Mark needed some positive elements in his perception of his father.

Massive clinging behavior to the therapist appeared in arriving an hour earlier, following her in corridors attempting to strike a conversation, and in trying to prolong the session by sticking his head in the door to say, "a very important statement." Setting limits was perceived as rejection. He blamed her for eliciting his sadness. Affect toward the paternal figure was projected onto the therapist. These issues were discussed with Mark. He readily understood interpretations and accepted limits. His motivation was "psychological improvement."

Seven months

A male adult stranger sexually assaulted him, two weeks before drawing Figure 17.2 and one week into his 10 days psychiatric hospitalization.

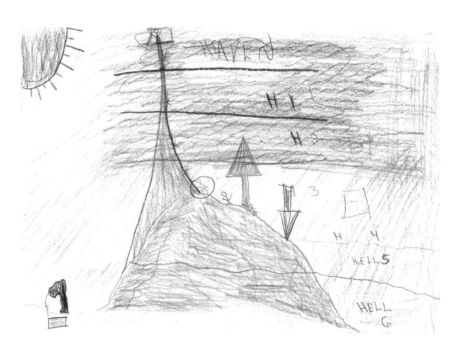

Figure 17.2

Mark's diagnosis was "Anxiety State secondary to rape with features of Post Traumatic Stress Disorder." He responded well to psychiatric therapy. He showed quick improvement in symptoms of Insomnia and Anorexia. The treating psychiatrist recommended continuation of individual psychotherapy.

He drew (Figure 17.2) a mountain on a green ground. It was horizontally divided into seven sections, with "Heaven" at the top and 6 degrees of "Hell" below. His father's grave was at Hell 6. "If I die now I'd be here," making a square between Hell 3 and 4. A quarter of a sun appeared at the left upper corner.

Mark perceived his improvement in therapy (the upward arrow) leading him upward toward normality (Heaven). He realized that he still had a way to go to reach his goal. There are vertical and horizontal distances between self and paternal graves' locations. This may symbolize separation-individuation from the paternal figure. The sun, as a paternal symbol, lost its aggressive feature (large teeth) found in Figure 17.1. It also occupied less space. Improvement within the father-son internalized relationship was demonstrated in drawing.

There was marked improvement in graphic quality, as compared to the previous drawing, in terms of line control and perception, probably an indication of psychological progress. Self-presentation (circled figure in Hell 3) was almost two-dimensional and identifiable as a human figure. This was an improvement compared to the unidentifiable human figures in Figure 17.1. Mark gained relatively better self-esteem and became more realistic as compared to his baseline.

His verbal associations about his father were relatively more positive than his initial ones. He would often say, in a relieved voice-tone, "I forgive him and I know he loved me but did not show his feelings." Simultaneously, therapeutic boundaries were maintained. Mark outgrew clinging to the therapist. He also gave up his persistent wish to become a "shrink" like her.

Two years

Mark, now 17 years old, was still entertaining a high level of aspiration. He drew a bank carrying his name, a most expensive car, and arrows going down from the words "books, education, work, action and result."

Yet in reality, "work vs. fantasy" ratio greatly improved compared to what he was like when he started psychotherapy. He invested much less time in daydreams about a prominent future compared to study and work time. Mark was now successful in a post-secondary vocational program. He was partly self-supportive, generating an income from a part-time job.

An almost smiling face appeared in the sun—a paternal symbol—as opposed to the sun with teeth in Figure 17.1. No strong negative comments about his father. He acknowledged paternal love, verbally expressed in several sessions.

Graphic quality had improved; lines employed in this figure were firm and well controlled. In life, anxiety was remarkably reduced and self-confidence increased. Mark was content and his general appearance became neat as opposed to his initial messy hair and clothes. Psychologically, he came a long way and had graphically documented his milestones.

2. James: Persistent castration anxiety

Background

James (Thomas, 1999) comes from an intact middle-class family. He had a younger sister. Parents cared a lot for their material needs. Love for children was mixed with overprotection. They eliminated children's exposure to strong feelings, such as pain, sadness, or explicit joy. A neutral emotional tone was maintained at home. Father needed quietness at home after a stressful working day. Mother was dainty, soft-voiced, and smiling lady. She undertook most of childcare activities. Behavioral boundaries and good manners were set for children, without physical punishment.

Kindergarten and grade one teachers described James as, "in his world, not paying attention, not participating and usually looked at the ceiling." His fantasy world dominated his life when he started individual psychotherapy.

Relevant events

Concealed information and emotions had adversely affected James. He was two years old when his mother was in her eighth month of pregnancy. His parents had planned to tell him about the expected baby in a couple of weeks to "Protect him from waiting for a long time." When his mother was hospitalized, James spent a week with his maternal grandparents, who also said nothing about the baby. The baby brother died two days after his birth. For six months, "James' cheerfulness helped me from day to day" as mother wrote in her detailed record-keeping notes. Yet, she did not mention anything about her own feelings. James was informed about the event *two years* later. But, his feelings were not shared or dealt with. Similarly, nothing was said about her two subsequent miscarriages.

At the time of the baby's death, James and his mother were looking at family pictures. She pointed at her grandmother, told him that she died. For three years, James had expressed intense fear of his own death. It is likely that concealed information and affect about the baby's death had filtered through a casual reference to an old woman's death he had no interaction with.

Six months later, James had a circumcision operation to prevent painful urination. Once more, his parents did not inform him that he would encounter pain. Fear, pain, and other emotions were not dealt with afterward, since "he did not bring up the topic," mother wrote. This operation involved invasion of his private body parts, which added yet another negative element to the situation. He was unaware that it was meant to be a remedy for his urination pain. Thus, James could have perceived the operation as if something was wrong in his body.

A year later, adenoids were to be removed. Unprepared for the event, James cried and tried not to go to the operation room. During this operation a tube was inserted in his ears.

At the age of four, James was sent to a day care only one day in two weeks. At this sporadic rate, James lacked frequent contact with other children. He preferred solitary play to group activities.

Next summer, he joined a French day camp to learn the language. James was five years old, without any knowledge of French. This experience is like "being thrown to the wolves." Children made fun of him and put candy and gum in his hair. His mother ignored his plea to withdraw from camp. Later, she went to "observe," found him, "miserable, standing around helplessly, not knowing what to do." A couple of months later, he started Kindergarten in a French Immersion Program.

James would look away when talking to people. Realizing that she was similar, his mother made serious efforts so that both would maintain eye contact.

Parents would, "drag him to play outside with children, ten minutes later he would return home." He wanted his parents to play with him and tried to construct the game, thus putting them in a child's place. Parents perceived his learned helplessness as "obedience." James would accept parents' prohibitions, without showing any resentment or attempted modification, as most children do.

He enjoyed affiliation to Scouts. His participation was well accepted by group leaders. His successes, as well as his love for his sister, were emotional assets.

Initial evaluation

James's responses to play therapy corresponded with life events. In choosing his play material and constructing interactions, human figures were poisoned and gas was used to combat bad guys. Nothing happened after to save them. These themes reflected his previous perception of his dangerous world, which was still vivid in his psyche.

Other evaluative methods; Thematic Apperception Test (TAT) (Murray, 1943) Rorschach (Ames, Metraux, Rodell, & Walker, 1952) and figure drawings also gave James the opportunity to reconstruct his memories and life events through symbolic forms.

Most stories made to the TAT were bizarre and irrelevant to stimulus cards. They were uncommon compared to those produced by children. For example, Card 2 depicts "a country scene with two women in the foreground and a man in the background holding the reigns of a horse." Children usually perceive persons as a family; James found them to be strangers. His story included, "he should put the horse away, maybe someone will take it and **eat** it." This most uncommon response reflected an uncommon fear of physical danger threatening one's live possession, a horse not being a commonly eaten animal in his culture. Similarly, human body injury was projected on Card 16. To this blank card, children chose what they want. Their stories generally tell their favorite past or desired future events. James said, "Treasure hunt, they'll take your heart and punch it up, you start dying."

A bizarre story was given to Card 6BM, which shows "a standing man and an elderly lady looking out of a window." His response was, "Marriage, a man is with a woman looking out of the window, it looks like marriage, they are friends but he's married and she's married, each has a husband or a wife."

Irrelevance to card stimuli appeared in another part of his response to Card 2, "I see the sea; they go there for a drink of water." A rarely noticed tiny background detail depicts a sea. Another part of his story to Card 16 was, "you always have to bring water in case there is a machine to kill people with knives, and so you have to throw water on top of it to make it break down." This response also included a projected dangerous world. Card 3BM "a young person's back, resting his or her head on a couch and what looks like a gun on the floor." He said, "a guy, very tired, wants to go home to rest, wants a drink of water." The gun was perceived but avoided. Water was uncommonly included in responses to these three cards.

James also projected anxiety and his perception of a hostile world on Rorschach cards. In content analysis, he responded to Card IV with, "a sea-otter, very close to extinction." To Card III, he said, "angry insect" and to Card X, "brown dragons with **tails on fire.**" The last response constituted a repeated theme in play therapy, which was directly linked to his pain and fear associated with his circumcision operation. His sadness was expressed in response to Card II, "a sad face, sad mouth, tears, and a boy."

At the age of seven, James's IQ was within the High Average level of intelligence, as assessed by a school psychologist. The general quality of the drawn Person (Harris, 1963) reflected emotional problems (Figure 17.3). Global impression is that of a scared child. Asymmetry between limbs reflected emotional problems associated with body image (Koppitz, 1968). Heavily shaded body as presentation of clothes may look like dirt. Interestingly, the left arm resembled a male organ. The traumatic circumcision experience surfaced in this drawing.

Based on James' constant mobility and wavy attention, the school psychologist reported Attention Deficit/Hyperactivity Disorder. The therapist referred James to a famous child neurologist. His report included, "there is an emotional origin for his hyperactivity." On the Conners scale (Goyette, Conners, & Ulrich, 1978), James scored (SD -1) on Hyperactivity Index and on Impulsivity. He departed more from average (SD -2 to SD -3) on Psychosomatics, Anxiety, and Learning Problems. His pediatrician tried medication, which had some positive impact on school achievement.

Early phase of therapy

James attended weekly sessions, nine months a year for three years. His main problems evolved around fear of body injury and associated defense mechanisms. The main goal of psychotherapy was to help him make connections between his emotional preoccupations and his psychological everyday reality. In

Figure 17.3

addition, to help him understand links between past painful experiences and his escape to a fantasy world and detachment from school work. Such connections appeared in symbolic forms in tests, techniques, play, and dreams.

James used a toy dog to construct his play, "a 7 year old dog like me, and sleeps near the fireplace. He's lazy, good for nothing." He projected on the dog his perception of himself as weak and helpless. "He found a stranger at home, who was dead millions of years ago, he turned back to life; he killed people by whacking them on their head. The dog scratched him; he flew out of the window." In fantasy, James's hero, the dog, overpowered a powerful fictitious adult, which may have represented the operating doctor. Displacement was used in the location of the assault. However, his account was emotionally flat, very similar to the emotional environment at home. His actions were smooth. He did not have a chance to discharge his anger in real life. So, the intensity of his repressed emotions had not yet surfaced, at this phase of therapy.

James reported this dream, "We were prisoners in class, and I saw kids, all boys, sitting on chairs. There were axes on a turn-table; some robots cut their heads with axes." Castration fear was clearly symbolized. "My turn was next with another group; I took control of the turn-table to exit from class." Control over body-threatening forces was attained in the dream.

It is very hard for a therapist to help a child improve, when parents resist change. James's mother was not "too convinced" that objective praise would enhance his self-esteem. She was satisfied with telling him, "He was a good person." Halfway through therapy, she told me that James started feeling "pompous" when she complied with my recommendation. Since being proud was not accepted in her family, she withheld praise.

Though children's punishments were rare in this family, they could occur without previous agreement with children and could be highly exaggerated. For example, James disobeyed his parents by allowing his younger sister to use his Nintendo. In response to his mother's emotional reactions, James "chose" his punishment of "five years confiscation." His mother agreed. Six months later, James verbally expressed his frustration, "this is too long, and I will not need it after five years." Mother accepted my logic, but she filtered it through her rearing principles. She would return the game after at least a month and upon receiving a better school report.

Late phase of therapy

A year and a half apart, the quality of James's body image improved in Figure 17.4, as compared to his earlier drawing in Figure 17.3, beyond what is due to maturity. The heavy body shading suggesting dirt disappeared. The body shape had become human, as opposed to the oval shaped body, seen in Figure 17.3. Here, clothes were present, instead of the undifferentiated dark area of the previous drawing. The fearful eyes expression also disappeared. Hair was added as an added realistic part of self-image. Ears were added; suggesting accepted auditory input as well as auditory curiosity, considering their size. However, the dots for eyes which reflected a tendency to shut off visual input, needed improvement. The figure also lacked a neck.

For two years, James insisted that he had experienced *no pain* after the circumcision operation. The subject bored him. He repeated what his mother had told him, "I had pain for a split of a second." In play, there was always a character who screamed, jumping up high, when another "set fire on his rear end". James symbolically re-acted his circumcision experience. He expressed the normal associative

Figure 17.4

affect by screaming due to intense pain in "his rear end." Thus, pain was expressed, which was an improvement compared with his earlier flat affect.

A mild variation to this theme reflected emotional improvement. He gained control by reversing roles. He chose a cat to be the therapist's play character. Upon hearing a loud alarm sound he made, the "cat" was to get startled and jump up high. James would have a good laugh. That is, he symbolically took the role of the offender. He exerted power. The offence was also much milder and was not associated with pain or fear.

Finally, James remembered the pain he had denied for so long. "When my mom pulled the bandage I cried, it was painful." Finally; he got in touch with his repressed emotion and was ready to accept it.

James would become very tense when he gave blood samples, which required several trials. This was interpreted in connection with his main operation as fear of body injury (castration fear). Toy syringes were used in play therapy, with exchanging patient and doctor roles, along with uttered soothing comments. This was intended as a concrete preparation for a temporary mild pain. James was also asked to draw a syringe. He attached an explosive to the syringe, to maintain his own control over a hurting object.

For Valentine, three months before termination, James described the card he drew for his mother, "a bomb was attached to a rope from 'behind,' and fire-like blew up 20 hearts." The familiar theme of "fire" attacking a "behind" location was altered. It resulted in a pleasant expression of love to the maternal figure, which was associated with the initial traumatic experience, as well as subsequent unpleasant experiences. Though the card was soon discarded, yet it reflected an improvement, at least internally in fantasy.

James used his Crazy Bones as aiming marbles in a game with the therapist. He enjoyed his figures knocking down hers in this age appropriate and socially accepted competitive game.

Five months prior to termination—as decided by his mother when James was 10 years old—specific improvements were reflected on other projective techniques.

His parents and teachers were concerned about the gap between his intellectual potential and his barely average school grades. James acknowledged the roles of work and motivation in his responses to TAT cards. To Card 1, "A boy looking at a violin," he said, "A boy, did not know how to "work" the violin; he put it in a closet, many years later he liked playing it. He should have asked how to use things." His initial response three years ago was, "he does not feel like playing." His recent response to the country scene, Card 2, was, "She wondered why her parents worked so hard, they had plenty of food, the crops did not grow this year, they almost starved, she should not have doubted about work." Three years ago, he perceived characters in this card as strangers not family, suggesting a present feeling of belonging to his family.

James got in touch with his sad feelings, to Card 6BM "a man and an old woman" he said, "a son, his mother was sad, she remembered her other son who died in hospital, the man was sad too." In his earlier response to this card, he avoided the expression of sadness by resorting to an irrational and bizarre theme. In the earlier phase of therapy, James would not talk about his deceased brother. He did not want to feel sad. Recently, he tolerated his sadness and added, "I pray for him." Figures in the recent story were perceived as two generations, in keeping with the card's stimuli and reality testing. In the previous story he perceived same generation characters.

James chose doing constructive and enjoyable activities, in his response to the Blank Card 16, "I am constructing a Lego city with my parents, I invent two characters, one runs for exercise, the other uses a skate-board for fun." The previous response was a life threatening treasure hunt.

Card 8BM consists of "a boy, a rifle, and two dim persons in the background with knives looking over a man lying down." James said, "The man was shot by one of the doctors who operated on him, a woman, she likes hurting people. The police found her and arrested her." Children usually perceive "doctors" as males. The hurting-healer may represent the maternal figure or the circumcision doctor. The story included the police as an external control. It is an age-appropriate response. So, James was able to express his repressed feelings of "being betrayed by his parents," connected with his circumcision operation and other early life events. It was interesting to find out that his mother confirmed the presence of such feelings of betrayal, expressed by James in real life situations.

On the Rorschach (Ames, Metraux, Rodell, & Walker, 1952; Klopfer, 1946) more contact with reality was projected. James responded to Card I with a real creature, "a butterfly." His earlier response was "a mask, like a bat" an artificial object. To Card II, the previous response of, "a sad face," which reflected depression and weakness, became, "volcano, tornado." Energy was used in momentum, along with violence. Since James was unable to express normal angry reactions in real life, this response reflected an improvement. The recent "observatory" response, for the same card, contributed to his ability to exert control on his life, on a symbolic level. It also suggested an age-appropriate curiosity.

His response to Card IV was, "a dancer," this human figure replaced the animal, "an otter, about to parish." It reflected a much better contact with the paternal figure.

The relationship with the maternal figure was still in need of improvement. The previous response to Card VII, "a cloud in the sky, nice, puffy" which portrayed a frail yet unattainable object, became, "a jelly fish" an unpredictable, potentially harmful object though apparently soft.

Conclusions

James came down to earth, got in touch with his sadness, pain, anger, and feelings of being betrayed by his parents. Such stored negative feelings toward his parents should have surfaced, in order to be normalized as human reactions. The use of denial and repression had tormented him and caused him to flee to a fantasy world. These feelings were explained in terms of his parents' well-intended motivations. He dealt with his problems and showed marked improvement, in behavior as well as inner feelings.

3. Nadine: Separation anxiety

Background

Nadine was seven years old when her mother sought child psychotherapy. She followed her mother everywhere at home, fixing her eyes on her. She was physically dragged to go to school. Separation anxiety started when Nadine was five months old. Up till this point, her mother was the sole caretaker, while her father worked at a distant location. Upon his return, her mother went back to work on a part-time basis. In spite of the father's serious attempts to care for her, Nadine would constantly cry. He was a complete stranger to her. After a couple of months, parents hired a baby-sitter for three years, and then a married couple took over for a year. Thereafter, she attended after-school services. Throughout, Nadine was fine with all her caretakers. It was only when her mother appeared on the scene that she would not let go.

Father-daughter relationship was gradually established, as he became part of family life. Nadine was able to tolerate his work-imposed occasional absence. When she was two-and-a-half years old her parents were divorced. It was a friendly arrangement; parents never argued or fought. Father would not participate in any decision, giving all power to mother. He probably meant to please her, but she resented making all decisions without his active participation. As if she was "looking in a mirror" as she put it. Father kept in touch with Nadine through visitations and phone calls. He had always fulfilled his financial responsibilities and maintained an active role in Nadine's life. She visited with him in his new location in another city. When she was six years old, he got married and had a baby boy a year later. Nevertheless, Nadine missed him a lot.

When Nadine was three years old, her mother's common-law partner lived with them for a year. He moved out since Nadine did not particularly like him. He occasionally visited with them and met her mother elsewhere. He was in and out of their life for five years before a final breakup took place.

Nadine was a well-disciplined child; she respected limits and learned good manners.

Self-presentation

Self-presentation, (Harris, 1963) projected on drawing, was made clear during the first session.

Nadine drew a seven-year-old girl in Figure 17.6, followed by a nine-year-old boy in Figure 17.5, then herself in Figure 17.7. One needs not be a projective drawing psychologist to see the sharp contrast between these figures. The

Figure 17.5

Figure 17.6

Figure 17.7

same-age female represented her ideal self (Figure 17.6). Both figures carried out the same activity: skipping rope. Engaged in a fun activity may suggest that she was a well-cared for child. Global quality of self-presentation was much inferior as compared to the female figure. It had gross body asymmetries, scribbles for clothes as contrasted to the well-decorated dress on the other girl's figure. Eyes in self-presentation were enlarged dots, not proper eyes that included pupils, as those in the girl's figure. The male figure's tilted legs depicted the movement of skating. Compared to self-presentation, similar differences may be noticed. Low self-esteem could be hypothesized.

Family relationships

Nadine started talking about her family relationships in an early session.

She drew a house with smoke coming out a chimney, a stick child flying a kite and a cloud.

There was no paternal representation, symbolized in the absence of the sun. Mother was "washing dishes inside the house," being a similar situation to her mother being at work, unseen but her absence is tolerated. Nadine's verbal explanation of her drawing had no indication of discomfort. The house was colorful, reflecting a lot of emotions, some bright others dark. Warmth at home, symbolized by smoke coming out of a chimney, may present her acknowledgement of mother's love. A considerable amount of anxiety in the family life however, was symbolized in a huge cloud, though bigger than the house, yet away from self-presentation.

Upon request, Kinetic Family Drawing (K-F-D, Burns & Kaufman, 1972) was done in the next session. Nadine was asked to draw all her family members including herself doing something. Though colors were available, she preferred to work with a pencil.

Here, a familiar fantasy to children of divorce was expressed. She drew representations of both biological parents holding ends of a skipping rope and self-presentation on its middle. Thus, parental figures were interacting with each other and focusing on self-presentation. Need stability was suggested as all figures, as well as house, leaned on the lower edge of the paper. Hands, as means of communication appeared on self, stretched toward each parent representation, yet hands were missing on both of them. That is, she is symbolically reaching out for them, but in her perception, they were not responding as much as she desired. In view of actual time and care her parents—though separately—offered her, it seemed that she needed to internalize more communicative parents. This could also reflect Nadine's need of her parents' joined communication with her.

The child, considered as self-presentation, was said to be five years old, a time preceding her father's second marriage. The sun as a paternal symbol had a face wearing glasses and its rays looked like messed hair. Projective drawings experts would not agree with Nadine's drawn face in the sun as "making it prettier."

This was an expression of anxiety added to the huge shaded cloud, symbolizing an obscure threat (Di Leo, 1983). More anxiety appeared in three birds, which produced an enormous amount of their secretions, though in tiny dots.

In her play with dolls, Nadine commented, "a baby was afraid that her mother would abandon her". This was the same kind of fear she experienced when five months old. Her mother's absence, at the time, could have been perceived as abandonment.

Nadine's confusion and anxiety were expressed in free drawings. The previous night she had a nightmare. Her mother had warned her against "talking to strangers." She did heavy scribbling with pencil and individual colors as well as crossed heavy lines. A hastily done cat's face was crossed and heavy lines also appeared in another drawing. These productions portrayed uncontrolled affect.

The last free drawing was done a month prior to termination, when mother's companion was completely out of their lives. It depicted a castle with a king and a queen inside. Glorification of parental figures in dreams interpretation could convey similar meaning in drawings. The castle had predominantly bright colors, much bigger than all previous houses. Yellow sun was conventional in size, with organized rayon and without a face; a more mature drawing characteristics. Anxiety-presenting clouds in previous drawings had considerably shrunk in one cloud and took a corner position. Some anxiety still appeared in birds, now being "clean," as compared to secretions produced by birds in a previous drawing.

Psychotherapy

Nadine attended nine sessions over a period of five months. It was suggested to mother to give Nadine a transitional object, such as a fluffy stuffed animal. Instead, mother gave her a family picture, which depicted Nadine with her biological parents. It worked wonders! Nadine called it "the magic picture" in play therapy. It chased away fearful feelings, which her doll had experienced hearing sounds made by wild animals. Nadine took the picture to school to look at when she missed one of her parents.

In make-believe play, she chose for herself as well as for the therapist dolls to impersonate. She "played" the situation of her first insecurity, at the age of five months. She chose a six-month-old doll for the therapist. Hers were two dolls as "mother and father ghosts." They were friendly ghosts who attended to baby doll's needs during parents' absence. They would often take baby on a flying trip. She whispered the therapist' lines, "I am hungry, I feel lonely." She would move ghost parents to attend to baby's needs. Additional whispered lines were, "I am afraid mom is dead," "she had abandoned me," and "dad cannot care for me." Then assuring words, "mom had gone to work to bring money for the family" and "she'll soon return." The therapist added, "Mom and dad live in baby's heart, so they are always present even when baby cannot see them."

During play in the last session, Nadine became father–doll who taught his doll–son (therapist), to do gymnastics. At home, she would wake her mother up so both would respond to a TV gym program. In addition to pleasant time spent with mother, rhythmic movements to music are considered a therapeutic technique, which was beneficial for her. She was eager to go to school; even ran on her way to school as opposed to being dragged to it, prior to psychotherapy.

After termination, her mother sent the therapist copies of teachers' positive comments and community newspaper clips showing Nadine's participation in extracurricular activities.

4. Amanda: Psychosomatic reactions

Background

Following a school-board decision, the sector of family's residence was moved to another school. On top of required adjustment to new environment and dealing with separation from old mates, Amanda hated her first-grade teacher. In her perception, the teacher did not like her. Her mother tried in vain to comfort her. For seven months she had stomachaches every morning, cried, and tried to skip school. Upon returning from school, she bitterly complained about her "unpleasant" teacher, whom she was "stuck with" almost all day. Amanda was six years old when she started individual psychotherapy.

Self and foe

To help Amanda externalize her feelings, she was asked to draw herself and the teacher.

Figure 17.8, shows both figures missing hands, probably reflecting lack of communication. Both figures also missed feet maybe suggesting difficulties in maintaining a grip on the environment. Teacher's figure had a straight, rather zigzag mouth giving the impression of a stern person. Self-presentation was rather slanted, depicting the child's feeling of emotional imbalance. The therapist asked Amanda to pretend she is telling her teacher all what she did not like about her, which was written below her drawing. It reads, "You are not nice, you give me too much trouble, you are way too strict, it gets me angry, you are too serious I cannot laugh, I hate you, I wish to have a better teacher than you, you scream at everybody, you never smile." Amanda added "She wears the scarf I gave her for Christmas,," which was drawn on teacher's figure. It seemed that Amanda expected teacher to like her as much as she liked her gift.

Amanda was then asked to think hard to find something good about her teacher. After a long pose she said, "She taught me to read." She was encouraged to tell this one positive comment to her teacher, which she did at a later date.

teacher   me

Figure 17.8

From foe to friend

Five sessions into psychotherapy, Amanda was asked once more to draw herself and her teacher. A remarkable improvement appears in Figure 17.9. The height of teacher's figure more than doubled, reflecting the amount of importance she held in the child's life. Both figures had hands, suggesting the presence of communication between them. Figures' feet and shoes were very well detailed for a child her age. Thus, negative implications of missed body parts, lack of communication and unmaintained positions in the environment, have diminished. Teacher's figure gained a smile, quite the opposite of grim/tight lips in Figure 17.8. The angle of slanted self-presentation had decreased, reflecting improvement in her sense of imbalance. Clothes on self-presentation had an ornament, which added a cheerful element to self-concept. Hair was better in style on both figures. Higher hair quality was another expression of positive feelings about self and teacher.

Amanda made great progress in a short-term psychotherapy. At termination, her mother reported that Amanda had remarkably changed. She was willing to

me

teacher

Figure 17.9

go to school and her physical pain symptoms had disappeared. Her anecdotes about school events included pleasant interaction with her teacher.

References

Ames, L. B., Metraux, R. W., Rodell, J. R., & Walker, R. N. (1952). *Rorschach responses: Developmental trends from two to ten years.* New York: Hoeber.

Burns, R. C., & Kaufman, S. H. (1972). *Actions, styles and symbols in Kinetic Family Drawing (KFD): An interpretative manual.* New York: Brunner/Mazel.

Di Leo, J. H. (1983). *Interpreting children's drawings.* New York: Brunner/Mazel.

Goyette, C. H., Conners, C. K., & Ulrich, R. F. (1978). Normative data on revised Conners Parent and Teacher Rating Scales. *Journal of Abnormal Child Psychology, 6,* 23–233.

Harris, D. (1963). *Goodenough-Harris Drawing Test: Manual.* New York: Harcourt, Brace & World.

Koppitz, E. M. (1968). *Psychological evaluation of children's human figure drawings.* New York: Grune & Stratton.

Murray, H. A. (1943). *Thematic Apperception Test manual.* Cambridge: Harvard University Press.

Thomas, A.D. (1999, July). A young boy. In S. Z. Dudek (chair), *The price of creativity.* Symposium conducted at the convention of the International Council of Psychologists, Salem, MA.

18

THE INTERSECTION OF ART THERAPY AND PSYCHOLOGICAL ASSESSMENT

Unified approaches to the use of drawings and artistic processes

Donna Betts and Gary Groth-Marnat

Introduction

Art therapists and psychologists can potentially benefit from collaborating in the clinical assessment and treatment planning process using drawing-based measures. The present chapter addresses this intersection. Recommendations for further refinement of respective approaches across these two disciplines are presented. Discussion of psychology's influence on the development of art therapy in the United States, and the influence of psychological assessment approaches in art therapy set the tone for the chapter. Mutually beneficial ways in which art therapists and psychologists can learn from each other in the context of assessment are explored, including a description of global ratings and formal elements as applied to scoring artwork, and consideration of important moderating variables such as artistic ability and experience with drawing.

Background

Influence of psychology on art therapy in the United States

The fields of psychology, psychiatry, progressive education, and art education provided the foundation for the development of art therapy as a distinct profession (Junge & Asawa, 1994). The *Bulletin of Art Therapy,* the first art therapy journal, was coconceived by psychologist Bernard Levy and art therapy pioneer, Elinor Ulman (Junge, 2010). Levy and Ulman also cofounded one of the first art therapy training programs in the United States in 1971, at George Washington University.

Influence of psychological assessment approaches in art therapy

Clinical assessment is considered integral to the training of art therapists and has been designated as a required course by American Art Therapy Association (AATA)-approved education programs (Betts, 2012; Horovitz & Eksten, 2009). Given the importance of assessment to art therapy practice and research, course material for teaching this topic often incorporates sources from the psychological assessment literature. This includes elements generic to assessment, including a strong emphasis on projective (or "performance-based") assessment.

Psychologists developed projective and drawing-based assessments and have used these tools for decades. The benefits and shortcomings of interpretation and analysis of patient art work have been widely discussed. Despite abundant criticisms of these tools, Klopfer and Taulbee (1976) concluded that psychologists would probably continue to develop, use, and rely upon projective instruments as long as they maintain an interest in the inner person and probing the depths of the psyche. More than 30 years later, Klopfer and Taulbee's prediction has come to fruition as evidenced by the resurgence of research on projectives in publications such as the *Journal of Personality Assessment*, and abundant projective assessment topics presented at annual meetings of the *Society for Personality Assessment*. These tools have provided a significant resource for the development of art therapy assessments. There has also been a movement to change the name from "projective" assessment to "performance-based" assessment (Meyer & Kurtz, 2006), clearly distinguishing it from self-report instruments in that participants perform some sort of activity, such as drawing a picture. This activity reveals how they perceive and organize their world.

Human figure drawings such as the House-Tree-Person (H-T-P) test (Buck, 1947) and the Goodenough-Harris Draw-A-Person (DAP) test (Harris, 1963) have been particularly influential for art therapists. Human figure drawings have been widely explored by practitioners in mental health professions. The literature has explored Human Figure Drawings (HFDs) with children (Allen & Tussey, 2012; Bruck, 2009; Deaver, 2009; Hagood, 2003; Milne & Greenway, 2005; Packman, Beck, VanZutphen, Long, & Spengler, 2003; Riethmiller & Handler, 1997), adolescents (Koppitz & Casullo, 1983; Yedidia & Lipschitz-Elchawi, 2012), and adults (Handler & Reyher, 1964, 1966). Five of these cited articles were published in an art therapy journal and six were published in a psychology journal, reflecting the mutual interest in both fields on the applications of HFDs.

The historical foundations of the use of projective and drawing-based assessments, derived from the field of psychology, established the development of similar techniques in the field of art therapy. Several art therapists integrated the psychological assessment literature with art therapy theory and approaches.

Some of the earliest standardized art therapy instruments include the Ulman Personality Assessment Procedure (Ulman, 1965), the Family Art Evaluation (Kwiatkowska, 1975, 1978), and Rawley Silver's tests (2002). The Ulman

Personality Assessment Procedure (UPAP) had its beginnings in the Washington, DC General Hospital's Department of Psychiatry. In 1959 the hospital's chief psychologist began sending patients to art therapist Elinor Ulman so that she could use art to derive diagnostic information (Ulman, 1965, 1975). The UPAP, a standardized series of four drawings on 18 inch × 24 inch gray drawing paper, became influential in the development of subsequent tools such as the Diagnostic Drawing Series (DDS; Cohen, J. Hammer, & Singer, 1988) (see *interviews and data integration*). Ulman did not develop a standardized scoring system for the UPAP, but she did recommend that validity might be increased by focusing on the ". . . form and its correlation with personal characteristics" (Ulman & Levy, 1975, p. 402) rather than the content of the drawings. This later influenced the development of the Formal Elements Art Therapy Scale: The Rating Manual (FEATS; Gantt & Tabone, 1998), a formal scoring system.

During her tenure at the National Institute of Mental Health, art therapist Hanna Yaxa Kwiatkowska (1975, 1978) developed a structured evaluation procedure for use with families. She was greatly influenced by Ulman's seminal work and stated that Ulman's ". . . exquisite sensitivity and broad experience allowed her to provide important diagnostic conclusions drawn from four tasks given to the patients investigated individually" (Kwiatkowska, 1978, p. 86). Her instrument, the Family Art Evaluation, consists of a single meeting of all available members of the nuclear family. The family is asked to produce (1) a free picture; (2) a picture of your family; (3) an abstract family portrait; (4) a picture started with the help of a scribble; (5) a joint family scribble; and (6) a free picture. Following completion, the art therapist facilitates a discussion with the family about the artwork and the process. Kwiatkowska's evaluation is significant in that it is one of the earliest standardized evaluation procedures developed by an art therapist.

Art therapist Rawley Silver developed the Silver Drawing Test of Cognition and Emotion (SDT; 1996, 2002) and the Draw A Story procedure (DAS; 1988, 2002). The SDT includes the following three tasks: predictive drawing, drawing from imagination, and drawing from observation. The DAS is a semistructured interview technique using stimulus images to elicit response drawings. Both tools have substantially influenced assessment in art therapy. Another assessment later developed by art therapists is the Person Picking an Apple from a Tree (PPAT; Gantt, 1990). The directive is to "draw a person picking an apple from a tree" (Gantt & Tabone, 1998, p. 13) on a 12 inch × 18 inch sheet of white drawing paper with 12 Mr. Sketch™ markers. Completed PPAT pictures are then scored using the Formal Elements Art Therapy Scale (FEATS; Gantt & Tabone, 1998). The PPAT has become quite popular among art therapists (Gantt, 2004; Cox, Agell, Cohen, & Gantt, 2000) because it uses a single drawing that examines "global" artistic elements and also because there are data on validity and reliability with diverse populations (Bucciarelli, 2007; Gussak, 2009; Munley, 2002; Rockwell & Dunham, 2006).

The content of a PPAT drawing includes the three basic elements of a person, tree, and an apple. The development of the PPAT was influenced by the Draw-A-Person (DAP; Machover, 1949) and House-Tree-Person (HTP; Buck, 1947) in that the drawings were considered to represent symbolic content expressed by the client. Because the instructions and content of the PPAT are standardized, raters can focus on formal elements of the drawings. Just as the DSM identifies disorders by clusters of symptoms, these 14 FEATS scales represent clusters of symptoms that correspond to diagnoses. In the process of developing the FEATS, Gantt developed this concept of the *graphic equivalent of symptoms*—which enabled assessors to see how certain FEATS scales dovetailed with DSM-III (American Psychiatric Association, 1980) symptoms. The FEATS is discussed in more detail and later in the section on *global ratings and formal elements.*

Neale and Rosal (1993) reviewed various issues related to the psychometrics and clinical use of drawings. As part of this review they articulated how the concerns of art therapists' developing and using assessments would be unique to art therapy and also distinct from projective drawing tests developed by psychologists. They identified the following themes: Can objective drawing characteristics be identified without losing the holistic view of the drawing (Wadeson, 1980)? How can optimal diagnostic indicators be determined (Shoemaker, 1982)? Can art be organized according to diagnosis (Gantt & Howie, 1979)? Can patient strengths, not just pathology, be identified through artwork (Anderson, 1978; Ulman 1975)? What is the most effective approach to developing a scoring manual (Chase, 1986; Sidun, 1986)? Should projective drawings be tied to a theoretical framework (Packard, 1978)? Can free drawings, as well as directed drawing tasks, be used in diagnosis and how should a free drawing be scored (Rubin, 1978; Ulman, 1975)? What are the implications of reliability and validity for clinical practice (Chase, 1986; Sidun, 1986)? What is the importance of well-designed studies in the investigation of projective art therapy tools (Cox, Agell, Cohen, & Gantt, 2000)? These questions and considerations continue to influence the use and research of art therapy assessments and drawing-based psychological tests.

Assessment in art therapy and psychology: Learning from each other

Art therapists have benefited from the foundations of projective assessment established in psychology. Conversely, psychologists can benefit from art therapists' extensive knowledge of art materials and art processes in the context of assessment. Levy and Ulman (1974) observed that "the art therapist makes unique and decisive contributions to diagnostic discussions of patients" (p. 25) which should include identification of patient strengths. Additionally, art therapists can identify formal art characteristics that reflect a patient's symptomatology, which is not always revealed through behavioral observation or other traditional means (Teneycke, Hoshino, & Sharpe, 2009). This has the potential to enhance the treatment team's conclusions. The above ideas underscore the unique skill set and valuable contributions offered by art therapists.

Approaches to the assessment process

In his presidential address to the 2010 annual meeting of the Society for Personality Assessment, Robert Erard emphasized the importance of gaining meaningful information about clients and encouraged the audience to "cook without a book"—to step outside the confines of measurement (Erard, 2010). "We know that clients derive considerable benefit, therapeutic and otherwise, from being understood and learning to understand themselves better, and that those who work with them ... can use such highly personalized, in-depth understanding to great advantage" (p. 10). This perspective on assessment has been expressed elsewhere in the literature, particularly relating to therapeutic and positive psychological assessment (e.g., Finn, 2007, 2009).

Since the success of an intervention is largely dependent upon the quality of the client-therapist relationship, assessment techniques that will foster this relationship are advantageous (D. Martin, Garske, & Davis, 2000; see Betts, 2012). Bornstein (2009) has elaborated on how therapeutically oriented assessment influences the assessor, assesses, and the outcome of a psychological test. This method emphasizes a collaborative approach to assessment that "can have a positive impact on patient insight, adjustment, and therapeutic engagement" (p. 6). Therapeutic assessment approaches psychological testing as a way to help clients better understand themselves, find solutions to their problems, and facilitate positive changes (Finn, 2007, 2009). Therapeutic assessment encompasses techniques of collaborative assessment (Fischer, 2000, 2001), a method based in humanistic and human-science psychology, whereby the power differential between the assessor and client is diminished as much as possible in a team approach to understanding the client's problems and establish new ways of thinking and being. In the art therapy literature, Dudley (2004) also emphasized the significance of the client-therapist relationship in the context of assessment and de-emphasized the traditional fact-finding approach to evaluation. Rather, she suggested, the initial meeting with a prospective client is an important opportunity to examine the "unfolding" of a relationship between the practitioner, the client, and the art" (p. 19). When considering drawing-based tests, other factors reviewed by art therapists and psychologists also have significance. These include the implications of color, and art materials and the art-making process, on assessment outcomes.

Color: Color is an important part of the art-making experience (Gantt, 2004); and a fundamental component of an art therapy assessment. It is assumed that the use of color reflects emotional expression (Groth-Marnat, 1997).

Because of the implications of using color in assessments, its effects warrant investigation. Milne and Greenway (1999) examined the influence of age and gender on color preference and identified a need for further research to gather normative data. Deaver (2009) investigated the implications of color in a normative sample, filling a gap in the effects of color in the human figure drawing research. She studied the HFDs of fourth graders and second graders. The drawings were scored with five scales modified from the FEATS (Gantt & Tabone, 1998): Scale I (Prominence of Color); Scale II (Color Fit); Scale III (Space); Scale IV (Developmental Level); and Scale V (Details of Objects and Environment; see Betts, 2013). Deaver's (2009) application of the FEATS scales to rate HFDs was an important departure from the traditional methods of scoring these drawings.

Koppitz and Naglieri, as well as many other researchers, focused solely on measuring the presence or absence of specific aspects of the drawn human figure, such as arms, hair, nose, and so forth (see Groth-Marnat, 1997), and did not attempt to measure formal artistic elements of the drawings such as color or the amount of space the drawing occupies on the paper (Deaver, 2009, p. 5).

Data for Deaver's study were analyzed according to the variables of gender, age, ethnicity, and mean scores on each of the five scales. Second graders used significantly more color and space in their drawings than fourth graders ($t = 3.3$, $p < .01$), typical of younger children's use of bold color and less refined motor skills. Gender differences were only significantly different on the Color Fit scale, ($t = 3.8$, $p < .01$), reflecting girls' more realistic use of color than boys.

Art materials and processes. Materials used for projective instruments include a pencil and a piece of letter-size paper, but art therapy tools provide a range of drawing materials, each one standardized with a specific type and brand of marker or pastel, for instance. The variety of tools available is discussed at length in Betts (2013). It is vital to consider how client media preferences affect assessment outcomes.

The Expressive Therapies Continuum theory (ETC; Kagin & Lusebrink, 1978; Lusebrink, 2010; Stuckey, 2012) provides a framework for understanding a client's mode of visual expression and information processing (Figure 18.1) while also identifying properties of specific materials and their influence on the client's performance when engaging in the art-making process. Simply put, the ETC provides a structure to describe the interaction between the individual and his or her experience with art materials and products (Moon, 2010b). The ETC emphasizes the importance of using appropriate art materials based on the client's needs in therapy, a concept widely discussed in the art therapy literature (Burns, 2009; Hinz, 2009; Henley, 1997; Moon, 2010a, 2010b; Robins & Seaver, 1994). The ideas of Horowitz (1970; 1983) provided the context for establishing a continuum between each level of the ETC (Hinz, 2009). Horowitz (1970; 1983) studied the idea that complex information processing allows an individual to hold an image, idea, or representation in his or her mind, even in the absence

273

of an object, and that this processing is additive in nature. Thus, healthy processing on one level serves as a catalyst to processing information on a more complex level. This progression is known as the "emergent factor" (Hinz, 2009; Kagin & Lusebrink, 1978), and provides the theoretical background for "parallels among imagery formation, cognitive processes, and art expressions on the different levels (of the ETC)" (Hinz, 2009, p. 30).

In ETC theory, differences in art materials are explained using a framework known as Media Dimension Variables (MDV; Kagin, 1969). The MDV system describes materials used in art therapy as moderated by media properties; quantity and boundary determined features; and implications of mediated and non-mediated materials (Burns, 2009; Hinz, 2009; Moon, 2010b; Somer & Somer, 2000). The spectrum ranges from most resistive media through most fluid, in this order: pencils, markers, soft pastels, chalk/charcoal, hard pastels, paint, finger paint, and wet clay. The resistive, more controlled materials tend to evoke a greater amount of cognitive processing on the ETC. Conversely, fluid materials, which are manipulated with ease, are more likely to elicit affective responding (Burns, 2009; Kagin & Lusebrink, 1978; Moon, 2010b; Robins & Seaver, 1994; Somer & Somer, 2000). In relation to assessments described in this chapter, the DDS (Cohen, J. Hammer & Singer, 1988) requires the use of soft Alphacolor chalk pastels, which possess both resistive and fluid qualities, and can thus bring forth an affective response. Conversely, the PPAT makes use of Mr. Sketch™ markers, which are more resistive than pastels on the MDV spectrum, and tend to elicit a cognitive response in the drawing process. Gantt and Tabone's (1998) choice of the markers was studied:

> In the early clinical trials we gave the artists a choice of felt-tip markers or pastels. A number of artists stated they did not like using pastels or refused to draw so we decided to use only markers. Using markers does make some rating tasks easier and the judges find it easier to count the number of colors used. We recognize the limitations of the materials but have found that, even with some restriction on expressiveness, we still obtain a great amount of useful information. (p. 13)

The Expressive Therapies Continuum and Media Dimension Variables are important to assessment in art therapy because therapists and researchers can use these theories to examine clients' processes and products in art therapy sessions (Hinz, 2009). Moreover, in order to establish appropriate treatment goals and work with clients successfully, the ETC is recommended for assessing a client's abilities and art material preferences. Research in art therapy has focused on integrating multiple sources of data during an assessment session, with consideration to global characteristics of art, emphasizing the process of how people make art, and behaviors observed during the process (Betts, 2012; Cohen & Cox, 1995; Hinz, 2009; Gantt & Tabone, 1998). Of importance is not only the art product and its formal elements scores, but also how individuals

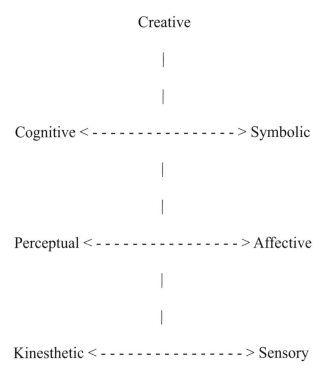

Creative

|

|

Cognitive < - - - - - - - - - - - - - - - - > Symbolic

|

|

Perceptual < - - - - - - - - - - - - - - - - > Affective

|

|

Kinesthetic < - - - - - - - - - - - - - - - > Sensory

Figure 18.1 The Expressive Therapies Continuum (ETC). The hierarchical ETC shows the levels kinesthetic/sensory, affective/perceptual, and cognitive/symbolic. The creative level is implicated throughout the continuum. Adapted from Kagin and Lusebrink, 1987.

interact with materials, and their comments and behaviors that are observed by the art therapist. This integrated approach appears to be more reliable than making inferences about an individual based solely on their art product.

Interviews and data integration. During interviewing and data integration it is often crucial to have the clients themselves validate interpretations based on their own associations, language, and metaphors. This is consistent with Therapeutic Assessment and Collaborative Assessment approaches. In addition, Betts (2012) recommended a "positive art therapy assessment" (p. 204) that identified the following commonalities shared by Collaborative Assessment (Fischer, 2000, 2001), Therapeutic Assessment (Finn, 2007, 2009), and integrative art therapy assessment, and an overall integrative approach to assessment that combines all sources of information and minimizes an over-reliance on test score (Groth-Marnat, 2009; Groth-Marnat & Davis, 2013; Harwood, Beutler, & Groth-Marnat, 2011); including strengths and hope in client reports (Snyder, Ritschel, Rand, & Berg, 2006); being cautious about test selection and interview questions to insure that assessments incorporate "inside" and "outside" environmental assets and weaknesses (Snyder et al., 2006); working collaboratively with the client (Bornstein, 2009; Fischer, 2000; Snyder et al., 2006); and focusing on the quality of the relationship (Dudley, 2004).

A good example of an interactive interview approach that uses many of the above components is the Diagnostic Drawing Series (DDS; see Cohen, Mills, & Kijak, 1994). The directions for completing a DDS are given prior to beginning each drawing, as follows: (1) make a picture using these materials; (2) draw a picture of a tree; and (3) make a picture of how you're feeling, using lines, shapes, and colors.

The DDS Rating Guide (Cohen, 2012) and Drawing Analysis Form provide illustrated and clearly defined criteria that address the structure, not the content, of the drawings, influenced by the "form as content" approach of art therapist and psychologist Janie Rhyne (1995). The DDS, designed for use with people 13 years of age and older, was the first art-based assessment to be systematically correlated with the classification system of the *Diagnostic and Statistical Manual of Mental Disorders* (DSM-III; American Psychiatric Association, 1980). Upon completion of the drawings, the client is asked to discuss them using the Drawing Inquiry Form, a semistructured interview that provides clients with an opportunity to reflect on and describe their drawings. For example, for the tree drawing, the client is asked whether the tree depicted is real or imaginary. The DDS Drawing Analysis Form is also used to assign scores on the nominal and ordinal scales of the formal elements of each drawing (such as use of space, color, line). The resulting data include the formal elements scores, the client's Drawing Inquiry responses, and the therapist's observations of client reactions to the pastels and other relevant behaviors. The evaluation system for the Bird's Nest Drawing (Kaiser, 1996; Kaiser & Deaver, 2009) also emphasizes the importance of assessors attending to their subjective responses, with its inclusion of an Overall Impression rating scale. In addition, Betts (2012) has encouraged therapists to engage in self-reflection to increase awareness of their own subjective biases that may affect their interpretations.

Approaches to interpretation and analysis: Signs, global ratings, and form

A crucial interpretive distinction is between specific signs on drawings versus more global ratings. The "sign" approach relies heavily on the meaning of drawing content that is then used to interpret aspects of the examinee. For example, an emphasis on eyes and ears may suggest hypervigilance, possibly reflecting paranoid processes. Underlying this approach is assumed isomorphy between the content of the drawing and the examinees' lives. This might be reflected in a human figure drawing that is off balance reflecting that the examinee's life is similarly "off balance." In contrast are more global ratings related to aspects such as the overall quality of the drawing or degree of distortion. A final strategy is the use of form that relates to drawing dimensions such as the size of the drawing and placement on the page.

In order to determine the degree of support for the above approaches, Kahill (1984) examined the literature published between 1967 and 1982 on the validity and reliability of human figure drawing tests with adults. Focusing on the assertions of Machover (1949) and Hammer (1954, 1958), Kahill (1984) discussed reliability estimates and evidence pertaining to the body-image hypothesis. Validity of form variables (e.g., size, placement, perspective, and omission) and the content of figure drawings (e.g., face, mouth and teeth, anatomy indicators, and gender of first-drawn figures) was addressed, along with the performance of global measures and the influence of confounding factors was described. He found that most interpretations based on content (e.g., large eyes suggesting hypervigilance) were not supported. In contrast, global ratings received more support. For example, he found that overall drawing quality was associated with better levels of adjustment.

Lally (2001) criticized both the "specific signs" and "global impressions" approaches to scoring HFDs, in the context of forensic assessment (p. 146). Although he asserted that these approaches may have no place in the courtroom; they "may arguably have a place in clinical practice" (p. 146). Even though drawings may not be psychometrically sound tests in and of themselves, validity may be increased by interacting with the client to establish the unique meaning the drawings has for them. In addition, composite global ratings of relevant drawing variables have also been found to have adequate reliability and validity. Whereas psychological approaches to projective drawings have often focused on the symbolic meaning of content, art therapy assessments have frequently relied on ratings based on more global and form-based approaches (see Gantt & Tabone, 1998; Lehmann & Risquez, 1953; Ulman & Levy, 1975). An important example of this is the Formal Elements Art Therapy Scale (FEATS; Gantt & Tabone, 1998). The premise behind the FEATS is that the focus on *how* someone draws as opposed to *what* they draw allows for meaning to be understood more objectively in the context of whole images that are assessed by taking into account formal elements (Gantt, 2004).

The FEATS is a "measurement system for applying numbers to global variables in two-dimensional art (drawing and painting)" (Gantt, 2001, p. 124). Its 14 scales address the following different formal elements of artwork: Color Prominence, Color Fit, Implied Energy, Space, Integration, Logic, Realism, Developmental Level, Problem-Solving, Details of Objects and Environment, Line Quality, Person, Rotation, and Perseveration. A sample page from the FEATS manual (Gantt & Tabone, 1998) (see Figure 18.2) illustrates the Developmental Level scale, which guides in scoring drawings based on Lowenfeld and Brittain's (1970) theories of artistic development in childhood through adolescence. Gantt proposed adapting the FEATS to score other drawing-based assessments as a way to test its validity and determine the extent of its applications (Cox, Agell, Cohen, & Gantt, 2000). The FEATS has been formally adapted to establish standardized rating systems for the Bridge Drawing (K. Martin & Betts, 2012) and the Face Stimulus Assessment (Betts, 2010).

To further substantiate the use of the FEATS, art therapy researchers have praised the collection of normative drawing data, and have called for more studies to take normative samples into account (Betts, 2006; Cox, Agell, Cohen, & Gantt, 2000; Gantt & Tabone, 1998; Gantt, 2001; Gantt, 2004; Kaplan, 2001; Silver, 2009). As a result, several researchers have included a normative comparison group in their investigations.

Bucciarelli (2011) explored characteristics of 100 PPAT drawings from a normative sample. An important outcome of this study was its conclusions that more art therapy assessment research needs to account for cultural differences, clearer definitions of normative participant characteristics, and especially the relationship between past artistic experience, artistic skill, and drawing-based assessment outcomes.

As described earlier, Deaver (2009) developed a normative sample of 467 children using the Human Figure Drawing (HFD) and used the FEATS scales to analyze the drawings. Though this research addressed developmental levels in relation to art-making, it also established much needed norms relating to art and drawing-based assessment.

In a discussion on scoring systems, rater characteristics must be considered. Personality differences may influence the accuracy of persons making interpretations based on artwork. For example, Scribner and Handler (1987) found that "subjects whose interpersonal orientation emphasized dominance, order, and precision were poor interpreters when using an approach that requires empathy and intuition" (pp. 119–120) and that such individuals' intellectual approach may not be conducive to an intuitive method of figure drawing interpretation. Their findings suggested that interview data may be effective in the selection of skilled interpreters, and that those who described themselves as affiliate rather than power-oriented were likely to be the best interpreters.

Artistic ability and experience

Many variables can moderate or confound scores on drawing-based projectives. Authors in both art therapy and psychology have addressed the effects of artistic ability on participants' performance in completing drawing-based projective tests. Gantt and Tabone (1998) emphasized the influence of an individual's artistic ability and previous artistic experience on their drawings. The same concern has been articulated in the psychology literature: "artistic skill may be a distinct influence on drawings" (Suinn & Oskamp, 1969, p. 130). On the one hand, *high* artistic skill might allow individuals to more accurately express core aspects of their functioning (Rostan, 1997). In contrast, such persons might obscure aspects of themselves by focusing on the aesthetics of the drawings. They might even use their command of their medium to disguise aspects of themselves that they would like to hide. On the other hand, persons with *low* artistic ability

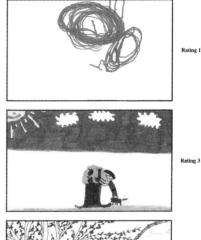

SCALE #9 - DEVELOPMENTAL LEVEL

How would this picture be rated according to Lowenfeld's developmental levels? Determining the developmental level is usually done with children's drawings. However, many people stop drawing in adolescence; therefore, many adults will draw in the style of adolescents, not having developed their artistic skills any further. The scale is used to give a rough estimate of the developmental level. If children's drawings were being studied, we would need a more finely gauged scale to rate them accurately.

CRITERIA	RATING
This variable cannot be rated because the individual elements cannot be identified.	0
The drawing consists solely of scribbles or masses of lines and shapes.	1
The drawing is like those of four- to six-year-olds (ex., no baseline, the person's arms appear to come from the head or neck, objects are composed of geometric shapes).	2
The drawing is like those done by latency-age children (with a baseline and/or a skyline; objects are lined up on the baseline).	3
The drawing is like those done by adolescents (with overlapping of objects and with realistic sizes for each object in relation to the others).	4
The drawing is an "adult" drawing and shows some artistic sophistication or training.	5

Gantt & Tabone, *FEATS Rating Manual*

Figure 18.2 The Formal Elements Art Therapy Scale: Developmental Level. Reprinted with permission from Gantt and Tabone (1998).

might have more difficulty hiding core aspects of their functioning. But then they might find it harder to express aspects of themselves due to a poor command of the medium.

Some art therapy studies have mentioned the possible effect art experience may have on art therapy assessments (Gantt, 2001, 2004; Kaplan, 2001; White, Wallace, & Huffman, 2004). For example, normal individuals with low artistic ability have sometimes been incorrectly diagnosed as patients, while individuals with psychiatric diagnoses and high artistic ability have been misidentified as nonpatients (Kaplan, 2001). This is consistent with Levy and Ulman's (1974) early study with participant raters who categorized drawings as either belonging to a patient category, or a nonpatient category. They found that the drawings by people with mental retardation were mistakenly identified by the participant raters as having psychopathology, and intelligent persons with schizophrenia were erroneously identified as nonpatients. Nonetheless, it is likely that the artistic skill of the people who did the drawings moderated the quality of the artwork.

Past research also shows significant differences in artists' and nonartists' choices in color and symbolic imagery (Cox & Frame, 1993). The sample included a normative control group with no artistic background beyond grammar school

(N = 70), and an artist group comprised of artists and art therapists (N = 70). Participants were administered the Mandala Assessment Research Instrument (MARI)® Card Test© (Kellogg, 1984). Artists were found to be more likely than nonartists to focus on and explore their inner conflicts and to also use creative expression to help resolve those feelings. Based on the above types of studies, authors have warned against over-pathologizing persons with poor artistic expression.

In the psychology literature, Handler and Reyher (1964, 1965, 1966) explored artistic ability using the stimulus of a car as a control drawing, compared to a figure drawing. Their findings indicated that the artistic differences between a figure drawing and a car drawing done by the same individual may be largely related to greater emotional content associated with the figure drawing. This supports a continued effort to acknowledge and further examine the role of artistic ability in the use of projective and drawing-based assessments.

Groth-Marnat and Roberts (1998) examined the concurrent validity of adult Human Figure Drawings (HFD) and House-Tree-Person (HTP) drawings as measures of self-esteem and found that neither the HFD nor the HTP quantitative composite ratings of psychological health related to the formal measures of self-esteem. They assessed for artistic ability but they neither found it to be a significant predictor of the two measures of self-esteem, nor was it related to age and gender of participants. However, the authors cautioned that the results were based on a somewhat small sample size.

It has been proposed that inviting participants to look at and draw a three-dimensional still life comprised of emotionally neutral objects (small boxes, cylinders) may be conducive to determining participants' artistic ability, when compared to their performance on a drawing-based assessment (Rabinowitz & Betts, 2012). The use of still life objects was determined to enable a greater degree of standardization as well as more appropriate assessment of technical drawing skills, such as rendering appropriate perspective, as opposed to drawing a picture from imagination. This suggests that future examination of artistic skill would benefit from the use of three-dimensional still-life objects.

Conclusion

This chapter discussed approaches to assessment across art therapy and psychology, and provided recommendations for their further refinement. The implications of color, art materials, and processes were discussed, with a focus on human figure drawings. In addition, methods conducive to interviews and data integration and approaches to interpretation and analysis were presented. This included a description of interpretive signs based on content, global ratings, and formal elements as applied to scoring artwork, and consideration of important moderating variables such as artistic ability and experience with drawing.

Art therapists and psychologists have co-examined many factors involved in assessment but this has often occurred without an awareness of each other's' important contributions. By increasing collaboration, clients will most likely be better served. This will ideally involve integration between psychologists' expertise in general assessment combined with art therapists' knowledge of art tools, art materials, and artists' processes. The result will ideally provide a well-rounded approach based on the assets of both disciplines that will result in accurate, nuanced, comprehensive descriptions of clients.

References

Allen, B., & Tussey, C. (2012). Can projective drawings detect if a child experienced sexual or physical abuse? A systematic review of the controlled research. *Trauma, Violence & Abuse, 13*(2), 97–111.

American Psychiatric Association. (1980). *Diagnostic and statistical manual of mental disorders (DSM-III)* (3rd ed.). Washington: American Psychiatric Association.

Anderson, F. E. (1978). *Art for all the children.* Springfield: Charles C Thomas.

Betts, D. J. (2006). Art therapy assessments and rating instruments: Do they measure up? *The Arts in Psychotherapy: An International Journal, 33*(5), 371–472.

Betts, D. J. (2010). *The Face Stimulus Assessment (FSA) rating manual* (1st ed.). Washington: Department of Art Therapy, George Washington University.

Betts, D. J. (2012). Positive art therapy assessment: Looking towards positive psychology for new directions in the art therapy evaluation process. In A. Gilroy, R. Tipple, & C. Brown (Eds.), *Assessment in art therapy* (pp. 203–218). New York: Routledge.

Betts, D. J. (2013). Art therapy assessment and evaluation. In R. Flaum Cruz & B. Feder (Eds.), *The art and science of evaluation in the arts therapies: How do you know what's working?* (2nd ed., pp. 266–306). Springfield, IL: Charles C Thomas.

Bornstein, R. F. (2009). Heisenberg, Kandinsky, and the heteromethod convergence problem: Lessons from within and beyond psychology. *Journal of Personality Assessment, 91*(1): 1–8.

Bruck, M. (2009). Human Figure Drawings and children's recall of touching. *Journal of Experimental Psychology: Applied, 15*(4), 361–374.

Bucciarelli, A. (2007). *Normative study of the PPAT assessment on a sample of college students.* Unpublished master's thesis, Florida State University, Tallahassee, FL.

Bucciarelli, A. (2011). A normative study of the Person Picking an Apple From a Tree (PPAT) Assessment. *Art Therapy, Journal of the American Art Therapy Association, 28*(1), 31–36.

Buck, J. N. (1947). The H-T-P, a projective device. *American Journal of Mental Deficiency, 51,* 606–610.

Burns, E. (2009). *Art material and anxiety: A study of art materials used with adults.* Unpublished master's thesis, Florida State University, Tallahassee, FL.

Chase, D. A. (1986). An analysis of Human Figure and Kinetic Family Drawings of sexually abused children and adolescents. *The Arts in Psychotherapy, 13*(1), 69.

Cohen, B. M. (2012). *The Diagnostic Drawing Series rating guide.* Self-published manual, Alexandria, VA (original work self-published 1985).

Cohen, B. M., & Cox, C. T. (1995). *Telling without talking: Art as a window into the world of multiple personality.* New York: W. W. Norton.

Cohen, B. M., Hammer, J. S., & Singer, S. (1988). The Diagnostic Drawing Series: A systematic approach to art therapy evaluation and research. *The Arts in Psychotherapy, 15*(1), 11–21.

Cohen, B. M., Mills, A., & Kijak, K. (1994). An introduction to the Diagnostic Drawing Series: A standardized tool for diagnostic and clinical use. *Art Therapy, Journal of the American Art Therapy Association, 11*(2), 105–110.

Cox, C. T., Agell, G., Cohen, B. M., & Gantt, L. (2000). Are you assessing what I am assessing? Let's take a look! *American Journal of Art Therapy, 39*, 48-67.

Cox, C., & Frame, P. (1993). Profile of the artist: MARI card test research results. *Art Therapy: Journal of the American Art Therapy Association, 10*(1), 23–29.

Deaver, S. P. (2009). A normative study of children's drawings: Preliminary research findings. *Art Therapy: Journal of the American Art Therapy Association, 26*(1), 4–11.

Dudley, J. (2004). Art psychotherapy and the use of psychiatric diagnosis. *Inscape, 9*(1), 14–25.

Erard, R. E. (2010). President's message: How to cook without a book (and how not to). *SPA Exchange: Newsletter of the Society for Personality Assessment, 22*(2), 1 & 8–9.

Finn, S. E. (2007). *In our clients' shoes: Theory and techniques of therapeutic assessment.* Mahwah: Erlbaum.

Finn, S. E. (2009). *How is Therapeutic Assessment different from other types of psychological assessment?* Retrieved April 5, 2010 from http://therapeuticassessment.com/about.html

Fischer, C. T. (2000). Collaborative, individualized assessment. *Journal of Personality Assessment, 74*, 2–14.

Fischer, C. T. (2001). Collaborative exploration as an approach to personality assessment. In K. J. Schneider, J. F. T. Bugenthal, & J. F. Pierson (Eds.), *The handbook of humanistic psychology: Leading edges in theory, research and practice.* Thousand Oaks: Sage.

Gantt, L. (1990). *A validity study of the Formal Elements Art Therapy Scale (FEATS) for diagnostic information in patients' drawings.* Unpublished doctoral dissertation, University of Pittsburgh, Pittsburgh, PA.

Gantt, L. M. (2001). The Formal Elements Art Therapy Scale: A measurement system for global variables in art. *Art Therapy: Journal of the American Art Therapy Association, 18*(1), 50–55.

Gantt, L. M. (2004). The case for formal art therapy assessments. *Art Therapy: Journal of the American Art Therapy Association, 21*(1), 18–29.

Gantt, L., & Howie, P. (1979). Diagnostic categories in art work. *Proceedings of the Tenth Annual Conference of the American Art Therapy Association.* Alexandria: AATA.

Gantt, L., & Tabone, C. (1998). *The Formal Elements Art Therapy Scale: The rating manual.* Morgantown: Gargoyle Press.

Groth-Marnat, G. (1997). *Handbook of psychological assessment* (3rd ed.). New York: John Wiley & Sons, Inc.

Groth-Marnat, G. (2009). *Handbook of psychological assessment* (5th ed.). New York: John Wiley & Sons, Inc.

Groth-Marnat, G., & Davis, A. (2013). *Psychological report writing assistant.* Hoboken, NJ: John Wiley & Sons.

Groth-Marnat, G., & Roberts, L. (1998). Human Figure Drawings and House Tree Person Drawings as indicators of self-esteem: A quantitative approach. *Journal of Clinical Psychology, 54*(2), 219–222.

Gussak, D. (2009). The effects of art therapy on male and female inmates: Advancing the research base. *The Arts in Psychotherapy: an International Journal, 36*, 5–12.

Hagood, M. M. (2003). The use of the Naglieri Draw-a-Person Test of Cognitive Development: A study with clinical and research implications for art therapists working with children. *Art Therapy: Journal of the American Art Therapy Association, 20*(2), 67–76.

Hammer, E. F. (1954). Guide for qualitative research with the H-T-P. *Journal of General Psychology, 51*, 41–60.

Hammer, E. F. (1958). *The clinical application of figure drawings.* Springfield: Charles C Thomas.

Handler, L., & Reyher, J. (1964). The effects of stress on the Draw-A-Person test. *Journal of Consulting Psychology, 28*(3), 259–264.

282

Handler, L., & Reyher, J. (1965). Figure drawing anxiety indexes: A review of the literature. *Journal of Projective Techniques and Personality Assessment, 29,* 305–313.

Handler, L., & Reyher, J. (1966). Relationship between GSR and anxiety indexes in projective drawings. *Journal of Consulting Psychology, 30*(1), 60–67.

Harris, D. B. (1963). *Children's drawings as measures of intellectual maturity: A revision and extension of the Goodenough Draw-A-Man Test.* New York: Harcourt, Brace & World.

Harwood, T. M., Beutler, L. E. & Groth-Marnat, G. (Eds.) (2011). *Integrative assessment of adult Personality* (3rd ed.). New York, NY: Guilford Press.

Henley, D. (1997). Expressive arts therapy as alternative education: Devising a therapeutic curriculum. *Art Therapy: Journal of the American Art Therapy Association, 14*(1), 15–22.

Hinz, L. D. (2009). *The Expressive Therapies Continuum: A framework for using art in therapy.* New York: Routledge.

Horovitz, E. G., & Eksten, S. (Eds.) (2009). *The art therapists' primer: A clinical guide to writing assessments, diagnosis, and treatment.* Springfield: Charles C Thomas.

Horowitz, M. J. (1970). *Image formation and cognition.* New York: Appleton-Century-Crofts.

Horowitz, M. J. (1983). *Image formation and psychotherapy.* New York: Jason Aronson.

Junge, M. B. (2010). *The modern history of art therapy in the United States.* Springfield: Charles C Thomas.

Junge, M. B., & Asawa, P. P. (1994). *A history of art therapy in the United States.* Mundelein: American Art Therapy Association.

Kagin, S. (1969). *The effects of structure on the painting of retarded youth.* Unpublished master's thesis, University of Tulsa, Tulsa, OK.

Kagin, S. L., & Lusebrink, V. B. (1978). The Expressive therapies continuum. *The Arts in Psychotherapy: An International Journal, 5,* 171–180.

Kahill, S. (1984). Human figure drawing in adults: An update of the empirical evidence, 1967–1982. *Canadian Psychology, 25,* 269–292.

Kaiser, D. (1996). Indications of attachment security in a drawing task. *The Arts in Psychotherapy: An International Journal, 23*(4), 333–340.

Kaiser, D. H., & Deaver, S. P. (2009). Assessing attachment with the Bird's Nest Drawing: A review of the research. *Art Therapy: Journal of the American Art Therapy Association, 26*(1), 26–33.

Kaplan, F. (2001). Areas of inquiry for art therapy research. *Art Therapy: Journal of the American Art Therapy Association, 18*(3), 142–147.

Kellogg, J. (1984). *Mandala: Path of beauty.* Lightfoot: MARI.

Klopfer, W. G., & Taulbee, E. S. (1976). Projective tests. *Annual Review of Psychology, 27,* 543–567.

Koppitz, E. M., & Casullo, M. M. (1983). Exploring cultural influences on Human Figure Drawings of young adolescents. *Perceptual and Motor Skills, 57,* 479–483.

Kwiatkowska, H. Y. (1975). Family art therapy: Experiments with a new technique. In E. Ulman (Ed.), *Art therapy in theory and practice* (pp. 113–131). New York: Schocken Books.

Kwiatkowska, H. Y. (1978). *Family therapy and evaluation through art.* Springfield: Charles C Thomas.

Lally, S. (2001). Should Human Figure Drawings be admitted to court? *Journal of Personality Assessment, 76*(1), 135–149.

Lehmann, H., & Risquez, F. (1953). The use of finger paintings in the clinical evaluation of psychotic conditions: A quantitative and qualitative approach. *The British Journal of Psychiatry: Journal of Mental Science, 99,* 763–777.

Levy, B. I., & Ulman, E. (1974). The effect of training on judging psychopathology from paintings. *American Journal of Art Therapy, 14*(1), 24–25.

Lowenfeld, V., & Brittain, W. (1970). *Creative and mental growth* (5th ed.). New York: Macmillan.

Lusebrink, V. B. (2010). Assessment and therapeutic application of the Expressive Therapies Continuum: Implications for brain structures and functions. *Art Therapy: Journal of the American Art Therapy Association, 27*(4), 168–177.

Machover, K. (1949). *Personality projection in the drawing of the human figure.* Springfield: Charles C Thomas.

Martin, K., & Betts, D. (2012). *The Bridge Drawing rating manual* (2nd ed.). Washington: Department of Art Therapy, George Washington University.

Martin, D. J., Garske, J. P., & Davis, M. K. (2000). Relation of the therapeutic alliance with outcome and other variables: A meta-analytic review. *Journal of Consulting and Clinical Psychology, 68*(3), 438–450.

Meyer, G. J., & Kurtz, J. E. (2006). Advancing personality assessment terminology: Time to retire "objective" and "projective" as personality test descriptors. *Journal of Personality Assessment, 87*(3), 223–225.

Milne, L., & Greenway, P. (1999). Color in children's drawings: The influence of age and gender. *The Arts in Psychotherapy, 26*(4), 261–261.

Milne, L. C., & Greenway, P. (2005). Children's behaviour and their graphic representation of parents and self. *The Arts in Psychotherapy: An International Journal, 32,* 107–119.

Moon, C. (2010a). A history of materials and media in art therapy. In C. Moon (Ed.), *Materials & media in art therapy: Critical understandings of diverse artistic vocabularies* (pp. 3–47). New York: Routledge.

Moon, C. (2010b). Theorizing materiality in art therapy. In C. Moon (Ed.), *Materials & media in art therapy: Critical understandings of diverse artistic vocabularies* (pp. 49–88). New York: Routledge.

Munley, M. (2002). Comparing the PPAT drawings of boys with AD/HD and age-matched controls using the Formal Elements Art Therapy Scale. *Art Therapy: Journal of the American Art Therapy Association, 19*(2), 69–76.

Neale, L. E., & Rosal, M. L. (1993). What can art therapists learn from the research on projective drawing techniques for children? A review of the literature. *The Arts in Psychotherapy, 20,* 37–49.

Packard, S. (1978). Techniques and tools for evaluation: A workshop for sensitive analysis of children's art products. In B. K. Mandel, R. H. Shoemaker, & R. E. Hays (Eds.), *Proceedings of the Eighth Annual Conference of the American Art Therapy Association* (pp. 94–99). Baltimore: AATA.

Packman, W. L., Beck, V. L., VanZutphen, K. H., Long, J. K., & Spengler, G. (2003). The Human Figure Drawing with donor and nondonor siblings of pediatric bone marrow transplant patients. *Art Therapy: Journal of the American Art Therapy Association, 20*(2), 83–91.

Rabinowitz, P., & Betts, D. (2012). A validity study of Formal Elements Art Therapy Scale scores derived from a sample of normative PPAT drawings. Unpublished manuscript, George Washington University, Washington, DC.

Riethmiller, R. J., & Handler, L. (1997). Problematic methods and unwarranted conclusions in DAP research: Suggestions for improved research procedures. *Journal of Personality Assessment, 69*(3), 459–475.

Robins, A., & Seaver, L. (1994). Materials. In A. Robbins (Ed.), *A multi-modal approach to creative art therapy* (pp. 206–211). Philadelphia: Jessica Kingsley Publishers.

Rockwell, P., & Dunham, M. (2006). The utility of the Formal Elements Art Therapy Scale in assessment for substance use disorder. *Art Therapy: Journal of the American Art Therapy Association, 23*(3), 104–111.

Rostan, S. M. (1997). A study of young artists: The development of artistic talent and creativity. *Creativity Research Journal, 10*(2–3), 175–192.

Rubin, J. (1978). *Child art therapy*. New York: Van Nostrand Reinhold.

Scribner, C., & Handler, L. (1987). The interpreter's personality in Draw-a-Person interpretation: A study of interpersonal style. *Journal of Personality Assessment, 51,* 112–122.

Shoemaker, R. (1982). Assessment and recordkeeping: Building bridges that communicate progress. In A. E. DiMaria, E. S. Kramer, & I. Rosner (Eds.), *Proceedings of the Twelfth Annual Conference of the American Art Therapy Association* (pp. 22–26). Alexandria: AATA.

Sidun, N. M. (1986). Graphic indicators of sexual abuse in adolescents' Draw-A-Person test. *The Arts in Psychotherapy, 13*(l), 69.

Silver, R. A. (1988). Screening children and adolescents for depression through draw-a-story. *The American Journal of Art Therapy, 26,* 119–124.

Silver, R. A. (1996). *Silver Drawing Test of Cognition and Emotion* (3rd ed.). New York: Albin Press.

Silver, R. A. (2002). *Three art assessments, Silver Drawing Test, Draw A Story, and Stimulus Drawings and Techniques*. New York: Brunner-Routledge; London, Taylor & Francis.

Silver, R. (2009). Identifying children and adolescents with depression: Review of the Stimulus Drawing Task and Draw A Story research. *Art Therapy: Journal of the American Art Therapy Association, 26*(4), 174–180.

Somer, L., & Somer, E. (2000). Perspectives on the use of glass in therapy. *American Journal of Art Therapy, 38,* 75–80.

Snyder, C. R., Ritschel, I. A., Rand, K. L., & Berg, C. J. (2006). Balancing psychological assessments: Including strengths and hope in client reports. *Journal of Clinical Psychology, 62*(1), 33–46.

Stuckey, A. (2012). *A normative study of the Expressive Therapies Continuum*. Unpublished capstone paper, George Washington University, Washington, DC.

Suinn, R. M., & Oskamp, S. (1969). *The predictive validity of projective measures: A fifteen-year evaluative review of research*. Springfield: Charles C Thomas.

Teneycke, T. L., Hoshino, J., & Sharpe, D. (2009). The Bridge Drawing: An exploration of psychosis. *The Arts in Psychotherapy: An International Journal, 36,* 297–303.

Ulman, E. (1965). A new use of art in psychiatric diagnosis. *Bulletin of Art Therapy, 4,* 91–116.

Ulman, E. (1975). A new use of art in psychiatric diagnosis. In E. Ulman & P. Dachinger (Eds.), *Art therapy in theory and practice* (pp. 361–386). New York: Schocken Books.

Ulman, E., & Levy, B. I. (1975). An experimental approach to the judgment of psychopathology from paintings. In E. Ulman & P. Dachinger (Eds.), *Art therapy in theory and practice* (pp. 393–402). New York: Schocken.

Wadeson, H. (1980). *Art psychotherapy*. New York: Wiley.

White, C., Wallace, J., & Huffman, L. (2004). Use of drawings to identify thought impairment among students with emotional and behavioral disorders: An exploratory study. *Art Therapy: Journal of the American Art Therapy Association, 21*(4), 210–218.

Yedidia, T., & Lipschitz-Elchawi, R. (2012). Examining social perceptions between Arab and Jewish children through Human Figure Drawings. *Art Therapy: Journal of the American Art Therapy Association, 29*(3), 104–112.

INDEX

Page numbers in *italics* followed by an *f* indicate figures, by a *t* indicate tables, and by a *d* indicate drawings to psychological assessment 271–2; assessment processes for outcomes 272–6; background of approaches 269–72; color 272–3; Expressive Therapy Continuum (ETC) theory 273–5, *275f*; Formal Elements Art Therapy Scale (FEATS): Developmental Level *279f*; Formal Elements Art Therapy Scale (FEATS) 270–1, 273, 277–8; interviews and data integration 275–6; signs, global ratings, and form 276–8; themes unique to art therapy/distinct from projective drawings 271; in the United States 268

Art Therapy-Projective Imagery Assessment (AT-PIA) with case illustration 131–47; 1. behavioral observations (case illustration) 136–7, *137–40d*; 2. drawings and titles table (case illustration) *140t*; 3. developmental level (case illustration) 140–1; 4. problems and concerns noted in the drawings (case illustration) 141–2; 5. strengths and coping mechanisms (case illustration) 142; 6. summary, conclusions, and diagnostic impressions (case illustration) 142–3, *143t*; 7. recommendations (case illustration) 143; administration guidelines 131, 133; background of AT-PIA 131; discussion about AT-PIA 143–5; documentation of AT-PIA 134–5; drawing directives for AT-PIA 133–4; drawing materials for AT-PIA 133; Favorite Weather Drawing (FWD) 132, *138d*, 141–2; Free Choice Drawing (FCD) 131–3, *140d*; Human Figure Drawing (HFD) 132, *138d*, 141; interpretation of AT-PIA 135–6; Kinetic Family Drawing (KFD) 132, *139d*, 142; Projective Scribble Drawing (PSD) 131–2, *137d*; Reason for Being Here Drawing (RBHD) 132, *139d*, 141–2; types of drawings in the AT-PIA 131–3

"Art Therapy-Projective Imagery Assessment, The" (Deaver and Bernier) 131–47

art therapy research, "Top Ten List" wish list for (Kapitan) 4–5

Asperger's symptoms, marital discord and 235–9, *237–8d*

Assessment: assessing adolescents 194–5; integrating assessment and therapy with the Squiggle Game 195–6; perception 22–3; performance-based 269; positive

art therapy assessment 275; processes and 272–6, 280; *see also* art therapy and psychological assessment; Art Therapy-Projective Imagery Assessment (AT-PIA); Human Figure Drawings in Therapeutic Assessment with Children; Squiggle Game case study for adolescent therapeutic assessment; test administration

AT-PIA *see* Art Therapy-Projective Imagery Assessment, Attachment styles 22

Attention Deficit/Hyperactivity Disorder (ADHD) 229, 252

Bardos, Achilles N. and Maria Doropoulou, "Draw-A-Person Screening Procedure for Emotional Disturbance Validity Evidence" 42–57

Bernier, Matthew 131–47

Betts, Donna and Gary Groth-Marnat, "Intersection of Art Therapy and Psychological Assessment, The Unified Approaches to the Use of Drawings and Artistic Processes" 268–85

Bird's Nest Drawing 276

Black children, DAP: SPED scoring 53

Blind drawing interpretations: doodling 214–16, *215*; free drawings 216–20, *218–19d*

Body image 77, 254–5, *255*, 262; *see also* anorexic House-Tree-Person (HTP) drawings

Body parts in drawings *see* sexually and physically abused children's drawings study

Borderline personalities 246; Draw-A-Person-in-the-Rain (DAP-R) test and 173, 175

Bulletin of Art Therapy 268

Burns, Robert, designer of Kinetic Family Drawing (KFD) 11, 13

CAAP *see* Child and Adolescent Adjustment Profile

Canadian Cree Indians and White Canadian children's abuse study *see* sexually and physically abused children's drawings study

Car drawings 164, 280

"Case Study: Jason, A Little Boy with a Lot Inside" (Finger) 240–5; diagnosis and treatment 244; discussion 244;